MOTHERING MULTIPLES

Breastfeeding & Caring for Twins or More!!!

KAREN KERKHOFF GROMADA

REVISED EDITION

Breastfeeding & Caring for Twins *or more!!!*

MOTHERING MULTIPLES

KAREN KERKHOFF GROMADA

REVISED EDITION

LA LECHE LEAGUE INTERNATIONAL
Schaumburg, Illinois

Cover photo by David C. Arendt
Book and cover design, Digital Concepts, L.L.C.

La Leche League International
1400 N. Meacham Road
Schaumburg, IL 60173-4840
www.lalecheleague.org

For my parents, Ed and Peachee Kerkhoff, who have shown, and continue to show, me what parental love is all about; For my husband, Joe, whose love allows me to believe I can do anything I try; For all five of my children (Elizabeth, Brandon, Tony, Joe, and Carolyn), who have taught me what is really important in life and who forgive me when I goof, but especially for my twins, Tony and Joe, without whose "help" this book would not have been possible nor would I have known it was necessary.

Contents

Introduction

If you are like most women, your emotions have seesawed since multiples were diagnosed! One minute the thought of multiples sounds exciting, and the next minute it seems frightening. Today you may resent getting more than you bargained for; tomorrow you may feel proud of your extra dividend(s). When you don't feel well, you may be overwhelmed with feelings of anxiety. At other moments, you feel in awe that your body can nourish more than one baby so well.

Questions may race through your mind. Will each baby be all right? How will multiples change the plan for labor and delivery? Can I manage the needs of two, three, or four newborns when one seems a handful? What preparation should I make? What extra equipment will I need? Can I still breastfeed although I'm having multiples?

How do I presume to know how you may be feeling about having multiples? I have felt the surprise and numbness myself. I have experienced the ambivalent feelings. And I have asked the questions. I am a mother of twins. I am also a La Leche League (LLL) Leader of a special group just for mothers who will be or who are currently breastfeeding and nurturing multiple-birth children.

I, and all the past and present Leaders of our Group, welcome you to our very special La Leche League (LLL) meetings. For more than 20 years, we have been meeting in Cincinnati to discuss the unique situation of breastfeeding and parenting multiple-birth children. All of the Leaders know what it is like to breastfeed and nurture multiples. Most of the women who attend are mothers of twins (MOT), but a fair number of mothers of triplets or quadruplets have also brought their babies to Series Meetings over the years.

A lot of the Leaders' work is done by phone—with expectant mothers confined to bedrest, with mothers recuperating from birth, with mothers pumping for preterm babies, and with mothers too overwhelmed to coordinate getting two, three, or four babies to meetings. Whether you currently are in contact with an LLL Leader by phone, attend "regular" LLL meetings, or even lead LLL meetings yourself, I hope you will find this revision of MOTHERING MULTIPLES helpful. It is a compilation of years of mothers' experiences, plus it discusses some of the science of multiple pregnancy and birth. There are frequent reminders that multiple babies are going to mean more adjustment and work for parents—no matter how they are fed.

Multiples do not plan to be born together. In spite of arriving as part of a set, each multiple is a unique individual. Parents must constantly remember that. Having one another can never replace the need of each for your mothering. Since babies cannot be expected to compromise their needs, you and your husband, as the mature members of the family, will have to give more. Because of this, there are chapters in this book that may seem to focus more on the negative aspects of mothering multiples. When I wrote the first edition, I felt very frustrated by this. Most of the mothers in our group would tell you that our experiences are very positive overall.

Then it dawned on me. A mother does not need a book to help her enjoy the fantastic feeling of being at the center of two, three, four, or seven babies' universe. You don't need another mother to explain the joy of seeing all those little arms and legs waving wildly in greeting as you approach them. No advice is necessary when it comes to savoring the intangible pleasure of having four tiny eyes focused on your face as you breastfeed two simultaneously. Do I need to describe the awe you feel as you watch your babies sleep side by side? You certainly don't need me to explain why you feel so proud when your babies' pediatric care provider congratulates you on the babies' good weight gains—all on mother's milk! It is an incredible feeling to be given the privilege of eavesdropping on nature's most perfect "environment versus heredity" study, but I don't have to tell you that. Certainly, you will experience enormous personal growth as a direct result of coping with this intense situation without someone telling you about it.

The positive aspects of mothering multiples are many and are to be experienced with joy. It is for the difficulties that assistance is required. When you are plagued with doubt or negative feelings, you may need a boost, some suggestions, or a reminder that you are normal—it is the situation that is not normal. Fortunately, it is in overcoming any difficulties and coping with ambivalent feelings that the most positive personal growth can be achieved.

Remember that you are not alone. There are 20+ years of other mothers of multiples cheering you on in this book, and LLL Leaders who have breastfed multiples are available if you ever want to talk in person to someone who has "been there." La Leche League International (LLLI) maintains an updated listing of LLL Multiples Groups and Leaders. We are here for you, so please feel free to get in touch with one of us. (To contact LLLI, see "Resources.")

Good luck as you begin one of life's grandest adventures and happy mothering—multiplied!

Karen Kerkhoff Gromada
1-99

Acknowledgements

A special thank you goes to Dee Keith, IBCLC, LLL Multiples Leader extraordinaire, and special friend, for reviewing the manuscript prior to edits. Thanks also to these wonderful women:

- Judy Torgus, Executive Editor, LLLI Publications Director, for her technical expertise and for her patience when this revision kept growing and growing and growing.
- Nancy Bowers, RN, BSN, mother of twins and President of Marvelous Multiples childbirth program, for her careful reading of the chapters about pregnancy, labor, and birth.
- Nancy Hurst, RN, MSN, IBCLC, Manager of the Lactation Support Program and Mother's Own Milk Bank at Texas Children's Hospital (Houston), for reviewing chapters about initiating breastfeeding with preterm or sick multiples, making up for a slow start, and full vs. partial breastfeeding.
- Martha Grodrian, RD, LD, IBCLC, for her help in developing a nutrition/food pyramid for multiple pregnancy.
- Mary Riker Kornick, MOT toddlers and LLL mother, for reviewing the chapters about toddler multiples to ensure the information fit the living experience.

I especially want to thank the mothers of multiples who contributed their personal stories and photographs for this edition. I hope they realize how their efforts will help other new mothers see that breastfeeding multiples is a realistic and wonderful way to feed babies—no matter how many arrive at one time!

Chapter One
It's Twins, Triplets, or More!

Congratulations! You've hit the jackpot! You are carrying two, three, or more babies! Whether you simply "got lucky" or the odds for you conceiving multiples were increased due to fertility-enhancing techniques, if you are like most parents of multiples, you never thought it would happen to you. Ready or not, here you are. You've now joined one of the fastest growing parent populations.

The number of multiple births in the United States (US) and in the United Kingdom (UK) rose significantly during the last decades of the twentieth century. The increase appears small when looking at the total number of births per year in the US. For example, the increase in twin births accounts for only an extra few tenths of a percent. However, those tenths of a percent represent a 35 to 40 percent increase in the number of twin births annually. The total number of annual births in the US decreased between 1984 and 1994, yet there were 25,000 more sets of twins born in 1994 than in 1984.

The increase in the number of higher-order multiple births, who also may be referred to as super multiples or supertwins, is even more dramatic. The number of triplets, quadruplets, and quintuplets born in 1994 represented only one-tenth of one percent of all US births that year. Yet this number reflects a 178 percent increase in these births since 1984.

Twin Types

Multiples come in two types—identical (one egg) and fraternal (two or three or more eggs).

Identical, or **monozygotic** (MZ), twinning occurs during an early stage of cell division for a single fertilized egg (ovum). Once the fertilized egg cell begins to divide it is called a zygote. At some point in the process of dividing to form twice as many cells, the single zygote splits completely to form two separate zygotes—each containing the same genetic material since each originated from the same fertilized ovum. Because their genetic make-up is essentially the same, identical twins are always of the same sex. They share the same hair and eye colors, basic body build, ear shape, and so on. Unless someone knows them well, identical twins often are difficult to tell apart. Identical twins are born at about the same rate worldwide—approximately one in every 250 births. The incidence of identical twinning appears to occur independently of a woman's age, ethnic group, or culture.

Fraternal twinning results from the fertilization of two (or more) separate eggs (ova) by two separate sperm, so it is referred to as **dizygotic** (DZ) twinning. (Three-egg triplets may be called trizygotes [TZ].) As with any siblings who share the same two parents, fraternal twins will have from 25 percent to 75 percent of their genetic material in common. They may look as alike or different as any two siblings in a family, and they may be of the same or opposite sexes. Many factors influence the likelihood that a woman will conceive fraternal twins, including:

- maternal family history of twins,
- previous fraternal twin pregnancy,
- history of several prior pregnancies,
- maternal age of 35 years or older at the time of conception,
- use of fertility-enhancing procedures to conceive.

Fraternal twinning occurs naturally most often in black ethnic groups and least often among Asian groups. Fertility-enhancing procedures, which also may be called reproductive-assisted techniques, are the main reason for an increase in the number of fraternal multiple births in white ethnic groups, at least in the US, and have especially influenced the increased number of higher-order multiple births.

Multiples occurring due to fertility-enhancing techniques generally are fraternal because most of these techniques involve the administration of ovulatory induction agents, which lead to the maturation and release of multiple egg cells (ova) during a single menstrual cycle. (Depending on the procedure, fertilization may occur inside or outside of the woman's body.) However, it is possible for one or more induced fertilized ova to split during cell division and create an identical pair.

*Breastfeeding is beneficial for a mother
and her multiples.*

All individuals within a higher-order multiple set will be identical if after splitting once, one or both of the two "new" zygotes splits again (and possibly again). All members will be fraternal if three or more mature egg cells are released and fertilized within a single menstrual cycle. Higher-order multiple sets may include a combination of identical and fraternal members. For example, naturally occurring triplet sets sometimes consist of an identical pair and a third fraternal member.

Yes, It's Really Twins (or More)

Less than a 25 years ago more than 25 percent of twin pregnancies went undiscovered until delivery. Today the birth of undiagnosed multiples is almost unheard of. When conception follows fertility-enhancement procedures, the possibility of multiples is always a consideration and health care providers* watch closely for signs of a multiple pregnancy. Yet naturally occurring multiple pregnancies also are being diagnosed earlier now. The development of simple but sensitive maternal blood (serum) tests, which are drawn in the first or second trimester of pregnancy, have helped.

---

* To simplify and be more concise the terms **health care provider, obstetrical health care provider,** and **pediatric care provider** are used in this book to avoid repeating a list of physician, nurse, or certified lay providers who typically provide health care to women and children.

Blood may be tested for the hormone human chorionic gonadatropin (hCG) during the first trimester; the results of a maternal serum alpha (α)-fetoprotein (MSAFP) are more accurate when it is drawn between 16 to 18 weeks of pregnancy. Higher levels for either test are associated with an increased likelihood of multiples.

Before the mid-1970s, x-ray was the only instrument able to definitely diagnose multiples and determine their positions in the uterus. Now a definitive diagnosis usually is made by ultrasound scanning—a method that creates moving "pictures" of the babies by bouncing sound waves off their body tissue in the uterus. (For more discussion of ultrasound, see Chapter 4, "What To Do If...")

Health Care with Multiples

A multiple pregnancy is monitored more closely, so it is more important than ever for you to have confidence in your health care provider(s) and in the health care setting where you will give birth. You need to be completely honest with health care providers about every aspect of the pregnancy and they need to be honest with you. Science still has a lot to learn about multiple pregnancy, and many medical recommendations and treatments for apparent complications of multiple pregnancy are unproven or controversial. Don't be afraid to ask questions—lots of questions.

You may feel more confident in your health care provider if soon after the diagnosis you schedule time for an in-depth discussion about many of the aspects of multiple pregnancy discussed in the first few chapters of this book. For instance, you could ask how many expectant mothers of twins or more a particular doctor or midwife has delivered. You may want to find out how many sets the provider has delivered vaginally and how many were surgically delivered, and what criteria are used to determine method of delivery. Ask whether the provider approaches multiple pregnancy differently than a single-infant pregnancy. If the answer is "yes," ask about the differences. A "no" answer should be followed up with a "why not?" since birth outcomes are not the same for multiples from a statistical standpoint. The physician or midwife who has always provided your gynecologic care, or who delivered your previous baby, may or may not be the best care provider for a multiple pregnancy and birth. If your care provider is a midwife, you will both very likely work closely with a physician specialist, such as an obstetrician or perinatologist.

Those who have been undergoing treatment for infertility may find they use this material to interview a new obstetrical care provider. Physicians working in the field of fertility treatment often do not provide obstetrical care once their clients have conceived. After building a relationship with one specialist, it is not always easy to start over again with someone new or with a care provider you haven't seen in awhile. It's okay to feel excited about the pregnancy yet feel sad that you will no longer be sharing your ups and downs with a provider you've learned to trust. You won't want to wait too long to find an obstetric care provider and your fertility specialist may pass on some recommendations, but you still may want to spend a little time with preliminary interviews. By speaking to potential care providers in advance, you are more likely to find one who best meets your and your unborn babies' needs for health care.

Early diagnosis gives you time to improve health habits that affect the babies' development. And once you know how many babies you are carrying, you will begin to form an attachment with each baby. It also means you and your health care providers can prepare for the special birth and subsequent breastfeeding and care of two or more babies. And more preparation is needed—physically and emotionally.

Chapter Two
Multiple Pregnancy as High Risk: Fact and Fiction

Multiple pregnancy shares many similarities with single-infant pregnancy, but multiple pregnancy also is different. Historically, the survival of the human species has depended on carrying and giving birth to only one offspring with each pregnancy. There is additional physical stress for a mother and her babies during a multiple pregnancy.

Because of the additional stressors most health care providers now label any multiple pregnancy as a "high risk" pregnancy. Putting it in proper perspective, the label of "high risk" only means that certain complications or conditions are more likely to occur with a multiple pregnancy than with a typical single-infant pregnancy. It doesn't mean a complication or condition **will** occur. Placing a label on multiple pregnancies merely reminds obstetrical care providers that they must screen more carefully for conditions or complications seen more often with multiple pregnancy.

Maternal Stressors

Even an ideal multiple pregnancy is more physically stressful than a single-infant pregnancy. Typical early pregnancy symptoms, such as nausea, fatigue, and constipation are often exaggerated during multiple pregnancies. Later in pregnancy, heartburn, backache, and quick tiring or shortness of breath with activity also occur more frequently. These symptoms are more common because of the higher levels of pregnancy hormones and volume of blood circulating within a woman's body and to the increased space two or more growing babies take up. During the last trimester of a multiple pregnancy many women find they've outgrown most maternity clothes and can no longer see their feet when standing upright. Even turning over in bed requires strategic planning!

To screen for the conditions seen more often in multiple pregnancy, your health care provider probably will want to see you more frequently, especially during the last half of pregnancy. Your blood may be drawn and monitored more often since pregnancy-related anemia is more common with multiple pregnancy. Your blood sugar may also be checked periodically because there is a slight increase in the incidence of gestational diabetes with multiple pregnancy. Pregnancy-induced hypertension (PIH), sometimes called preeclampsia or toxemia, occurs more often with multiple pregnancy, which means the doctor or midwife will carefully check for sudden increases in your blood pressure and weight and for protein in the urine. (See Chapter 4, "What To Do If...")

Physical stress isn't the only kind you may experience. Many expectant mothers feel ambivalent about a multiple pregnancy. Whether your multiple pregnancy was a complete surprise or required years of treatment for infertility, it is normal to have mixed feelings about getting more than you bargained for! The thought of multiples may sound exciting one minute, and only a few minutes later the thought of caring for two or more newborns may lead to feelings of mild panic. A concern about giving birth too early may alternate with a sense of awe that your body is nourishing two or more infants so well within it. You sometimes might wonder how multiples will affect your birth plans, how you will manage breastfeeding, how your older children will react, and how much two or more babies will strain the family budget. Don't be surprised if your feelings about the pregnancy and the thought of having multiple babies fluctuate not only from day to day, but also from minute to minute. If you find your emotions about the pregnancy and being the mother of multiples vacillate, you are in good company. Such feelings are very common!

Infants' Stressors

Sharing a uterus is physically more stressful for babies, too. Multiples are more likely to be born early. The average length for a twin pregnancy, or gestation, is approximately 36 weeks compared with 39½ weeks for a single-infant pregnancy. Length of gestation averages about 34 weeks with triplets and 31 weeks for quadruplets. Multiples also tend to weigh less than single babies at the same week of pregnancy, also called the same gestational age. At least 50 percent of all twins and more than 90 percent of higher-order multiples weigh less than 2500 gm, or 5 lb 8 oz, at birth compared with only six percent of single-born infants. It isn't surprising then that a disproportionate number of newborn multiples spend some time—hours to weeks—in a newborn intensive care unit (NICU). Your obstetrical care provider probably will begin watching closely for any signs of preterm labor or a slowing down in the growth rate of any of the babies after 24 weeks of pregnancy.

One large or two or more separate placentas take up more uterine space, and placenta problems occur more often with multiple pregnancies. A problem with the placentas may affect the mother, one or more infants, or a mother and infant(s).

Think Positive

There is every reason to think positive when multiples are discovered during pregnancy. Many women have healthy multiple pregnancies and deliver two, three, or more healthy babies. Almost 15 percent of twin pregnancies are full-term. It is not unusual for a woman to give birth to twins having average birth weights of 3175 to 3400 gm, or 7 to 7½ lb. Occasionally each of a set of twins weighs 3629 to 4309 gm, or eight to nine and one-half pounds at birth. And many multiples born only a few weeks early, but who are small for gestational age, still are very healthy at birth.

Improving the Odds

There's no point in ignoring risk factors. As the saying goes, "Forewarned is forearmed." However, you can take action to decrease some risks. The earlier a diagnosis of multiple pregnancy is made, the earlier you can start working to improve the outcome.

Some risk factors are beyond your control, but you can improve the odds of going full-term, or close to full-term, and having babies within normal weights for gestational age, if you do your part to maintain your health and the health of the babies and their placenta(s).

A placenta's job is to keep a baby supplied with essential oxygen and nutrients. It depends on a mother's healthy cardiovascular system to provide it with the oxygen and nutrients the baby needs. A decrease in placental function, which may affect one or more placentas in a multiple pregnancy, is associated with preterm labor and slower growth rates in affected babies. You can take an active role in keeping the placentas as healthy as possible by eating well, avoiding harmful substances, exercising as your pregnancy allows, and relaxing as needed.

Chapter Three
Multiple Pregnancy: Caring for Three, Four, or More before Birth

Many women have essentially normal, uncomplicated multiple pregnancies, labors, and births. Many multiples are born at term and are of average birth weights or close to term and close to 2500 gm (5 lb, 8 oz). And many multiple sets and their mothers are eager and able to breastfeed within an hour or two of birth. There are actions you can take to improve the odds of a good outcome for your babies and minimize both the risk of complications and their consequences, so you and your babies can get off to the best breastfeeding start.

Don't wait and simply hope that all goes well during your multiple pregnancy. Take an active role in promoting good health for you and your babies. There are several contributions only you can make, which can affect all of you during pregnancy and after the babies are born.

Good Diet

You already have an advantage if you are: 1) 25 years or older, 2) at average or slightly higher weight for height, and 3) not anemic when you conceive multiples. Continuing to eat well if you meet these pre-pregnancy criteria or improving your diet if you do not, which means eating more in either case, throughout pregnancy is the most important thing you can do to take care of yourself and your babies. Although there still is much to learn about the association between diet and a healthy outcome for multiple pregnancy, a link has been found between mothers' weight gains during twin or triplet pregnancies and babies' birth weights and possibly the length of pregnancies as well. Making positive diet changes, even during the last 12 to 15 weeks of a multiple pregnancy, has had positive effects on the eventual outcome for mothers and babies.

It takes a lot of good food to support the growth and development of two or more unborn babies, and keep one or more placenta(s) healthy! A woman's nutritional requirements are higher during any pregnancy, but those nutritional requirements continue to multiply along with the number of babies a woman carries. Pre-pregnancy general health and weight-for-height also influence pregnancy nutritional requirements.

Pre-pregnancy guidelines suggest that a woman of average height and weight should take in at least 1800 to 2200 calories from food a day. Most current calorie recommendations for twin pregnancy suggest a daily minimum of 2700 calories and some recommend consuming as many as 4000 calories daily.

Various sources advise anywhere from 300 to 600 extra calories per day for each additional multiple. If you aren't a calorie counter, eating more of the right kinds of foods and including frequent protein and carbohydrate snacks between meals should help you meet multiple pregnancy weight gain goals. (See "Nutrition Hints" below.)

The goal is to gain an average of 450 grams, or one pound, a week for the first 24 weeks and at least 680 grams, one and one-half pounds, for each week of a twin pregnancy after that. The weekly weight gain goal increases by about 115 to 340 grams, or one-quarter to three-quarter pounds, for higher-order multiple pregnancies.

Although some women gain weight at a fairly steady pace, many women don't gain so consistently. Some gain more than the average during certain weeks of the pregnancy and less than the average during others. Unless a larger weight gain is associated with symptoms indicating some health problem for mother or babies, weight gain variations in any given month generally should be considered appropriate for an individual expectant mother of multiples—as long as she continues to progressively gain weight. Small weight gains for two consecutive months, a failure to

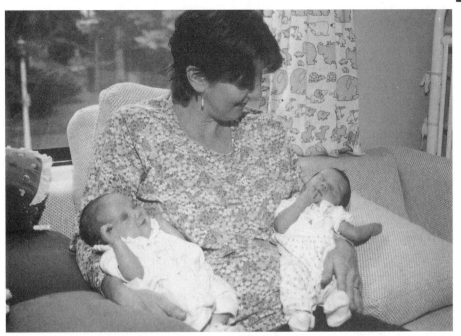

Eating well during pregnancy helps you grow healthy babies.

gain any weight during one month, or an actual weight loss in any given month should be looked at carefully by health care providers.

No matter how different the individual patterns of gain, gaining **at least** 40 to 50 pounds, or 18.5 to 23 kg, throughout twin pregnancies, with an additional 10 pounds, 4.5 kg, for triplet pregnancies, is associated with multiples who are born closer to term and at greater weights. Women in Cincinnati's La Leche League Multiples' group who delivered at full term and whose twins were of average birth weight typically gained 23 to 27 kg, or 50 to 60 pounds, during their pregnancies.

For single-infant pregnancies it usually is enough to recommend expectant mothers "eat to appetite." This suggestion can backfire when given to someone expecting multiples. Feelings of nausea may be exaggerated early in multiple pregnancies. Later in multiple pregnancy some women experience feelings of extreme fullness after eating even small amounts of food.

Although quantity is important when working toward a weight gain associated with better outcomes, the emphasis should be on the **quality** of the foods you eat if eating the recommended quantity is impossible. Ideas for eating quality foods and meeting nutritional requirements during multiple pregnancy follow in "Nutrition Hints." Acupuncture also has been used to relieve some pregnancy-related diet difficulties, such as severe pregnancy-related nausea or vomiting.

Another problem can occur in Western cultures where "thin is in," because it may be difficult to remember that pregnancy weight gain is very different than other weight gains. The babies' weights make up only a percentage of the total pregnancy weight gain. Other necessary physical adaptations to the demands of multiple pregnancy and the fact that your body is planning ahead for breastfeeding add important pounds. It's not unusual for mothers of multiples to lose two-thirds or more of the weight they gain during pregnancy within the first week of delivery. The rest may "fall off" within weeks of giving birth or melt away more slowly during the first year of breastfeeding.

If you or others sometimes lose sight of the importance of a large weight gain during a multiple pregnancy, post signs around your home to help you maintain the proper perspective. They might say: "I'm eating for three (four, or more)!" or "I'm not getting fat; I'm growing healthy babies (and keeping their placentas in good working order)."

Many large medical centers now employ dietitians who specialize in pregnancy and postpartum nutrition. Consulting with such a dietitian is important for any woman expecting multiples, but it is **crucial** if you:

- are carrying higher-order multiples;
- were significantly under or over weight-for-height prior to pregnancy;
- are anemic;
- are vegetarian;
- are currently breastfeeding an infant or toddler (see "Breastfeeding while pregnant" in this chapter);
- have a history of an eating disorder (or think you ever had);
- smoke (or your partner does);
- have a family history of allergies (or your partner does);
- have a pre-existing health condition that is affected by diet in any way;
- develop a health condition that is or may be affected by diet, such as gestational diabetes or pregnancy-induced hypertension (PIH/preeclampsia);
- are preoccupied with your body size or weight gain;
- often find it difficult to eat enough for whatever reason.

Nutrition Hints

What to Eat

Foods high in protein are especially important for building babies' bodies and keeping placenta(s) working well. In addition to adequate protein, many of the calories you take in should be in the form of complex carbohydrates, such as pastas, rice, and whole grain breads or cereals.

MINIMUM Number of Daily Servings*

	Pre-pregnancy	Single Pregnancy	Twin Pregnancy	Triplet Pregnancy**
Grains Group: Bread, Cereal, Rice & Pasta One serving= 1 slice bread, ½ oz. pasta, rice 1 oz./1C. cereal 1 oz.=30 ml/30 gm	6-11	7-11	8-12	9-12
Vegetable & Fruit Groups One serving= 1 whole/ 1 C./8 oz. raw ½ C./4 oz. cooked ¾ C./ 6 oz. juice	3V & 2F	4V & 3F	4-5V/3-4F	5V/4F
Dairy Group: Milk, Yogurt & Cheese One serving= 1 C./8 oz. milk 1 C./8 oz. yogurt 1 oz. cheese	2-3	3-4	4-5	5-6
Meat, Poultry, Fish, Eggs, Dry Beans & Nuts Group One serving= 2 oz. meat, poultry, fish 2 eggs 1 C./8 oz. dry beans 4 Tbsp. peanut butter	2-3	3-4	4-5	5-6
Fats Group: Oils, Processed Snack Foods & Sweets	Use sparingly.	Get from meat, eggs & dairy products as needed for adequate gain.		
Non-alcoholic, uncaffeinated beverages One serving= 8 oz./1 cup	6+	Enough so that urine remains pale yellow		

Number of servings is approximate.
**Increase servings in each food group by ½-1 serving for each additional fetus.*

MULTIPLE PREGNANCY

Your body uses the energy from carbohydrates to fuel its usual functions, which frees the protein to "build" healthy babies and maintain the placenta(s). Fats also are used for fuel, plus they are a crucial building block in each baby's brain and nervous system development. A fat-free diet is not a goal during multiple pregnancy.

Certain nutrients help minimize maternal anemia, which in turn help maintain the health of your babies and their placentas. Most doctors and midwives recommend a multi-vitamin and mineral supplement during pregnancy. Sometimes higher doses of certain vitamins or minerals are suggested during a multiple pregnancy. Since there is divided opinion on whether extra supplements are helpful, do not take additional vitamins or minerals without first discussing it with your health care provider. You also may want to discuss it with a dietitian specializing in nutrition during the childbearing year.

Whether or not additional vitamins and minerals are advised during your multiple pregnancy, such supplements **do not** replace the essential nutrients and calories in food. Also, some vitamins, especially the fat-soluble ones, and minerals can be toxic in higher doses. If your health care provider does recommend supplemental vitamins or minerals, continue to eat a well-balanced diet that enables you to gain necessary weight.

The food pyramid was developed by the US Departments of Agriculture and Health and Human Services as a guide to making food choices. It illustrates the types and amounts of foods that should be eaten daily for optimal nutrition. Meeting daily pyramid guidelines is simpler than counting calories for most people. The following chart compares pre-pregnancy and single pregnancy nutrition with that for multiple pregnancies. (The amounts indicated are only an approximation.)

Don't panic if the amount of food to be eaten during a multiple pregnancy seems overwhelming. Most single-serving sizes on the chart are small compared to the servings many persons usually eat. For example, a typical bowl of pasta would meet the requirement for three to four servings from the grain group.

Make the most of meals and snacks by eating foods in as close to their natural states as possible. Focus on whole grain breads, cereals, pastas, lean meats, low-fat dairy products, fresh fruits, vegetables, and 100 percent juices. Foods rich in animal protein, including dairy products and eggs, usually will supply most of the daily requirement for fats. However, don't be afraid of a little extra fat intake during a multiple pregnancy. Simply eat fewer processed or canned foods, which often are higher in (saturated) fats, salt, or refined sugars, and have lost vitamins and minerals in the manufacturing process. Sauté or fry foods in unsaturated vegetable oils instead of in a saturated fat, such as lard.

Try eating smaller amounts frequently—nibble all day long! This is especially helpful if you regularly experience nausea, quickly feel overfull, or are put on bedrest. Even if you enjoy eating several larger meals, be sure to snack between meals. A healthy snack could consist of a half sandwich of lean meat, liverwurst (braunschweiger), peanut butter, or egg salad on whole grain bread or crackers. Follow the high-protein snack immediately, or about an hour later, with a fresh fruit or vegetable or its juice.

Women often lose weight when put on bedrest. If you are on bedrest, have a helper fill a cooler with healthful snacks and beverages each morning. Keep the cooler within reach so you can continue to work on growing healthy babies.

A liquid food, such as soup, often is easier on a stomach having little extra room. Meat, poultry, fish, lentil, split pea, and bean soups are good choices because they are rich in protein. A salad containing a variety of greens, and other vegetables or legumes, is another nutritious but lightweight meal. Toss slices of lean meat, poultry, fish, tofu, or cheese in with salads for extra protein. Middle Eastern and Asian cuisines generally are highly nutritious, light on the stomach, and known for many complete-protein vegetarian dishes.

Don't forget the nutritional power packed in every egg. Eggs are an excellent source of protein and iron. Cook eggs first—whether scrambled, fried, or boiled—because raw egg may carry bacteria that can cause food poisoning.

Blending milk or yogurt with fruit makes a nutritious, high-protein shake drink that should not overfill. Some women add powdered milk, wheat germ, or a protein powder to boost the nutrition in shakes or smoothies without adding volume in their stomachs. If you've thought about buying a protein powder or one of the flavored high-protein, high vitamin and mineral beverages, be aware that not all brands are created equal. And these beverages can only supplement your diet; they do not replace the nutrition in well-balanced meals and snacks. Before you try one of these commercially prepared drinks, discuss the potential advantages and disadvantages of different brands with your obstetrical health care provider, or with a dietitian specializing in perinatal nutrition.

Getting enough fluid also is important during a multiple pregnancy. You are less likely to experience constipation, urinary tract infections, and preterm labor if you drink enough liquid each day. As long as the color of your urine appears pale yellow, you probably are getting enough liquid. Add more fluid to your diet if your urine becomes dark yellow in color. However, some vitamins or medications pass into urine and may change its color.

You might find it helps to keep a large sports mug that has a self-contained straw nearby during the day and on a bedside table at night.

Fill it with water and squeeze in the juice of lemon or lime wedges for extra vitamin C. Or alternate lemon water with 100 percent juices. This large mug will become indispensable during the early months of breastfeeding. (See Chapter 23, "For Mothers Only")

Taking Charge in Other Ways

Exercise

Ask your doctor or midwife about exercise during multiple pregnancy. Normal activity can increase your appetite and improve your general health. However, you probably will have to curtail many activities earlier with a multiple pregnancy. Avoiding strenuous aerobic exercise, any exercise that makes you feel short of breath or causes you to break into a sweat, may be recommended much earlier. Such exercise puts more stress on a cardio-respiratory system that already is working harder to accommodate multiples. It also raises core body temperature, which can have harmful effects throughout pregnancy. You may be told to avoid hot tubs while pregnant for the same reason. Your obstetrical care provider may recommend taking an earlier leave of absence from your place of employment if your job is strenuous or if you are unable to take periodic rest breaks during the last 10 to 15 weeks of pregnancy.

Pregnancy-related physical changes affect fine and large motor skills, especially during the last trimester. Multiple pregnancy often has a greater effect on motor activities. Your center of gravity shifts earlier and more significantly during multiple pregnancy, which can affect your balance. And you are receiving multiple doses of those pregnancy hormones that are floating around loosening your ligaments.

Women expecting multiples often tire more easily or feel short of breath with activity. If you're anemic, this tiring or shortness of breath often is exaggerated. Also, two or more babies "take over" space in your upper abdomen that usually is occupied by the lungs—among other organs in the vicinity—giving the lungs less room to expand at a time when you're breathing for three or more.

Most women continue to perform normal daily activities throughout twin, and some triplet, pregnancies. However, most also find their bodies tell them to slow down considerably during the last 10 to 15 weeks. If you are used to an active lifestyle, it may seem strange to "allow" yourself frequent rest breaks during the day. Some women even say they feel guilty taking these very necessary breaks!

You may be more comfortable during the last trimester of pregnancy if you wear a wide **maternity support "belt"** under your clothes and around your lower abdomen. Expectant mothers have reported that these belts decrease aches in the lower back and pelvic area by supporting, or "holding," some of the weight of the growing babies. Ask your obstetric care provider to discuss the possible advantages or disadvantages about using such belts in your particular case before investing in one.

Listen to your body when it tells you to sit down and prop your feet up. It is telling you what you and your babies need at that moment. Intermittent rest breaks take the weight of the babies off of your pelvic area, which usually feels better. And they can help your body use food energy more efficiently.

Breastfeeding while Pregnant

If you are currently breastfeeding an infant, toddler, or older child, immediate weaning generally is advised once multiples are diagnosed. Breastfeeding during pregnancy, in and of itself, is not considered to be a risk factor for preterm labor. However, it is considered an additional risk in the presence of any other factor associated with preterm labor and birth, and multiple pregnancy is highly associated with preterm labor and birth. Also, continuing to make milk for the current nursling "competes" for nutrients that a mother's body would use to meet the additional physical demands on her body due to two growing babies and their placentas.

It is vitally important to the health of your unborn babies, the current nursling, and yourself that you be completely honest with your obstetric and pediatric care providers about the current nursling's breastfeeding pattern and needs. If you are concerned about an abrupt weaning, you might discuss with your care providers the risks and benefits of a more gradual weaning process during the first half of an apparently healthy twin pregnancy. (Gradual weaning is less likely to be considered a possibility during higher-order multiple pregnancy.)

A natural weaning often occurs before the second trimester because as the placenta(s) assumes production of the hormones that maintain pregnancy, milk production often decreases. You and your child's pediatric care provider must also consider the nutritional needs of the current nursling, especially for an infant, when twin pregnancy is making so many demands on your body.

If immediate weaning seems warranted after weighing the risks and benefits with care providers, contact a La Leche League Leader or an International Board Certified Lactation Consultant (IBCLC) for ideas that can minimize any physical or emotional discomforts for you and your nursling. (See "Resources.") Should a more gradual weaning be considered as safe, you still may want to speak with a Leader or IBCLC for ideas to begin decreasing the daily number of breastfeedings. You also may need to include an additional several hundred calories and extra protein daily to the twin pregnancy diet until weaning is complete.

What to Avoid

You'll want to keep the babies and their placenta(s) free of all harmful substances. Tobacco, alcohol, and street drug use are associated with preterm delivery and low birth weight newborns for single pregnancies, so it isn't difficult to imagine their effects on multiple pregnancies. Never take a medication unless you've checked on its relative safety with your doctor or midwife. It is extremely important to let your health care provider know if you or your spouse regularly smokes or drinks alcoholic beverages, or if either of you recently used or took any prescription, over-the-counter, herbal, or street drugs.

Tobacco use is the most common among harmful substance abuses. Smoking decreases the amount of oxygen reaching the placenta(s), and therefore, the babies receive less oxygen, too. Smoking can interfere with appetite and it reduces your body's ability to absorb or use many vitamins and minerals, so it also affects the kinds and amount of nutrients the babies and the placenta(s) receive and contributes to maternal anemia. Over time areas of the placenta(s) deteriorate due to the decreases in oxygen and necessary nutrients.

You won't want to expose yourself and your unborn babies to secondhand smoke either, since it also interferes with placental blood flow. Ask persons who smoke to do so outdoors. Babies and young children exposed to secondhand smoke are more likely to suffer from colds, croup, bronchitis, and other respiratory illnesses. If you insist on a smoke-free home to improve the health of you and your babies during pregnancy, it will have become a habit by the time you bring your babies home. And feel free to lovingly remind those who must step outside to smoke that they are to become role models for two or more curious children. Of course, they won't have to go outside at all once they quit.

Mind-Body Connection

Is it possible that women expecting multiples deliver prematurely more often than need be partly because their health care providers, family, and friends keep telling them it will happen? No one has studied whether it might contribute to the creation of a self-fulfilling prophecy. But it certainly can't help. Many mothers mention the anxiety they felt due to a constant repetition of this message. Instead of imagining a joyful birth followed by early breastfeeding and interactions with babies in the immediate postpartum, there often is an expectation of pregnancy and birth problems with newborn intensive care unit (NICU) stays for the babies.

It is possible to be prepared for potential problems without becoming preoccupied by them. If you are eating well, avoiding potentially harmful substances, and being sensible about exercise and rest, you are doing all that's within your power to give birth to healthy babies. Worrying about

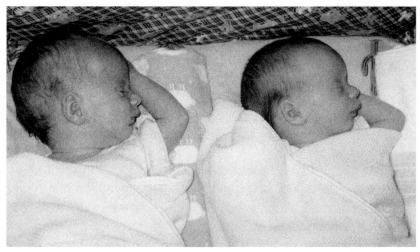

Taking good care of yourself during a multiple pregnancy can help you give birth to healthy newborns.

what **might** occur wastes mental energy on factors beyond your control and improves nothing, even if you do experience a sign of some complication.

Instead of worrying, invest a few minutes several times a day on relaxation and visualization exercises that often decrease anxiety and improve the function of your cardiac and respiratory systems. This in turn increases the amount of oxygen and nutrients available to the babies via their placenta(s). Take advantage of frequent rest breaks to practice these exercises. Most women prefer to close their eyes while practicing relaxation and visualization, but it isn't always essential. Many can "see" with the mind's eye when their other eyes are wide open—a useful skill if taking a rest break during the workday. There are many relaxation and visualization scenarios, but this one is fairly simple. It will take longer to read the following example than to actually practice it.

- Take two or three deep breaths, breathing in through your nose and out through your mouth.
- Beginning with the crown of your head, work down your body and check for muscular tension—face to neck and back to upper extremities to abdomen to pelvis, and finally to lower extremities. Consciously relax tense muscles. Let it melt away and move downward, until all built-up tension exits through the bottoms of your feet.
- Figuratively watch the air you breathe in as it enters your nose, travels to your lungs, passes into your circulation, and moves throughout your body—picking up different-colored nutrients from your food as it flows through your intestinal tract.

- Follow the flow of oxygen and nutrients as they leave your circulation, enter placental circulation, and spread through the placenta(s)—keeping the tissues healthy.
- Visualize oxygen and nutrients entering each baby's cord. Watch each multiple literally grow within your uterus as the oxygen and nutrients circulate and are used by their bodies.
- Talk to your babies—mental conversations work. Tell them how much you love them and that you are doing everything you can to help them grow and develop.
- When you are ready to leave them, travel back to your lungs. Become aware of your breathing again. And as you breathe out through your mouth, release with each breath any worry or anxiety you've been feeling.
- Once you feel calm and relaxed, open your eyes if they've been closed, stretch and move around again.

If you believe in a higher spiritual power, place yourself and your babies in the "hands" of that being. Ask that higher power to take on your tension and worry for you as you pray or meditate. You literally may feel your tension and worries let go or lift away. Many expectant mothers say this method has helped reduce anxiety about any risks of multiple pregnancy.

Chapter Four
What to Do If...

It would be wonderful if you could be assured of giving birth to full-term multiples, each weighing more than 2500 gm (5 lb, 8 oz), rooting eagerly at your breast soon after birth, simply by eating well and gaining sufficient weight, exercising sensibly, and avoiding harmful substances. However, there are no guarantees. A woman can do everything "right" during a multiple pregnancy and still experience a complication, because many aspects of multiple pregnancy are beyond the expectant mother's control.

If you're now asking, "What's the point of doing everything right?" it may help to know that the consequences of complications may be minimized by health habits that maintain your health during pregnancy, build strong baby bodies, and provide for optimal function of the placenta(s). Following diet and exercise recommendations presented in the previous chapter still should lead to the healthiest outcome possible for you and your babies—even if the pregnancy or birth includes a complication. You will also have the satisfaction of knowing you did everything that you possibly could for you and all your babies.

Recognizing the early signs of common complications can also make a difference, since reporting symptoms and getting immediate treatment will often stop or slow the progress of several of the most common complications, such as preterm labor and delivery, and allow the pregnancy to continue longer. Sometimes an extra week or two of pregnancy makes a big, positive difference for the babies' health. For other complications, the obstetrical care provider may recommend delivering multiples early as immediate treatment. For instance, little or no growth of one or more of the babies for days to weeks may mean that it is safer for the babies to be outside the uterus than in it.

Signs to Watch and Report
Preterm Labor
Labor occurring before the 37th week of pregnancy is one of the most common complications of multiple pregnancy. When such labor progresses and is followed by preterm birth, it is associated with the most complications for the babies because their immature physical systems are not ready to function optimally outside the uterus. The earlier preterm labor is followed by birth, the more likely infant complications are to occur. Fortunately, early intervention can often halt preterm labor or at least postpone delivery.

Fetal fibronectin. Your obstetric care provider may recommend testing vaginal secretions for a protein called "fetal fibronectin" (fFN) every other week from about the 24th to 34th week of pregnancy. This protein essentially "glues" the amnion, or bag of waters, to the inner wall of the uterus. It is common in vaginal secretions until about the 22nd week of pregnancy, but fFN should not be found in secretions after this time until at least the 34th week of pregnancy. Research has shown that an increase in fFN between the 22nd and 34th week of pregnancy is associated with a significant incidence of preterm labor within two weeks of the testing.

Obtaining a sample of the vaginal secretions is similar to the procedure for any pelvic exam. The care provider inserts a speculum into the vagina and wipes the secretions with special swabs, which are then tested for fFN. While obtaining the sample, the care provider may also check to see if the cervix has begun to thin out or dilate. A negative sample is considered reassuring, and in the absence of cervical dilatation, a woman is usually able to go about her business for the next two weeks. When a test is positive for fFN, the care provider may want to initiate interventions for preterm labor.

Know the signs. Contact your obstetrical care provider **immediately** if you experience **any** of the following warning signs of preterm labor:

- four or more uterine contractions in an hour—entire uterus is tight, hard, "balled up" to the touch; may or may not feel painful;
- intermittent or persistent/constant low backache;

- intermittent or persistent/constant pelvic pressure-may "spread" to the back or thigh area(s);
- intermittent or persistent/constant menstrual-type cramping;
- increased vaginal discharge—whether mucus, blood, or water (leaking of amniotic fluid or definite rupture/burst).

Painless uterine contractions, called Braxton-Hicks contractions, occur throughout any pregnancy. Studies have shown that Braxton-Hicks contractions occur more frequently in multiple pregnancies, and they may be more noticeable in a uterus stretched by multiple babies. Because you may be more aware of such contractions, you may want to wait and see what happens before "bothering" your doctor or midwife. Don't wait.

If you have or think you are having more than two or three contractions an hour: 1) begin timing how often one occurs and how long each lasts, 2) empty your bladder, 3) drink several glasses of water, and 4) lie on your left side. Once you've had four contractions within an hour, whether you feel any pain with them or not, call your care provider right away. Do not wait to see if they stop, increase in number, or get stronger.

Should you experience any bleeding, with or without contractions, call your care provider immediately. Bleeding may be associated with certain complications of the placenta(s). Such complications are more common in multiple pregnancy because the placenta(s) take up more space.

Treatment for Preterm Labor

Generally physicians recommend immediate hospitalization for suspected preterm labor. They will want to determine whether the contractions are true labor contractions—contractions that cause cervical change, particularly cervical dilatation. Bedrest, fluids, often given intravenously (IV), and special tocolytic medications to decrease the "irritability" of the uterus usually are used to stop true preterm labor. Also, you may be given an injection of a corticosteroid that has been shown to enhance the maturity of babies' lungs.

Blood will be drawn to see if you should be treated for anemia, a common development for women during multiple pregnancy. In addition, if true labor occurs early in pregnancy or a woman has a history of preterm labor, physicians may advise stitching the cervix closed in a procedure known as a cerclage.

Most women are discharged once contractions stop, but many continue on bedrest and tocolytic medications at home. These treatments have been found to prolong a pregnancy after a confirmed episode of preterm labor. Home treatment usually includes a system to monitor further contractions or uterine activity, such as bringing in a home health nurse to make regular calls or home visits. The nurse often becomes a wonderful resource for answering questions and a sounding board for sharing your concerns.

Routinely prescribing bedrest or tocolytic medication during the last few weeks, and even months, of a multiple pregnancy in an effort to prevent preterm labor is common in some areas. However, the use of these treatments prior to a confirmed episode of preterm labor is very controversial. The thinking is that bedrest shifts the weight of the babies to decrease the pressure against the cervix and increase blood flow to the uterus and the placenta(s). Routine tocolytic use is thought to lessen uterine activity, and therefore contractions, during the remainder of the pregnancy. Yet there is no solid evidence to support the use of either bedrest or tocolytic medication as preventive measures for preterm labor and birth during twin pregnancy.

The preventive effect on higher-order multiple pregnancies is less controversial, but bedrest has not been found to be helpful unless it is initiated before the 28th week of pregnancy. Still, there is much to learn about the effectiveness of routinely prescribing either bedrest or tocolysis without a confirmed episode of preterm labor even in higher-order multiple pregnancies because of the profound side-effects associated with both of these treatments.

Long-term bedrest is associated with maternal muscle weakening, diminished appetite with decreased food intake, and feelings of being "down" or "blue." Any of these side-effects may affect a woman's physical and mental health for the remainder of the pregnancy and her physical and emotional ability to care for her babies after delivery. Tocolytic medications are associated with mild to severe side-effects, which differ depending on the action of the particular drug or combination of drugs.

It is crucial to discuss all aspects of preterm labor treatment with your health care provider. Ask why tocolysis or bedrest is recommended and whether there are alternatives. Ask to see the research reports that support the recommended treatments. Discuss the potential benefits, risks, and possible side-effects of any treatment plan. Be sure you understand the signs and symptoms of all possible side-effects.

When bedrest is prescribed, find out what your care provider means by this term. Different health care providers define "bedrest" differently. It might mean anything from restricting physical activities and propping your feet up for one or more extended rest periods each day to lying on your left side and staying off your feet completely. Sometimes brief bathroom breaks and visits to the doctor are the only activities allowed. Most definitions of bedrest include a recommendation to begin a leave of absence from a woman's place of employment, since few job descriptions can accommodate long rest breaks with feet propped.

If bedrest becomes important to continue the pregnancy after preterm labor is diagnosed, ask your care provider to provide the names of other mothers who have been on bedrest during pregnancy. These mothers often can provide tips that help you maintain perspective, accomplish work, and make the time seem to go faster. A local support group for parents of multiples often has information or contacts. There is even a USA organization with a related web site for mothers who are or have been on bedrest during a pregnancy. (See "Resources.") Ask to be referred to a facility that specializes in sports medicine so you can learn exercises that will help you avoid the loss of muscle mass and related physical strength.

Women often are given extra fluids when admitted to the hospital in preterm labor. This is because dehydration is associated with contractions. Quickly hydrating a woman often helps decrease contractions for the time being. Some women think it then follows that preterm labor and delivery can be avoided and pregnancy weight gains safely limited as long as they drink large amounts of fluid. Wrong! Poor diet and inadequate food intake are also associated with preterm labor contractions. You, your babies, and their placenta(s) depend on your nourishing diet—one that includes varied nutrients, plenty of calories, and sufficient fluid.

Fetal Well-Being

Fetal Growth Restriction

Multiple babies essentially "compete" for space and nutrients during pregnancy. Sometimes one receives more nutrients and grows better than a multiple sibling(s) because of where or the way the placenta(s) or umbilical cord(s) attach or develop. When a baby is not growing as well, it is said to be affected by fetal growth restriction (FGR), which may also be called intrauterine growth restriction (IUGR). Differences, or discordancy, in babies' growth rates typically begin to show up at 28 weeks of pregnancy or later—about the time growth rates slow down for twins or triplets when compared to a single baby during later pregnancy. (This may occur earlier for higher-order multiples.) Because of this, health care providers want to keep a close eye on each baby, which gets rather tricky when one may be hiding behind, below, or above another.

Twin-to-Twin Transfusion Syndrome (TTTS)

TTTS occurs only in identical twins who share a placenta. Of the approximate 75 percent of identical twins who share a placenta, about 15 percent will develop abnormal blood vessel connections within the shared placenta that affect the amount and direction of blood flow. Depending on the type of vascular connections, identical sets may be affected to different degrees, but the one receiving increased blood flow is always called the **recipient** twin and the one receiving less is termed the **donor** twin.

The recipient twin receives too much blood, which may overload his cardiovascular system and lead to congestive heart failure in severe cases.

Since the donor twin receive less blood, he is affected by anemia, which may vary from mild to severe. Identical twins affected by TTTS look quite different on ultrasound. The recipient twin is significantly larger and there may be too much fluid in his amniotic sac. The donor twin is growth-restricted and his amniotic sac may contain too little fluid. In severe cases one or both babies may die, so twins suspected or known to have TTTS will be followed closely during pregnancy. Some TTTS symptoms may be treated during the pregnancy, but if staying in the uterus becomes more of a danger for the babies, it may be necessary to deliver them early.

Diagnostic Testing during Multiple Pregnancy

Ultrasonography

When an early prenatal physical examination and evaluation of certain factors in a woman's blood sample indicate multiples, an ultrasound exam is usually recommended to confirm whether a woman is carrying two or more. Ultrasound allows obstetrical care providers to "see" the babies by "bouncing" ultrasonic sound waves off the babies' body tissues. This creates a "picture" of the developing babies which can help care providers determine the number as well as measure the growth and development of the babies while in the uterus.

Ultrasound has confirmed multiple pregnancies as early as five to six weeks. First trimester diagnosis has resulted in an interesting side-effect of ultrasound's role in the early confirmation of multiple pregnancy—the discovery of a **vanishing twin** syndrome in which at least one multiple confirmed early in a pregnancy has "disappeared" on a later ultrasound. Some instances of early pregnancy bleeding now are thought to be related to the miscarrying of a multiple, but not all cases of "vanishing" multiples are associated with bleeding. Some instances probably are related to errors in the interpretation of an early ultrasound, so a repeat ultrasound within weeks of the first one is often suggested when a diagnosis is made early in pregnancy. When a multiple does "vanish," the development of the remaining multiple(s) usually progresses normally, but many women still experience feelings of disappointment or deep sadness and loss.

Once multiples are definitely diagnosed and the babies' initial measurements taken to help establish gestational (pregnancy) age and a "due date," additional ultrasounds often are postponed until after 24 weeks of pregnancy. At this point care providers may recommend **serial ultrasounds**—ultrasound examination at regular two to three week intervals. Serial ultrasounds may be recommended earlier for higher-order multiple pregnancies, and more frequent ultrasound will be suggested if an extreme change is seen in the growth rate of one or more babies.

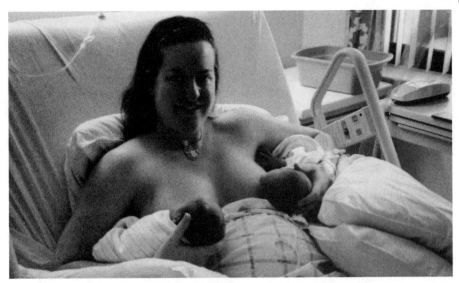

Healthy babies are ready to breastfeed soon after birth.

During the last 10 to 12 weeks of pregnancy an in-depth ultrasound exam, referred to as a **biophysical profile** (BPP), can help health practitioners evaluate the babies' breathing and body movements, the amount of fluid in their amniotic sacs, the function of the placenta(s) and umbilical cord(s). Ultrasound also may be used for doppler flow studies, which allow health practitioners to visualize blood flow in a baby's umbilical cord. These studies can help them determine how well the placenta(s) is functioning.

There has been some controversy regarding the routine use of ultrasound during pregnancy since its widespread introduction in the USA in the mid to late 1970s. However, ultrasound is considered a valid and important diagnostic tool during multiple pregnancy, since early confirmation and monitoring of the individual babies' growth later in pregnancy can have a significant effect on the health of the babies and mother.

Nonstress Test

Another test care providers may recommend during the last 10 to 12 weeks of pregnancy as a way of keeping an eye on the babies' well-being is called a nonstress test (NST). During a NST you recline in a semi-sitting position and belts equipped with special monitors are fastened around your abdomen. One belt picks up uterine contractions and babies' movements. The other belts, and the number depends on the number of babies you're carrying, record babies' heart rates. The belts are attached to a nearby machine that translates the information coming from the monitors into a written recording. The test usually takes about 20 to 40 minutes of sitting fairly still while the machine records information.

Care providers then look at the tracings of babies' heart rates and compare them with uterine and baby activity. This gives them an idea of how the individual babies' are responding to change. Certain heart rate patterns are associated with a baby's healthy response to environmental changes; other patterns may indicate that one or more babies are having some difficulty. Depending on the perceived problem, a repeat NST or an immediate BPP ultrasound may be advised to get more complete information.

A similar test deliberately induces uterine contractions by using a synthetic oxytocin (Pitocin) or nipple stimulation. It is called a contraction stress test (CST). When oxytocin (Pitocin) is used, CST may be referred to as an oxytocin challenge test (OCT). CST using breast stimulation to induce contractions is called a breast self-stimulation test (BSST). Because of the risk of inducing preterm labor, CST is not recommended during multiple pregnancy.

Counting Fetal Movements

You can help care providers keep an eye on your babies' development during pregnancy by becoming aware of each baby's movements. This is referred to as a "Kick Count." You may already have noticed that each seems to move in a certain spot and has a particular pattern of movement during the course of a day. If you haven't paid attention to this yet, you may be surprised how easy it usually is to identify each baby.

At about 28 weeks of pregnancy, and possibly a little earlier with higher-order multiple pregnancies:

- count each baby's movements at about the same time each day until each has moved 10 times;
- track, on a separate sheet for each baby, how long it takes each to move 10 times;
- chart the types of movements noticed for each, such as vigorous "kicking" versus a more rhythmic turning.

If you notice that any of the babies is taking longer each day to reach the 10 movements, contact your obstetrical care provider. Should you ever notice one suddenly making very strong movements, which are then followed by a sudden stopping of movement, **call your care provider immediately.** Difficulty counting a baby's movements may mean that one or more babies are napping at the time you've chosen to count their movements or one simply may be harder to identify because of the babies' positions in the uterus. If you can't distinguish which baby is which, you probably can develop sensitivity to their general patterns of movement at certain times of the day. Report any real change in the babies' patterns. It never hurts to report questionable findings and it may really help.

Maternal Issues
Pregnancy-Induced Hypertension (PIH)

PIH, or the development of high maternal blood pressure during pregnancy, used to be called toxemia, and it is the most common maternal complication of multiple pregnancy. It occurs two to three times more often in multiple pregnancies. The cause(s) of PIH and why it is more common in multiple pregnancy still are not well understood. It also may be referred to as **preeclampsia** or **eclampsia,** according to which category it falls into. Eclampsia is the most severe form, but PIH rarely progresses to this stage in developed countries where an increased awareness of the early signs of PIH has led to earlier diagnosis and intervention.

Obstetrical care providers check for PIH during each prenatal visit by weighing you, testing your urine for protein, taking your blood pressure, and checking your reflexes. However, PIH can develop between prenatal visits, so it can help to know that the **warning signs** of mild PIH are:

- sudden but sustained increase in an expectant mother's blood pressure;
- sudden swelling or puffiness in the face and hands related to extreme fluid retention;
- swelling of the ankles or lower legs that is unrelieved after propping the feet and legs up;
- sudden and excessive weight gain that is related to the fluid retention.

The development of any of these symptoms should be reported to the care provider immediately.

Severe PIH is associated with the warning signs listed above and often one or more of the following is also present:

- headache, blurred vision, or seeing spots in front of the eyes;
- pain in the area of the stomach or left, upper abdomen;
- nausea and vomiting;
- shortness of breath or "wet" breath sounds;
- exaggerated feelings of tension or irritability.

It is crucial to **contact your care provider immediately** if you experience any symptom of severe PIH whether or not you have had or been treated for milder PIH. At times PIH progresses quickly, and milder signs don't always occur before a warning sign of more severe PIH. Severe

PIH increases the risk of maternal seizures (eclampsia), which can affect the babies' oxygen supply.

Treatment for PIH depends on its severity. Mild PIH often is treated at home. Bedrest may be recommended and your diet may be reviewed for adequate protein. Severe restriction of salt or the use of diuretics to decrease swelling have been found ineffective in treating PIH and are no longer used. Your care provider probably will want to see you more frequently and measures for testing the babies' well-being might be recommended more often.

Severe PIH is treated with bedrest in the hospital and IV medications to decrease the risk of a seizure. Depending on a woman's blood pressure, a medication to lower blood pressure may be prescribed. Sometimes a sedative is suggested if feelings of tension or irritability continue. The babies' well-being will be monitored closely.

Preterm Delivery

Unavoidable Preterm Birth

Sometimes preterm labor cannot be halted or prenatal tests may indicate that the babies can no longer safely remain in the uterus. Unless labor is progressing rapidly or compromised babies must be delivered immediately, it is likely that your care provider will recommend additional tests or treatments in either of these cases. When birth can be delayed for at least 24 hours, care providers usually recommend that you receive an injection of a steroid that has been found to quickly advance lung maturation in unborn babies.

Doctors may want to do an **amniocentesis** in which a small amount of amniotic fluid is withdrawn from each baby's sac to test for substances that indicate whether the babies' lungs are mature enough for them to breathe without assistance outside the uterus. By using ultrasound and then injecting a small amount of a harmless dye into a sac from which amniotic fluid already has been drawn, doctors can be sure they do not miss testing the fluid of any baby or retest the same baby. Some research indicates that the stress of competing for nutrients may help some unborn multiples' lungs mature a little earlier in pregnancy than those of single-born infants.

If the tests show that the lungs of one or more babies are not yet mature, obstetric and neonatal care providers should include you in a discussion to weigh the risks of preterm delivery with those of remaining in a less safe uterine environment.

It can be scary to think about the possibility of complications. However, it is even scarier to be faced with a complication after missing the early warning signs that might have minimized the consequences. When it comes to your health and that of your unborn babies, you are likely to be the first one who becomes aware that something is not "right."

Trust your knowledge of yourself and your babies. You know your body, its response to the pregnancy so far, and the behaviors or responses of your unborn babies better than anyone. If some change occurs, whether it is obvious, "just a feeling," or a sense that something isn't quite right, contact your obstetrical care provider right away. And if your care provider recommends a treatment that you don't yet feel comfortable with, advocate for yourself and your babies. Ask questions, discuss benefits and risks, and explore possible alternatives until you clearly understand how a test or treatment is in your and your babies' best interests.

Chapter 5
Getting Ready to Breastfeed Two, Three, or More Newborns

Breastfeeding is the ideal way to feed and nurture a human baby whether that baby comes alone or as part of a set. There is no reason to change your decision to breastfeed simply because multiples are expected. Many mothers have breastfed multiples in sets of two, three, or more babies.

No matter what the circumstances of your babies' births, it is possible to breastfeed. Women have breastfed multiples after having surgical deliveries, a "surprise" extra baby, preterm births, multiples requiring long-term special care, personal complications, other small children at home, little or no household help, employment outside the home, or combinations of the above. Have confidence in your body's ability to adapt no matter what your particular situation.

Advantages of Breastfeeding Multiples

Breastfeeding provides numerous benefits for babies and their mother. The advantages of breastfeeding one baby are even more important and intense for multiples. Babies tend to be happier when they are healthy, and human milk is associated with better infant health. Caring for two or more multiples is bound to be easier when they are in optimal health.

Human milk is the most nutritious and balanced food available for human infants. It contains everything babies need for growth and development during the first several months, and it continues to provide important nutrients as other foods are added to the diet. Because human milk is made for human babies, sensitivity to a mother's milk is highly unlikely. Breastfed babies also tend to develop fewer allergies. Companies producing infant formulas strive to make their products more like human milk, but they will never be able to make a perfect match. A mother's milk keeps adapting to her own particular babies for however long they breastfeed.

Babies digest human milk more easily and quickly, and they use the nutrients in it more completely. For instance, the fats in human milk are tailor-made for human brain and nervous system development, and they are in a form that a baby's body can easily use—even if born preterm. Human milk is easier for all their little systems to use, or metabolize—from heart and lungs to intestinal tract and kidneys—which is especially important for preterm or sick newborn multiples, but is beneficial for all young babies. It is rare for fully breastfed babies to become constipated or suffer from diarrhea. Once each establishes a weight gain and breastfeeding is going well, you can quit keeping the charts that let you know which had a stool and when.

Immunity (antibody) factors in human milk help protect babies against many illnesses. Your milk will contain antibodies to any disease you've ever been exposed to. This aspect is important for multiples that have had to share antibodies passed through the placenta(s) before birth. It is even more important when multiples are preterm or when uterine conditions were less favorable for one or more babies. And since one sick multiple usually means the other(s) soon will catch whatever it is, you will appreciate the antibody protection of breastfeeding more than most. It can save quite a few dollars that might have been spent on visits to the babies' pediatric care provider or for prescription medications as well.

Breastfeeding ensures maximum skin contact with each baby. This advantage is particularly important with multiples whether they are fully or partially breastfed. It even applies when two babies always breastfeed simultaneously. No matter how hard you try, it is difficult, if not impossible, to give each multiple the time and attention you could give a single baby. Yet each multiple has the same needs as any single baby. Breastfeeding is the perfect way to meet the babies' need for food and their mother's arms.

It is more than twice as nice to curl up at night for feedings in your warm bed, rather than wake to crying babies who must wait for you to heat

A father's support can be essential to a mother who is breastfeeding multiples.

their meals. Breastfeeding is a one-handed task, which means you still have a free hand to tend to one multiple when another is feeding or you can feed two at once.

Cost is another important consideration. You will save twice (or more) the cost of infant formula and feeding equipment. The estimated cost of powdered formula is about **$100 per baby** per month; ready-to-feed varieties cost more. In general the less preparation involved, the higher a product's cost. If one or more babies has a sensitivity to an infant formula, you may end up using different products for each one, which adds to the cost and preparation time.

When mothers are surveyed, they often complain about the time it takes to prepare double, triple, or quadruple the amount of bottles and the work involved in keeping equipment clean and ready to use. Breastfeeding takes a lot of time too, but your time is directly invested in the babies instead of in preparation and cleanup.

Breastfeeding Goals

Have you thought about your goals for breastfeeding multiples? You may not have thought about it, but you probably do have goals. A breastfeeding goal is more likely to be achieved if you are aware of that goal. A goal is like a destination for a trip. If you haven't chosen a destination, it's going to be difficult to get there.

Committing a goal to paper is like marking your destination on a map. Once you decide on "how much" breastfeeding and for "how long," it helps to have a plan to reach the goal. You are more likely to reach your breastfeeding destination if you plan your route. Otherwise, you may come to some dead-ends or find yourself on the long and scenic route when you wanted the super highway.

Early postpartum is a time of confusion after the birth of even a single baby. It can be even more chaotic when bringing home two or more newborns. If one or more babies requires special care in a NICU for any length of time, you may feel pulled in several directions at once.

Many mothers question the decision to breastfeed during the early weeks when they and their babies are still learning to coordinate at least twice as many breastfeedings each day. Sleep deprivation may fog thinking and make it difficult to remember that caring for two, three, four, or more newborns takes more time no matter how they are fed.

A commitment to breastfeeding may be the single most important element in reaching your final breastfeeding destination. No one would say, "I'm going to try to make it to the city for my family reunion, but if something comes up, I'll stop or turn around." Travel often includes unexpected glitches, so once committed to making the trip, the traveler anticipates and prepares to handle a detour, flat tire, or some other difficulty that may occur.

To reach a breastfeeding destination, be positive about making the trip. Say to yourself and others, "I am going to breastfeed my babies," instead of, "I want to try to breastfeed." Plan the trip and prepare for a few obstacles along the way. You may be surprised at how much more confident you feel when you have a positive attitude and a plan.

Planning a "trip" with multiples involves developing short-term breastfeeding goals. These are like stages of the route that mark specific distances toward the final destination. On a day when reaching the final destination seems overwhelming, traveling one stage, or leg of the journey, usually appears manageable. Short-term breastfeeding goals keep a mother moving—another day, another week, another month. Achieving one goal motivates one to stay on the route until the next stage is reached.

An initial short-term goal may be to establish and maintain milk production for multiples, whether babies are able to go directly to breast or milk must be expressed for preterm or sick babies. Each multiple will have an individual approach to breastfeeding, and as the babies begin to breastfeed and you start to decipher their individual styles, your next goal may be to continue for a certain number of weeks before re-evaluating the route. The second goal should allow enough time for you and the babies to learn to breastfeed well.

Most mothers of multiples suggest setting an initial breastfeeding goal of at least six weeks. They say it takes at least that long to recover from the birth and give everyone involved time to learn to breastfeed. Other mothers set a shorter initial short-term goal. They commit to breastfeeding (or expressing/pumping breast milk) for one week. When they meet the one-week goal, they re-establish that same goal for one more week, and so on.

Put your short-term goals in writing and sign it like a contract. It may help even more if the "contract" specifies how you plan to reward yourself each time you meet a short-term goal. You should invest at least some of the money you save by breastfeeding multiples to reward yourself for providing your babies with nature's perfect food.

It's best to anticipate that you may face an occasional detour or wrong turn when multiple babies are along for the trip. Check out alternate breastfeeding routes in advance by reading this book and others on the subject. You'll want to be free to concentrate, especially for the first leg or two on the journey. Arrange ahead of time for someone else to take over household tasks, such as cooking, doing laundry, or caring for an older child. It also helps to have extra arms to hold a baby or two at times. (For more ideas on the aspect of preparation, see Chapter 7, "Getting Ready: Preparing for Multiples.")

Family and friends can make travel easier or more difficult. To gain their support, share information about breastfeeding with them and let them know how important breastfeeding is to you and the babies. When passengers understand the route and why you wish to take it, they are more likely to help you navigate and to cheer you on if an obstacle arises.

There are "mechanics" available if you want help with a mechanical problem or if you feel lost after taking a wrong road. La Leche League (LLL) Leaders and lactation consultants help mothers with breastfeeding questions or problems. (You will read more about them in the next section.) Post their numbers near a convenient telephone. In addition, it's always helpful to talk to a mother who has traveled the same road. Talking to someone else can help you regain "big picture" perspective on days when you worry that one or more baby will never learn to breastfeed well or when babies stage a breastfeeding marathon.

Once you develop your basic plan, refuse to listen if anyone tells you the trip can't be made. It can and it has. Many, many times. You know the route is flexible. If a detour pops up along the route, you can revise the plan to fit the circumstances. Who knows? You may have two, three, or even four storybook babies who are happy to adapt to any realistic breastfeeding routine. Then again, you may have to adapt the plan, perhaps only temporarily, if two, three, or four babies need extra time to learn to breastfeed or they consistently stagger feedings around the clock. Wait and see.

Additional Tools for Mapping Your Route

Written Information

There are numerous books and pamphlets containing good, general information about breastfeeding and lactation—the bodily process of producing milk. THE WOMANLY ART OF BREASTFEEDING published by La Leche League International, has been a popular breastfeeding guide for more than 40 years. The basic process of breastfeeding is the same no matter how many babies you will be feeding, so read, read, and read some more. Be sure to share written information with your husband, family, and friends.

Many childbirth classes incorporate breastfeeding information as part of the curriculum. Others offer separate breastfeeding classes. As much as your multiple pregnancy allows, take advantage of any such opportunities.

La Leche League (LLL)

The most valuable breastfeeding help is available at La Leche League (LLL) monthly meetings. In many areas an LLL meeting is the only place where a woman can actually see babies breastfeed and hear real mothers discuss the joys of nurturing babies this way. You can also watch mothers handle babies and see how they position them for breastfeeding. It can be reassuring to observe how babies of the same age are as different as they are similar, which may be of particular interest if your multiples are fraternal.

Begin attending LLL meetings early—before 20 to 24 weeks if possible, because your activities may be restricted later in pregnancy. If for any reason you are unable to attend meetings, contact a local LLL Leader and talk. The Leader will have information that will help you begin breastfeeding multiples. She may also know of a Leader or mother who has already breastfed multiple infants. It is really helpful to talk to someone who has "been there."

Being Prepared for Anything

Multiples are more likely than single infants to be cared for initially in a newborn intensive care unit (NICU), so there is a greater chance that you will have to express your milk for one or more of your babies during the early postpartum period. To prepare for this possiblility, ask your obstetrical care provider if the hospital where you are to deliver has automatic self-cycling breast pumps and double milk collection kits available. The double kit will allow you to pump milk from both breasts at once, which can save time and increase milk production. LLL Leaders usually know about equipment available in local hospitals. You could also contact the hospital and ask to speak with a lactation consultant or nurse on the postpartum unit. Either should have this information.

Ideally, the hospital will have an International Board Certified Lactation Consultant (IBCLC) on staff. She can give you an idea of what to expect at the hospital and how to get the help you need when you are on the postpartum unit. You may want to ask if nurses routinely apply a breast pump when a mother's condition initially makes it difficult for her to do so or whether you need to include that request on a birth plan. The LLL Leader or IBCLC will also know where you can rent a breast pump or buy a collection kit if you must continue to pump after hospital discharge. If the hospital does not have an IBCLC on staff, you might want to locate a lactation consultant who practices in your community. An LLL Leader usually is aware of IBCLCs working in an area or you can contact the professional organization for lactation consultants listed in "Resources."

Physical Preparation

A breast assessment specific for breastfeeding and lactation can be helpful in identifying potential physical factors, such as flat or inverted nipples, that might affect breastfeeding initiation. Many such factors resolve without treatment by the end of pregnancy. Also, treatments currently recommended for flat or inverted nipples or as prenatal preparation for breastfeeding are controversial during a single-infant pregnancy and are potentially dangerous during multiple pregnancy.

Due to the increased risk of preterm labor and delivery during multiple pregnancy, **avoid** prenatal nipple care and all nipple "exercises" or techniques that involve any type of nipple stimulation or nipple stretching. Nipple stimulation may stimulate uterine contractions. This warning also applies to the use of breast shells, which are devices that exert a gentle but steady suction pressure to draw out flat or inverted nipples. In addition, prenatal nipple care has been found to be of no value in the prevention of sore nipples and may actually damage a protective layer of cells on the nipples and areola.

A physical factor, such as a flat or inverted nipple, that persists into postpartum usually can be overcome with appropriate support from someone knowledgeable about breastfeeding and lactation. Sometimes multiple babies can be part of the solution. A factor that causes a problem for one multiple may create no impediment for another. Actually, the "work" of one multiple often helps another breastfeed better.

Many mothers have breastfed multiples and you can do it, too. Determine your goal, or "final destination," for breastfeeding and then develop a flexible plan to reach it. You can learn about possible routes by reading information about breastfeeding, going to special classes, and attending La Leche League meetings. Achieving short-term goals, or stages, may be motivating on days when the final destination seems out of reach. It also helps to know where to get help if you meet an obstacle in the road.

One final note about reaching the final destination—your multiple passengers will have a great deal of influence about the ultimate route that is followed, but you don't really get to meet them until you begin the trip. Therefore, you may as well accept that it is impossible to anticipate everything that could come up. There's no point in wasting time now worrying about potential problems that may, but then again may not, be far down the road. You've done what you can to get ready for the trip. La Leche League Leaders and lactation consultants* are prepared to assist you if a contingency plan becomes necessary. So relax and enjoy the rest of your pregnancy.

For an extensive discussion of the physical benefits of breastfeeding, read THE WOMANLY ART OF BREASTFEEDING, published by La Leche League International. Also, check the "Resources" section at the end of this book for information about obtaining other reading material, contacting LLL Leaders and lactation consultants, renting or purchasing breast pumps or other breastfeeding aids or devices, etc.

---

*This book uses the term lactation consultant to refer to a Board Certified Lactation Consultant (IBCLC).

Chapter 6
Getting Ready: Birth Preparation

A diagnosis of multiples has been made, your initial questions about multiple pregnancy have been answered, and you know you are doing all you can to help your babies grow while they reside inside you. To learn more about the "how-to" of breastfeeding multiples, you have been attending La Leche League meetings or you are talking to an LLL Leader by telephone. Now your thoughts may turn toward giving birth and other baby care issues for two or more newborns. What can you expect? How do you get ready?

Preparation for Birth

Obstetric care providers often view the labor and delivery of multiples differently than a single-infant birth. You, your partner, and your care provider may have to spend more time discussing possible labor and birth scenarios if you are to work together to achieve an optimal birth experience as well as optimal physical outcomes for you and each of your babies. The first step you can take is to learn more about the process of childbirth and explore your thoughts and feelings about labor and birth. Share information and feelings with your partner. Determine the kind of birth experience you consider to be ideal or meaningful. Discuss your views about birth with your doctor or midwife and ask for her/his view, especially for multiple births. If the care provider's view is not compatible with yours, ask for explanations. You and your partner will want to understand the rationale when the care provider's approach to multiple birth differs from the one you hold. It is your task to clear up any questions related to what you believe would be a safe and meaningful childbirth experience.

Vaginal vs. Surgical Birth

Surgical, or cesarean,* delivery is more common with multiple births. Almost 50 percent of US twin births are surgical deliveries; in another 10 percent, the first twin is delivered vaginally and the second is a surgical birth. Some increase in surgical births for twins would be expected because there are more instances of complications for babies and mothers, but such a high rate of surgical delivery for twins has been questioned. It seems to be due mostly to an increase in the "routine" surgical delivery of twins by some care providers.

The routine surgical delivery of twins appears to be unnecessary. Vaginal delivery is a reasonable consideration and outcomes are unchanged for the second twin in otherwise complicated twin pregnancies when:

- gestational length is at least 32 weeks,
- each baby is estimated to weigh at least 2000 gm (4 lb, 7 oz),
- the first baby presents in the vertex, or head down, position.

(The first twin is vertex in about 80 percent of sets.) However, research indicates that surgical delivery leads to better outcomes when the first twin is non-vertex (breech or transverse) and for the small percentage of identical twins that share an inner sac, or amnion. (Most identical twins do share the outer sac, or chorion.) Surgical delivery also is associated with improved outcomes for all higher-order multiple sets.

Birth Setting

A hospital birth generally is recommended for all multiple births. Even when a twin or triplet pregnancy is full-term, all babies are estimated to be over 2500 gm (5 lb, 8 oz), and the first baby is well "engaged" in a vertex presentation, there are increased risks for babies and mother during a multiple labor and birth. Because of the unpredictability of any subsequent (second or third) baby's position, the potential for pressure on its umbilical cord, and a concern about maternal bleeding, obstetric care providers prefer to deliver multiples where they are prepared for any emergency.

---

* This book uses the term "surgical" birth or delivery instead of cesarean birth. It is more accurate and it reminds all involved that the mother is recovering from major surgery while assuming the care of two or more infants

The precise presentation of the second (and third) baby cannot be determined until after the previous multiple's birth. Although few second (or third) babies do a complete flip of position during labor, it is fairly common for the second (or third) baby to find itself in a somewhat "cockeyed" position as it enters the birth canal. Such "malpositions" can increase the physical stress for an unborn baby and its mother.

An umbilical cord prolapse is always a serious concern with each multiple after the first. A prolapsed cord results in compression of the baby's umbilical cord, which decreases that baby's oxygen supply. It is more common if a multiple is in a breech or transverse position but it can occur as a second (or third) baby is becoming engaged in a vertex position.

Maternal blood loss is a concern with the expulsion of one large or two (or more) placenta(s). Also, the distended, or "overstretched," uterus may have difficulty contracting effectively after a multiple birth. (Of course, breastfeeding, or pumping, soon after delivery helps the distended uterus do a better job contracting, which should help decrease some bleeding.)

Many care providers will monitor labor and "catch" twins in a hospital birthing room. Unmedicated birth can be ideal for the vaginal birth with twins or triplet sets. You, your contracting uterus, and gravity can work together to push out each baby, thereby minimizing the need for artificial manipulation, especially for the second (and third) baby.

You may want to find out what level of nursery care is available in the hospital where you are considering giving birth. Multiples are much more likely than single-born infants to spend a few hours to several weeks in a newborn intensive care unit (NICU) because of complications associated with multiple pregnancy, labor, and birth. Not all NICUs provide the same level of care. It simply is not cost-effective for every hospital to equip and staff a high level NICU. Smaller hospitals and those with a limited number of births usually have lower to medium level NICUs. When very sick or very low birth weight (VLBW) preterm babies are born at a hospital that provides a lower level of newborn special care, they must often be transported to a hospital with more extensive services.

It usually is difficult for mothers when one or more babies must be moved to a different hospital. Since the mother is recovering from a more demanding pregnancy and birth, quite often a surgical delivery, it may be more difficult for her to travel to be with her babies. Frequently babies are "divided" between two different hospitals, one (or more) remains in the birth hospital while the other(s) are transported to a high level NICU. These mothers feel as divided emotionally as their babies are physically.

You may want to discuss the option of delivering in a higher level medical center with your care provider. A lower level medical center may be reasonable for a healthy twin pregnancy. However, you may want to reconsider birth sites if you experience symptoms of any infant or maternal complication. Most care providers prefer to deliver higher-order multiples in high level, or regional, health care centers.

Childbirth Classes

More and more cities in the US now offer childbirth classes designed for parents expecting multiples. Ask your obstetrical care provider or look for "childbirth classes" in the yellow pages of your telephone book. Most groups offering classes are aware if special classes are offered by others and usually will provide you with the appropriate telephone number when possible. If there is no special class in your area, attend childbirth classes anyway. The basic process of birth and how to cope with labor don't change. Let the instructor know that you are expecting multiples. Many will adapt class instruction to accommodate your needs.

It also is a good idea to sign up for a class that discusses surgical delivery. This class (or series) usually explains the procedure(s), the types of anesthesia and post-delivery pain medication used, and what to expect in the first weeks after the surgery. Ideas for getting a good breastfeeding start after surgical delivery are often included.

You probably will feel more physically comfortable, and you are more likely to make it to every class, if you atend childbirth classes during the second trimester of a multiple pregnancy. You will want to attend a series of special multiple birth or surgical delivery classes even earlier if higher-order multiples are expected. Some childbirth educators provide weekend "intensive" courses and others are willing to provide in-home, private instructions. (See "Resources" for information about childbirth classes for expectant parents of multiples.)

Birth Plans

A written birth plan can be very helpful in ensuring that as many as possible of the aspects you find meaningful are included in your multiples' births. Birth plans should include your preferences for:
• labor and birth interventions,
• medication and anesthesia,
• immediate mother-babies interaction,
• breastfeeding after birth.

Of course, it can help to prepare optional plans that take into account common variations for labor and delivery with multiples, which means expecting the unexpected. You may want to plan for the uncomplicated, full-term (or close to term), vaginal births of all babies; surgical birth of all babies; and a vaginal-surgical birth combination.

Discuss your plan with your partner, your obstetrical care provider, and any other labor-birth support person who is planning to be with you. When obstetrical providers understand that you appreciate the need for flexibility during multiple labor and birth, most will do what they can to fulfill the birth plan and help to make the birth experience as satisfying as possible. Seeing it on paper can help gain agreement for plan items before labor. Take several copies to the hospital with you. Your partner and your care provider will each need to keep a copy nearby. Another copy should be attached to your chart. Any additional support person also should be given a copy. (See Chapter 8, "Happy Birthday," for other aspects of labor and delivery to be considered while developing birth plans.)

Doula Support

A doula is a woman with knowledge and experience about the childbirth process who provides physical and emotional support to the laboring and birthing mother and her partner. Doula support for birth is a "new" old idea! Throughout human history most women have had other experienced women to support them during labor and birth. New research among women having single births reinforces the old idea that the support of an experienced woman is of benefit to mothers and babies—labors tend to be shorter, less medication is required, and surgical births are fewer.

The support of a doula during multiple birth is an idea worth considering, although her role might be slightly different. You would want to find someone knowledgeable about multiple births or who is willing to learn and adapt to the situation. However, the support of a woman you've come to know—and one who knows what you want of the birth—could prove invaluable. A doula could help you and your partner develop a birth plan and will work with hospital care providers to see that it is fulfilled insofar as possible after admission. Most doulas remain with mothers during the initial recovery period, so she can help you begin to breastfeed your healthy babies. (See "Resources" for information about locating qualified doulas in your area.)

Baby Care Classes

First-time parents may not feel sure where to begin with multiple newborns. Today many new parents give birth with no prior experience handling a newborn or young infant. You will feel more comfortable cuddling your own babies if you spend time during pregnancy observing other parents and holding and changing others' babies. La Leche League meetings are a great place to gain some experience.

Baby care classes for expectant parents are offered in many areas. As with other classes, it is a good idea to attend classes during the second trimester of a multiple pregnancy. The dolls often used in these classes don't squirm like the real thing, but they do allow fledgling diaper-changers or baby-bathers to get some idea of how to handle basic baby care tasks. Many expectant parents of multiples also feel more confident after taking an infant cardiopulmonary resuscitation (CPR) class. (See "Resources" for US agencies offering baby care or CPR classes. Children's hospitals and hospitals with large NICUs often hold classes to learn infant CPR.)

Pregnant Memories

You may think that once the babies arrive, you would just as soon forget the details of your multiple pregnancy. Many mothers of multiples say they don't want photographic reminders of their extremely pregnant waistlines, but many of them are the same women who later express regret that they didn't get photos of themselves late in pregnancy. Be sure to take a photographic series of your expanding profile during the last 10 to 12 weeks of pregnancy. As the memory of how it looked and felt to carry multiples fades, these photographs may become a cherished treasure of a special time in your life. Older multiples, curious about where they came from, will enjoy seeing what Mommy looked like when they were inside you.

Chapter 7
Getting Ready:
Preparing for Multiples

You're reading birth and breastfeeding books, attending classes, watching "caring for multiples" videos, and speaking to an experienced mother about breastfeeding multiples. What else needs to be accomplished before your multiples are born?

Pediatric Care

Pregnancy is the time to "shop" for pediatric care for your babies. Many pediatricians, family physicians, or pediatric nurse practitioners offer a free office interview visit. Others will schedule telephone interview time. Take advantage of these opportunities, but be sure to speak to the care provider directly. Office personnel are not acceptable substitutes. Your obstetrical care provider, LLL Leaders, and IBCLCs may be able to recommend local pediatric care providers who are supportive of breastfeeding. If you already have a child, you probably have a pediatric care provider. However, you will want to discuss the impact multiples might have on the type of care provided, especially if this will be your first breastfeeding experience.

Interview Questions

Interviewing "homework" is especially important since you plan to breastfeed multiples, because the care provider's support and encouragement can affect your confidence. You will want to ask each pediatric care provider you interview what she or he knows about breastfeeding in general, and breastfeeding multiples specifically. If your goal is to breastfeed two to four babies completely for several weeks or months, what kind of support can the care provider offer? Does the provider work with LLL Leaders and IBCLCs in the community? How many sets of completely and partially breastfed twins and higher-order multiples has the provider seen? How long did the multiple sets breastfeed? Does the provider believe multiples, especially twins, can be fully breastfed for several months? What are the provider's thoughts about complementing, or "topping off," and supplementing breastfeedings? Will the provider support a decision to express milk and feed it to preterm or sick newborn multiples if any of the babies require NICU care? What does the provider think about "kangaroo care," skin-to-skin parental care when babies are in the NICU? What plan does the care provider recommend to help transition preterm or sick newborns to direct breastfeeding?

Other Questions

Check the provider's business hours and ask about the "call" schedule and how long it usually takes for a phone call to be returned. You'll want to know how long you can expect to spend in the waiting room with multiple—sometimes fussy— babies. Ask if you can avoid a long wait if you schedule your babies to be seen at certain appointment times. You may want to know whether an office has an "isolation" waiting area, so your babies aren't exposed to children with contagious illnesses unnecessarily. Look into the fee structure. Some care providers charge less for each additional multiple's office visit after the first baby; although each immunization or treatment usually is a set fee.

Location, Location, Location

Actually visit each care provider's office or clinic to check the location as well as to interview providers if possible. Unlike a mother of one baby who has a free hand to open doors or hold a stairway handrail, mothers of multiples can't maneuver two or more babies in or out of a car and building as freely. Depending on an office's accessibility, you may be able to get by with only your multiple stroller or a baby carrier, or you may need to take another adult with you for every trip. Look for a safe play area in the waiting room—it won't be long before your babies are curious and fast-moving toddlers.

Baby names x 2, 3, 4, +

Pregnancy is the ideal time to begin thinking of your multiples as separate, unique persons. And what is more reflective of an individual than the name that person carries? Consider carefully the names you give each multiple. Naming provides a clue to others, and eventually to the multiples themselves, how you view these children. Is each considered special in his or her own right or are they seen as more special because they arrived as a "packaged" set?

Some adult multiples think "twin" names—close-sounding, rhyming, alliterated, or "famous couple/trio" names—are fun. Others resent such names. Naming each from the same category, such as ethnic, Biblical, traditional, or unisex names, or using family names can give the impression that the babies "go together" yet may avoid the appearance of a "set."

There is no "right" or "wrong" answer for naming multiples. Some parents have regretted bestowing "twin" names on their babies, but others have never felt it caused a problem. However, you might imagine yourself as a multiple and explore your feelings about having a name that "matches" one or more others. Then bestow on your babies the names that you and your partner like best.

Household Help

Having household help before and after a multiple birth is not a luxury; it is a necessity. Mothers of multiples often say in hindsight, "I should have gotten more help," or "I wish I'd had help longer." In cultures stressing feminism and self-reliance, it can be difficult for women and their partners to accept the need for help in the household during a multiple pregnancy and after babies are born. Incorporating a single newborn into a family requires a major investment of time and energy. Multiply the amount of adapting required when bringing multiple babies into the family. Few mothers of multiples can manage the household routine alone and still feel rested and ready to manage baby care times two, three, or more. Planning for household help will decrease postpartum pandemonium.

You should be free to get to know your babies and recuperate from multiple pregnancy and birth when you first bring multiples home, so arrange to have at least one full-time, supportive household helper in your home during the first few weeks after discharge. Part-time helpers can also take over some household chores. The more babies you have, the more helpers you will need and the longer you will need them.

Determine the kind of help you will need. This varies depending on the circumstances, however, most new mothers need someone to cook, clean, and run a washing machine while they take care of the babies. If your

An extra pair of hands can help to soothe a fussy multiple.

multiples are first children, you may also want someone who can help you learn to handle, bathe, and change them. An experienced mother probably will want someone who can help care for older children and keep them occupied. All mothers of multiples can use an extra pair of hands at times to help cuddle fussing babies.

Examine household help options realistically. If dad can take a couple of weeks off work and knows his way around the kitchen and laundry room, he may be the ideal full-time helper. If housework is not his specialty, recruit him to hold babies and run errands, but look elsewhere for someone to cook, clean, and do laundry. The babies' grandparents or new aunts and uncles often are willing and eager to lend a hand. If husband or relatives are likely to be more hindrance than help, look elsewhere!

Hire someone to take over household tasks when family members or friends are unable to stay full time. Hiring help is cost-effective when you consider that it frees you to breastfeed, which in turn saves money. You'll be healthier long term and ready to resume more of the household tasks sooner if you've been given time to recover from multiple pregnancy and birth and to develop a breastfeeding and baby care routine.

Women have found help through housecleaning and nanny agencies. Others have posted notices or received names for full- or part-time help at churches, senior citizen centers, and junior or senior high schools. Another excellent source of help might be through a postpartum doula service. (See "Resources" for information about finding doula services.)

When full-time help is no longer needed, don't be surprised if you still require part-time help for years. Housecleaning service once or twice a week still may be a sanity saver when two or more toddlers or preschoolers are finding creative uses for household items. You may also want to have a mother's helper come in to help with older children or babies for a few hours several times a week.

Families with freezer space may want to get a head start on postpartum meal planning by doubling recipes or going on a day-long cooking binge now to freeze dinners for later use. Extended family members and friends may also want to contribute to the stockpile. Many mothers of multiples say they appreciate a "supper shower" more than a regular baby shower. Guests at this shower bring meals that can be frozen or it can take the form of coupons to be redeemed at a later date if freezer space is minimal.

Employment Issues

Many women combine parenting, breastfeeding, and outside employment—and many do it well, but anticipating a return to work after giving birth to multiples adds to the challenge of combining the roles of mother and employee. Multiple pregnancy often results in a woman taking an earlier than anticipated leave of absence. This can add pressure to return to work at an earlier date after a more physically demanding pregnancy and delivery.

You probably will need more time—not less—to recuperate after a multiple pregnancy and birth. Of course, you are more likely to get less rest instead of more, since multiple babies will require more daytime and nighttime care. Because of the increased complexity of returning to work after giving birth to multiples, you may want to spend time during pregnancy considering options for several work-related issues.

Leave of Absence

Ideally, mothers of multiples can extend a leave of absence due to the lengthier recovery period. If multiples were preterm and discharge was delayed, the family will need more time to adapt. In addition, each multiple has the same need as any single infant to develop a strong bond with his or her mother, but it takes more time to get to know and learn to love the individuals within a multiples set. The pressure of returning to work within weeks of delivery also can interfere with establishing breastfeeding. Many mothers think they have to "hurry and get it right" when, in reality, most multiples and their mothers need more time to learn to breastfeed as a team.

If a lengthier leave is possible but only if it is an unpaid leave, don't dismiss the idea until you have done some calculations. To consider the effect on the family budget, deduct the costs of child care, transportation to and from work, work clothing costs, and meals during the work day from your salary. This may give you an entirely new perspective.

Alternative Work Plans

Returning to part-time employment is another option to working full time on top of mothering multiple babies during their first year or two. If dad takes over baby care during mother's work hours, this actually may provide comparable income to a full-time salary with child care costs deducted. Some mothers find they can combine part-time hours at the work site with "at home" hours for paperwork. New computer and Internet technology has made it more realistic to combine work on site and at home or entirely from home. Another idea is to join the increasing number of women sharing one full-time job or who arrange to work flexible hours, or flex-time, in order to meet both personal and professional responsibilities.

Examine aspects of your present job during pregnancy. If you find there is potential for a more flexible return-to-work schedule, now is the time to develop and present a plan that outlines how it would work. An idea is more likely to be favorably received if you've considered all the details in advance of the proposal presentation.

Child Care for Multiples

Finding quality day care for multiples is not always easy. Most parents must balance the increased cost of care with a child care provider's ability to meet the physical and emotional needs of two or more babies. Many providers charge less for each multiple after the first, but figure that quality care will be costly—sometimes about the same or even more than one parent's salary after deducting other job-related expenses, such as transportation, clothing, and meals. Child care is not, however, the place to trim your budget. Also, some providers may have to be eliminated because they or their facilities are unable to handle multiple infants.

If you will be or are considering returning to work during the multiples' first several weeks or months, begin interviewing day care providers during pregnancy. To learn whether an individual care provider's or providing agency's philosophy of child care is compatible with yours, ask each to share beliefs about meeting infants' and children's physical and emotional needs. Agencies also should have written mission and philosophy statements available. When considering day care to be provided outside of your home, ask how many other babies are in the care of each care provider. Providing agencies should also explain how they "divide" care for multiples.

You may want to ask potential providers if they often have other breastfed children in their care and whether they are comfortable with having expressed milk brought in for your children. Let potential care providers know if you will be taking breastfeeding breaks with your babies, and that in either case, you intend to drop in unannounced at times to check on your children. Quality care providers welcome parents at any time. You will also need to ask what arrangements must be made if any of your multiples is sick. Since multiples often share childhood illnesses with one another, parents can lose a lot of sick days when each child becomes ill one at a time.

Consider what type of child care will work best in your situation—care in your home, day care in an individual provider's home, or a day care center. If you make arrangements for day care near your work site, you might be able to take a breastfeeding break with your babies once or twice a day. You will also be separated from the babies for less time each day. Care in your own home means the babies are in a familiar environment and there is no exposure to other children and their illnesses.

During pregnancy it may seem difficult to imagine that your babies will ever arrive. Yet they will be here before you know it! Any postpartum preparation that you can accomplish now will help you meet your own and your family's needs later. And it probably will decrease the postpartum pandemonium that is so common after multiple births.

Chapter 8
Happy Birthday

Today's the day! Ready or not this is your babies' birthday. You've taken childbirth and breastfeeding preparation classes. You've toured the maternity unit. Your obstetrical care provider has reviewed your birth plan(s) and given the go-ahead. What can you expect when rehearsals end and the actual performance begins?

Labor

The **stages of labor** are essentially the same whether one baby or multiples are born. The uterus, or womb, is a muscle and the establishment of regular contractions of that muscle identifies the **first stage** of labor. Contractions dilate, or open, the lowest portion of the uterus, which is called the cervix. The contractions increase in strength and number as labor progresses until the cervix is completely dilated (about 10 cm) so that the first baby's presenting part can enter the vagina, or birth canal. The cervix dilates only once for a multiple birth.

During the **second stage** of labor you work with your contractions to push the first baby through and out of the birth canal. Although the cervix usually remains dilated, the process of pushing begins again once the second baby is in position. When the second baby is born, the process is repeated when a third baby is born vaginally. However, pushing to give birth to the first baby generally takes longer than pushing for each subsequent baby. No matter how many babies you push into the world at the end of a multiple pregnancy, it is considered a single second stage of labor. It's not referred to as two or three second stages!

The **third stage** of labor begins when the last baby is born and ends when the last placenta is delivered. Rarely does expulsion of the first baby's placenta precede the birth of the second baby. About 75 percent of identical twins share one large placenta. The remaining 25 percent of identical twins and all fraternal multiples have individual placentas. Sometimes two (or more) placentas grow until they join along their borders, which can give the appearance of a single, large placenta.

The first one to four hours after birth compose the **fourth stage** of labor. During this time the uterus begins to adapt to the "loss" of its recent occupants and the mother's body must adjust rapidly to the sudden change in hormones that is initiated with expulsion of the placenta(s).

Women are often told to expect a longer labor with multiples. It is thought that a uterus distended with multiples may contract less effectively or that the contracting uterus cannot exert as much downward pressure against the body of the first baby. The length of labor for women in the Cincinnati LLL Multiples Group tended to be typical for whatever number labor and delivery experience the multiple pregnancy represented. First labors were longer but the first and second stages of labor usually are longer for first pregnancies. The length of labor for women who had given birth before generally was consistent with what would be expected, depending on the length of previous labors. (The first stage of labor typically lasts 12 to 18 hours with first pregnancies and about half that time for subsequent pregnancies. You can expect to push for about one to two hours—and occasionally longer—during the second stage of labor with a first pregnancy and for about 15 to 60 minutes for subsequent pregnancies.)

Vaginal Birth

The birth of a first multiple in the vertex, or head down, position is essentially like the birth of a single vertex. On some labor and delivery units, women may give birth to full-term, vertex multiples in a birthing room. This is more likely when the room can be adapted for an emergency surgical delivery or a surgical suite is within several steps if a problem arises during the birth of the second (or third) baby. When this flexibility is not available, care providers generally prefer that multiple births take place in a delivery room with the mother on a delivery table. Depending on how you feel and the condition of the first baby, you may be able to hold Baby A before labor resumes in earnest with the second baby.

Once the first (or second) baby is born, obstetric care providers will want to continue to monitor any multiple remaining in the uterus. As the second (or third) baby moves into position for birth, it may be necessary to readjust external monitoring belts. Because of the increased risk for delivery with the second (and third) multiple, care providers usually want to apply an internal monitoring electrode once that baby is engaged in the pelvis. The need for medical intervention with the birth of any subsequent multiple depends on that baby's position in the birth canal and whether there is any sign of fetal distress.

Surgical (Cesarean) Birth

Surgical delivery is common with multiple births. (See Chapter 6, "Getting Ready: Birth Preparation.") Surgical delivery may be planned when a first twin is in the breech or transverse position, two babies are in the same sac, a placenta covers part of the cervical opening, or there are higher-order multiples. A "repeat" surgical birth is not always a necessity when a twin pregnancy follows the surgical delivery of a previous pregnancy. Many women have had twins by vaginal birth after cesarean (VBAC).

A "trial of labor" may be considered first for some of the complications that may occur in multiple pregnancies. These may include maternal conditions, such as pregnancy-induced hypertension (PIH) or gestational diabetes, or when there is greater risk of fetal distress for one or more babies, as with a poorly reactive nonstress test (NST) or a second twin in a breech or transverse position. (See Chapter 4, "What to Do If...") Should fetal distress develop during labor for any multiple or if a mother's condition suddenly worsens, an emergency surgical delivery can be performed.

During a surgical birth each baby is delivered through an incision, or cut, made in a woman's abdominal area. The outside, or skin, incision may run vertically from the umbilicus to the pubic hair line, or it may be a horizontal cut (Pfannenstiel) along the pubic hair, or bikini, line. The skin incision does not reflect necessarily the direction of the uterine incision. Generally a horizontal incision is made in the lower segment of the uterus; however, some care providers prefer a lower segment vertical incision for multiple births, especially if one or both are in unusual positions or when a placenta covers part of the cervical opening.

Multiples delivered surgically are lifted out one at a time, and the time between births usually is closer than during a vaginal birth. There may be a slightly longer time between births when the first multiple is born vaginally and a subsequent one is surgically delivered. Depending on the babies' conditions, some mothers ask that a nurse or a doula massage the babies after delivery to provide skin stimulation in place of that received during passage through the birth canal.

Hospital Routines and First Stage Interventions

Interventions are recommended more often during labor and delivery with multiples, and it was for the special situations more likely to occur with multiples that many interventions were developed. However, all interventions also have consequences or side-effects. Sometimes parents and care providers must weigh the potential consequences of a complication or condition with those of an intervention. This makes it more important for you to understand the reasons for and the potential consequences when labor and delivery interventions are recommended.

Admission. A prenatal/antenatal form usually is sent to the labor and delivery (L&D) unit so the personnel will have pertinent information about your pregnancy. Often it is sent during the second trimester. It probably won't include the birth plan(s) you and your partner developed, so tuck an extra copy or two in the bag you've packed to take to the hospital.

In most areas a prep, or shave, of the perineum prior to a vaginal birth is no longer a routine. Likewise, studies have shown that there is no need to administer an enema to a laboring woman. Mother Nature has done a good job of taking care of both jobs herself.

When admitted for a planned surgical birth, an abdominal prep, in which the abdomen is cleansed with antibacterial soap and then shaved, will be completed before surgery—often during the admission process. Also, a catheter is inserted into the bladder to continuously drain urine for the first day or two after birth. Sometimes catheterization is postponed until a woman is anesthetized. These procedures can be performed later in labor if a surgical delivery becomes necessary.

The admission procedure with any labor includes asking a lot of questions and checking maternal temperature, blood pressure, and pulse. Usually the nurse or midwife will also do an initial vaginal examination to check the dilatation of the cervix. Blood will be drawn to make sure blood counts are within normal range. With multiple pregnancies it is common for a portable ultrasound machine to be brought in to check for the babies' and placenta(s)' positions in the uterus.

Early in labor you may be encouraged to walk, because activity has been shown to accelerate labor naturally. Walking will be discouraged if the first baby's presenting part is not firmly engaged in the pelvis, especially if that baby's membranes (amniotic sac or bag of waters) already ruptured, or broke, spontaneously—referred to as spontaneous rupture of membranes (SROM). When labor is preterm, this is called premature rupture of membranes (PROM).

Intravenous line (IV). Because of the extra risks associated with multiple birth, obstetrical care providers may want to insert an IV or a heparin lock during active labor even when an unmedicated birth is planned. The idea is to have a vein already available for infusing medication if a complication or emergency develops. The IV only provides extra fluid during an unmedicated labor and birth.

If you plan to have analgesic, or pain, medication or an anesthetic is to be given, obstetric care providers may insist on an IV before administering medication, because these medications include some additional risks. An epidural, which is considered both an analgesic and an anesthetic, should never be given unless an IV is in place. Medication used to induce or to "speed up" labor can be better controlled when given IV. An IV is essential for surgical delivery.

Labor Induction and Augmentation (Acceleration)

Induction of labor means that uterine contractions are stimulated before spontaneous contractions occur in order to achieve cervical dilatation and birth. Labor augmentation, also called acceleration of labor, is used to speed the progress of spontaneous labor. Both procedures are common during labor with multiple pregnancies.

Some experts recommend inducing labor at 37 to 38 weeks gestation for twin pregnancies, since some studies indicated that multiples born a couple of weeks before their due dates had better outcomes than those delivered at or after due dates.* (The same recommendation is made in triplet pregnancies for which vaginal birth is being considered.) Apparently the placenta(s) mature and begin to deteriorate earlier in multiple pregnancy. Placental deterioration can affect the babies' growth and oxygen supply.

Induction may be recommended when there are maternal complications, such as pregnancy-induced hypertension (PIH) or gestational diabetes. Baby-related reasons for induction may include placental insufficiency that is affecting the babies' growth. If you experience PROM and begin to run a fever or you have a SROM that is not followed by spontaneous contractions within several hours, induction of labor may be suggested. Augmentation

---

* No study has yet followed a group of women through multiple pregnancies while closely watching diet and weight gain. Most studies of multiple pregnancy have involved surveying mothers months to years after multiple pregnancy and birth.

may be recommended for a prolonged first stage of labor; however, "prolonged" can be a subjective term.

Maternal **nipple stimulation** may be all that is needed to induce or augment labor when a woman's cervix already is very soft or thin and has begun to dilate. Nipple stimulation is safe and non-invasive, so it is a good procedure to start with. However, do not use it without the care provider's agreement before the 38th week of a multiple pregnancy.

Obstetric care providers may suggest artificial rupture of the first baby's membranes as a means to induce or augment labor. **Artificial rupture of membranes** (AROM) is considered controversial by some care providers, as the amniotic fluid contained within the membranes cushions a baby's head, body, and umbilical cord during labor. (The amniotic sac should never be ruptured intentionally before the first baby is firmly engaged in the pelvis.) Once the membranes have been ruptured, the risk of maternal infection increases, so most care providers want full- or close-to-full-term babies delivered within 24 hours of a rupture of the first baby's membranes.

Oxytocin is the hormone most responsible for spontaneous contractions. To induce or augment (accelerate) labor a synthetic oxytocin, such as pitocin, is used alone or with AROM. As a consequence of using pitocin or a similar drug, the uterus may contract too often or for too long. This then decreases the amount of oxygen the babies receive, which can lead to "fetal distress." If fetal distress is not resolved quickly, an emergency surgical delivery would be necessary.

The usual procedure for induction or augmentation is to slowly increase the amount of IV pitocin. Women who have had labors both with and without a pitocin drip say contractions can become closer and stronger too quickly and peak more abruptly, which makes it difficult to keep pace and adjust breathing techniques.

Labor Monitoring

Both you and your babies will be monitored throughout the course of labor. If you are admitted to the hospital during the early phase of first-stage labor, a nurse or midwife will time your contractions and feel the strength of one or two about every hour. **Vaginal examination** is performed intermittently to monitor the progress of cervical dilatation. How often depends on the labor pattern or any sign of a potential problem. The timing of exams may be influenced by medications, including medications used for induction or augmentation, and for analgesics/anesthetics. Often a woman is examined before a medication is given. Afterward it depends on her response to the drug.

The nurse or midwife will listen to and count each baby's heart rate two or more times an hour. A **fetoscope,** which looks like a strange stethoscope, or a **doppler,** which allows you to listen too, may be used. You will have to lie flat or in a low semi-sitting position until each baby's heart rate is counted. Since this tends to be an uncomfortable position during contractions, most nurses try to count all the babies' heart rates between two contractions. Occasionally, the nurse might need to listen to one baby during the beginning of a contraction or soon after a contraction peaks and the uterus begins to relax.

Electronic Fetal Monitoring

As labor progresses it is likely that **electronic fetal monitering** (EFM) of the babies' heart rates will be recommended. There are two forms of EFM: external monitoring and internal monitoring. Both types measure how each baby is responding during, and between, contractions by measuring each one's heart rate and the differences for each from one heartbeat to the next. Nearby machines translate information coming from monitoring devices, which in turn create ongoing written recordings, or tracings, of your contraction pattern and the corresponding heart rate with heartbeat variability of each baby. The routine use of EFM is controversial, yet many obstetric care providers believe its use is appropriate for labor with multiples because of the increased risks with multiple births.

If you've already had an NST (see Chapter 4, "What to Do If..."), you will be familiar with the belts equipped with special devices that are fastened around your abdomen during external monitoring. One device, a transducer, picks up uterine contractions and babies' movements. The device on each of the other belts—the number of belts depends on the number of babies you're carrying—records each baby's heart rate. Prior to very active or the transition phase of first stage labor, intermittent external monitoring may be an option if all the babies appear to be responding well to labor (during monitoring) and you have not received medication. During intermittent monitoring the belts will be attached for 10 to 20 minutes every hour to hour and a half. If labor is to be induced or augmented, you receive analgesic medication, or there is a question about any baby's response to labor, continuous monitoring will be recommended.

External monitoring is a non-invasive technique, but tracings are prone to disruption because your movements and those of any baby can affect the ability of the devices to pick up and record information. However, belts usually can be repositioned easily. Some women report discomfort associated with pressure from the belts during contractions.

Internal monitoring produces a more accurate tracing of the presenting baby's heart rate with beat variability. Only the multiple currently engaged in the pelvis can be monitored internally. (External monitoring is done for the other babies.) In addition, insertion of an internal transducer may be recommended when an accurate tracing of contraction intensity is desired.

Internal monitoring devices cannot be applied without SROM or AROM for the presenting baby and the cervix is dilated at least 2 cm, about one finger width. During a vaginal exam a spiral or clip, thin-wired electrode is attached to the skin on the presenting part—usually the back of the baby's head, which produces a continuous and clearer tracing of that baby's heart rate. It may occasionally produce a small scab on the baby's head, and there is a slight risk of infection at the electrode site. A slim, flexible plastic transducer may be inserted to monitor contractions.

Applying an internal monitoring device is a more invasive technique and once begun it restricts the laboring woman's movements to the bed or near the bed. It is more likely to be suggested during labor for any multiple pregnancy because of the increased risks, especially if the active labor phase has begun when contractions are five or fewer minutes apart and each lasts 40 or more seconds. Care providers may recommend initiating internal monitoring sooner for induction or augmentation, the administration of analgesic or anesthetic medication, and any sign of fetal distress.

Analgesia/Anesthesia

Labor hurts. But so do many physical activities. Many exercise workouts are painful yet women continue—not only for the physical benefits but also for what they learn about themselves. Pushing oneself beyond former physical limits teaches a person to believe she (or he) can do anything. If marathoners are celebrated for their achievement with the chant, "No pain, no gain," why in many industrialized cultures are women who choose an unmedicated birth treated as pariahs? **Unmedicated birth** achieves the same personal gains as those learned by coping and transcending other kinds of pain.

An unmedicated birth is feasible when full- or close-to-full-term twins (or triplets) meet the criteria for vaginal birth. However, you may have to put up with a few "just in case" interventions because of the increased risks that usually aren't associated with labor and birth of a single baby, such as an IV or EFM. Also, you may have to be given a general anesthetic if an emergency arises.

You may have to search during early pregnancy for a care provider who has experience delivering multiples without anesthesia. You can learn alternative methods for coping with the pain of contractions by attending classes that "specialize" in teaching coping skills for unmedicated labor. (See "Resources" for information.)

Analgesia. Medications that relieve pain are called analgesics. Most analgesics that are given once a woman is in active labor are some form of narcotic. Women have varied responses to these drugs, which usually are given intramuscularly (IM) or intravenously (IV). Some women report good pain relief after receiving medication. Other women say these drugs had little effect on the actual pain, although many report feeling drowsy between contractions or losing a sense of time passing. Nausea and vomiting are also common side effects of narcotic analgesics.

All narcotics affect the babies, because these medications pass through the placenta(s). These medications can contribute to fetal distress—which already is more of a risk for multiples. Also, one or more babies may be sleepy and less responsive at birth. Since it takes a newborn's system longer to eliminate these drugs, a baby's ability to breastfeed can be affected at delivery and for several days after.

Epidural block. A continuous epidural block may be used as analgesia during labor and then continue to serve as an anesthetic during an episiotomy repair or if a surgical birth becomes necessary. When manipulation of the second (or third) baby is anticipated because of breech or transverse positioning, an epidural might be suggested. It may also be used as an anesthetic for a planned surgical birth.

During an epidural block a thin, plastic catheter is inserted in the epidural space of the spinal canal in the lumbar region on the lower half of the back. The anesthetic agent is delivered through the catheter tubing and acts on nerves that branch off the spinal cord which serve the abdomen, perineum, and legs. In some areas a "one shot" epidural, or one dose of an anesthetic agent, is administered directly into the epidural space for surgical births. An epidural may provide consistent relief or it may work better—or only—on one side of the body. At times certain areas may remain unaffected by the anesthetic.

Typically a local anesthetic agent, such as novocain (procaine), xylocaine (lidocaine), or bupivacaine (marcaine) is used. Some of these drugs are short acting and others produce a long-lasting effect; some reach the placenta(s) in minute amounts and others cross the placenta(s) and into the babies' circulations for long periods. A drop in maternal blood pressure is common with epidurals, so it is monitored closely because it can affect the babies' oxygen supply. Allergic reaction to a local anesthetic agent is rare but can occur. Using a narcotic as an anesthetic agent, alone or with a local agent, in a continuous epidural infusion pump is fairly new and considered controversial by some.

In several studies a significant number of babies exposed to epidurals that used longer-acting local anesthetics demonstrated poorer neuromuscular behaviors for several weeks after birth. Although this research did not test babies' sucking ability, sucking is a neuromuscular activity so breastfeeding could be affected by exposure to these agents. Although continuous infusion allows for smaller doses of both narcotic and local agents to be given, babies may demonstrate the side-effects of each type of agent.

Second Stage Interventions

Second Stage Anesthesia

Anesthetics are given to block the pain associated with giving birth, and for cutting and repairing an **episiotomy**—an incision made in the perineum to enlarge the opening of the birth canal. Usually anesthesia is given for assisted deliveries using forceps or vacuum extraction. Anesthesia is unnecessary when no episiotomy is performed and no assistance is required. Except for continuous epidural, anesthetics generally are given when a baby's presenting part is visible and birth is imminent—whether it's the first or a subsequent multiple.

Local anesthesia: local infiltration and pudendal block. Infiltration of a local anesthetic agent and a pudendal (nerve) block can provide anesthesia in the physical area of birth—the perineum—if an episiotomy becomes necessary during an otherwise unmedicated birth or for delivery in conjunction with narcotic analgesia during labor. Because of the risks associated with multiple births, an episiotomy is more likely to be performed to "speed up" the delivery of a multiple, particularly for a second (or third) baby.

With **local infiltration** an anesthetic agent is delivered directly into the perineal tissue immediately before an episiotomy is cut. Local anesthesia rarely affects babies. However, it sometimes begins to wear off in one or more spots before episiotomy repair is completed.

A **pudendal block** is given late in the second stage of labor. It affects the nerves that supply the perineum as they branch off the pudendal nerve. It may also provide anesthesia if low forceps or vacuum extraction is needed for a more rapid delivery of one or more babies.

Saddle/spinal block. Saddle and spinal blocks are administered just prior to birth when a local anesthetic agent is injected into the spinal fluid, producing numbness from above the waist (spinal) or below the waist (saddle). Most care providers prefer a saddle block for vaginal deliveries, which may be given prior to the birth of the first or a subsequent multiple. A spinal is often given as anesthesia for surgical deliveries. Since the second (or third) multiple is more at risk, care providers may opt for a spinal even when vaginal birth is anticipated for both (all). This anesthetic can also cause a drop in a woman's blood pressure. In this case it is more likely to affect the oxygen reaching the second (or third) baby, since the first baby should be ready for birth when the saddle block is given. You may be told to lie flat for several hours after delivery to prevent spinal headaches during the first postpartum (postnatal) week.

General anesthesia. Few doctors today routinely put woman to sleep to give birth. However, general anesthesia is occasionally used in emergency situations. For instance, it provides rapid anesthesia if an unmedicated mother requires immediate assistance in the form of midforceps or an emergency surgical delivery for the birth of the second (or third) baby. General anesthetics may be injected through an IV, inhaled from a mask over a woman's nose and mouth, or the two methods may be combined.

General anesthetics cross the placenta(s) and affect babies within minutes. Care providers must be prepared to deliver any baby still in the uterus quickly to prevent or minimize the need for resuscitation. It may take several days for a newborn to eliminate these anesthetic agents, which can affect a baby's ability to breastfeed and interact with his or her mother. After delivery increased maternal bleeding, which is already more likely after multiple birth, is common due to the muscle relaxation associated with general anesthetic.

"Assisted" Vaginal Delivery

Forceps delivery. Forceps are metal instruments used to expedite the birth of one or more multiples by providing traction that helps guide the head out. Most forceps-assisted births are "low" or "outlet" forceps births, and the forceps are not applied until a baby's head is crowning. Occasionally midforceps are used to help rotate a baby's head to a more advantageous position—a situation more likely to occur with the second (or third) baby—before guiding that baby's head through the birth canal. Special forceps may be used to help deliver the baby's head during a breech birth of the second (or third) baby.

Forceps may be used when fetal distress occurs during the second stage of labor, and the baby's head is crowning or close to crowning. Forceps assistance is more often needed after the administration of an epidural block, a spinal or saddle block, and general anesthesia, since these anesthesias can interfere with a woman's ability to effectively push to deliver the babies. Occasionally low/outlet forceps are offered to hasten birth if a woman becomes exhausted after a long first or second stage of labor.

Side-effects are minimal for a baby delivered with the help of low/outlet forceps. Occasionally forceps application results in a small amount of bruising or swelling in the cheekbone area. Rarely, a hematoma or a short-term facial paralysis occurs with the application of midforceps; however, it is doubtful midforceps would be used unless there is a greater risk of consequences due to fetal distress.

Vacuum extraction. Vacuum extraction is similar to forceps assistance except that a "cap" is placed on the back of a baby's head through which suction is applied to help guide the baby out of the birth canal. The reasons for using vacuum extraction are similar to those for low/outlet forceps. The area covered on the baby's head by the suction cap may be slightly swollen for a few days or bleeding between the scalp and bone—usually mild—may develop in that area. This may contribute to jaundice.

Third Stage of Labor

The obstetric care provider will be watching for signs that the one large or two (or more) placentas are beginning to separate from the uterine wall even as the last baby's cord is cut. When placental separation begins, you may feel an urge to push again if you are unmedicated, and you may be asked to push if you've had an epidural or saddle block. The placenta(s) are delivered through the abdominal incision during a surgical delivery. Ask to see your babies' placenta(s) and cords. They have done a truly amazing job looking after two or more babies during your pregnancy.

Because excessive maternal blood loss is more likely after a multiple birth, you probably will receive IM or IV pitocin to help your uterus contract. Breastfeeding soon after delivery, or breast pumping if the babies must spend time in a special care nursery, also contracts the uterus to minimize bleeding.

What Are They? Once all the babies are born, parents of multiples often ask, "What are they?" They probably are asking if the babies are identical or fraternal rather than about the babies' sexes. Of course, asking about the sex of each baby often clears up both questions at once. Whatever combination of identical and fraternal twinning the multiples are, wanting to know "twin type" is as much a part of who each multiple is as its sex and it is a valid question to ask.

A single, shared placenta often is sent to the hospital laboratory for further examination, which includes a microscopic inspection to determine twin type. Because this examination can identify only those identical twins that shared a placenta, it cannot rule out the possibility of identical twinning when there are two separate placentas. Blood taken from the umbilical cords can be sent to the hospital's hematology lab to determine the babies' blood type(s) and subtypes, or genetic studies can be done to examine the DNA in each baby's blood or saliva. DNA testing is the most accurate for determining twin type, but it also remains the most expensive method. (See "Resources" for information about lower-cost DNA-zygosity testing.)

Chapter 9
Beginning Breastfeeding

The best time to begin breastfeeding healthy, newborn multiples is almost immediately after birth. Multiples born at 36 or more weeks of gestation usually are eager to breastfeed within 30 to 90 minutes of birth. Until one or more is ready to feed, enjoy just getting to know your babies. Often the reality of multiples doesn't actually sink in until you see them together.

Get a good look at each baby and begin putting the new faces with their new names by laying the babies "chests down" on your chest. Take your gown off and clothe them only in diapers so you have lots of skin contact. If the birthing or recovery room is cool, the babies can wear the knit caps many hospitals provide, and someone can place a blanket or two over all of you. Direct body contact helps newborns regulate body temperature, heart and breathing rates, and blood sugar level.

It's easier to tune in to your babies' feeding cues when they are in close bodily contact with you. You will know each is ready to first breastfeed when she roots, or searches with her mouth for food, and puts her hands to her face or mouth. She may begin to squawk to let you know she really means it. These are called **feeding cues.** Crying is a late feeding cue.

Newborns tend to latch on more easily if they are put to the breast when they demonstrate early feeding cues. When one begins rooting or bringing her hands toward her face, you may notice she inches her way toward the breast to latch on. You may need to ask your midwife, a nurse, or doula to help you position that baby to latch on to the breast. Most new fathers willingly hold the other(s) while mother and one baby begin to learn to work together. Alternate breasts and babies until each has had a turn.

After a Surgical Birth

Breastfeeding one baby at a time within 30 to 90 minutes of a surgical birth is ideal, since the epidural or spinal block keeps you comfortable. If you had an epidural block, you will be able to sit up to breastfeed. You can cushion your incision with a pillow if necessary when using the cradle or cross-cradle position to breastfeed. Many mothers say the "football," or clutch, position feels better initially because it avoids contact with the incision. (See Simultaneous Feeding Positions in Chapter 12, "Coordinating Feedings.")

The midwife or nurse can help you roll to one side to breastfeed if you must lie flat after a spinal block. Pillows or a rolled blanket can be placed at your back to help support you in this position. If you are on your right side, position one baby on her side facing you. She can lie in the crook of your right arm, or on the bed, to feed at your right breast. When the first baby is finished, prop the second on a pillow facing you slightly lower than or at the level of your left breast so he can latch on more easily. A third baby could assume the same position as the first baby and at the right breast again once the second one is satisfied. (Triplets and other higher-order multiples are likelier to be preterm and go directly to the NICU for evaluation after birth.)

Early breastfeeding can be a very effective way to minimize postpartum blood loss after giving birth to multiples. Multiple babies overdistend the uterus, interfering with its ability to contract after delivery. This poor uterine contractibility, or decreased uterine muscle tone, and the greater area covered previously by placenta(s) often results in greater maternal blood loss. Breastfeeding causes and strengthens uterine contractions, which constrict blood vessels at the placental site(s) and enhance uterine involution, or shrinking.

During the Hospital Stay

Early, frequent, effective breastfeedings are the best way to let the breasts know that double, triple, quadruple, or more amounts of milk must be produced. They are also a wonderful way to begin to know the two or more unique persons who have joined your family. If you and your babies cannot be together because they were born early or are affected by another

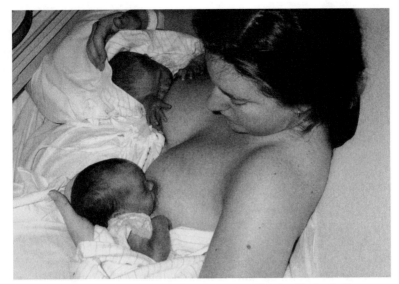

These newborn twins are breastfeeding in the double-football or double-clutch hold soon after birth.

complication, see Chapter 11, "Multiples in the Newborn Intensive Care Unit." Beginning to breastfeed when at least one baby can be with you or you are recovering from a pregnancy-related condition is included later in this chapter.

What to Expect the First Few Days

Most healthy babies will be awake, alert, and "cueing" to breastfeed at least several times during the first 24 hours after birth. By their second day expect them to breastfeed at least eight and up to 12 times a day—a pattern they probably will continue for several weeks to months. Alert babies will latch on and suck almost continuously for several minutes, pausing only to take a breath.

Breastfeeding each baby on cue now lessens the chances of breastfeeding problems later. Unless one or more requires a stay in the NICU, ask that all babies be brought to you for all feedings—day and night—to establish adequate breast milk production. No matter how many times multiples were seen on ultrasound scans prior to birth, many mothers find it difficult to believe more than one baby actually was growing inside them until they see the babies together. This is reality. The time to start handling and feeding all your babies is now.

You may find different feeding positions are more comfortable or work better with the different babies. Don't be concerned if breastfeedings initially seem a bit awkward for all concerned. It takes time for any mother-baby breastfeeding couple to learn to work together, and you are learning to work in more than one mother-baby breastfeeding partnership.

The basic mechanics of breastfeeding each multiple are the same as for a single infant, but every baby approaches the mechanics of breastfeeding somewhat differently. Most mothers know when breastfeeding feels "right." If it hurts or you aren't sure that a baby is latched on and feeding properly, ask that a lactation consultant, midwife, or nurse watch each baby breast-feed. The mechanics of effective breastfeeding and typical feeding patterns are discussed in more depth in Chapter 10, "Effective Breastfeeding."

Feeding on cue also continues to help your uterus contract and keep bleeding to a minimum, which is particularly beneficial for mothers after a multiple birth. Say "hooray" if you feel menstrual-like cramping soon after a baby begins to breastfeed. These "afterpains" mean your baby's sucking has caused the release of the hormone oxytocin, which is responsible for the milk-ejection, or let-down, reflex. This cramping proves that your uterus is contracting and that your baby probably is breastfeeding effectively. You are more likely to feel afterpains if you've given birth before, but first-time mothers often also feel them after a multiple birth. (They still occur yet may not be felt in other first-time mothers.) Afterpains usually subside within a few days of giving birth.

Simultaneous Feeding

Breastfeeding two babies at the same time is called simultaneous feeding. Some mothers and multiples are ready for simultaneous feedings the day of birth, but often it is several weeks before mother or babies are ready. Feed each multiple separately at first. Wait to breastfeed two at once until you feel comfortable positioning and helping the individual multiples latch onto the breast one at a time, and until at least one baby can latch on with little help. When you or the babies are still learning, feeding two at once may result in or reinforce poor techniques that can lead to problems, such as sore or cracked nipples and ineffective breastfeeding for babies.

A lactation consultant, nurse, or midwife can help you learn to position the individual babies for feedings, and she can show you simultaneous feeding positions. You and the babies can practice using different simultaneous feeding positions whether or not the babies are ready for simultaneous feedings. She can also demonstrate ways to handle more than one baby at the same time. Simultaneous breastfeeding is discussed in more depth in Chapter 12, "Coordinating Feedings."

Rooming-In

Rooming-in means that the babies stay with you in your hospital room for all, or most, of the day and night. When you and your newborn multiples are in good condition after birth, full-time rooming-in is the best way to ensure frequent and effective breastfeedings. The more time you and all your multiples spend in each other's company, the more you can get to know them and develop sensitivity to each one's feeding cues. Each baby will benefit from having access to you for frequent feedings.

Partial rooming-in is usually possible during the first day or two after a surgical birth or when you are recovering from a pregnancy-related condition and cannot yet care for your babies full time. If babies can spend only minimal time in your room, still ask that all babies be brought to you for all feedings when possible.

Visitors

Many hospitals now have liberal visiting policies for the postpartum/postnatal unit, and the birth of multiples draws visitors like butterflies to flowers. This can be a blessing or a curse. When visitors support breastfeeding and help hold and cuddle one (or more) while you feed another baby, they are a blessing. If their presence interferes with the newborns' frequent feedings, they are a curse.

Getting to know your babies and making sure they are off to a good breastfeeding start is much more important than introducing multiples to guests. If a baby cues to feed and you are not yet comfortable breastfeeding with others in the room, visitors should be asked to go to the hospital cafeteria for a while or to leave.

Limit visitors to a few helpful ones. You may want to ask someone to stay with you and the babies if your husband is unable to remain around the clock. Rooming-in may be more feasible with a support person to help you day and night. You might suggest that other friends and relatives postpone their visits until you and the babies have settled in at home—a process that may take days or weeks.

Supplementing or Partial Breastfeeding

Avoid giving any multiple a supplementary bottle of artificial baby milk (ABM), also called infant formula, or a pacifier during your hospital stay unless there is a diagnosed medical reason to do so. (Such reasons are addressed later in this chapter and in Chapter 10, "Effective Breastfeeding.") Also, there usually is no reason to complement, or "top off," with ABM after breastfeedings. You'll produce more milk sooner if you simply allow all multiples to feed as often as they cue. Giving any baby something other than mother should be taken seriously, because there are always implications that can affect long-term feeding behaviors and milk production.

Sometimes hospital personnel think they are doing new mothers of multiples a favor by letting them sleep through a feeding or two, or by bringing one baby alone for a feeding while the other(s) is supplemented. Feeding all the babies for all feedings now means you soon will produce the amount of breast milk needed for the number of multiples you gave birth to. When one or more is not included in feedings during the first postpartum/postnatal days, you will have to play "catch up" later. Few mothers want to deal with two or more lethargic, sleepy babies who stop "asking" to eat often enough and are losing weight or with two or more hungry, screaming babies who require round-the-clock breastfeedings for several days.

Introducing the babies to artificial bottle nipples/teats and pacifiers may lead to babies becoming "nipple confused," which can result in ineffective breastfeeding for a baby and sore or cracked nipples for mother. They also interfere with learning to "read" babies' feeding cues and with establishing adequate milk production. Although these problems can be reversed, they easily undermine a mother's confidence, and contribute to an over-reliance on supplements and early weaning from the breast.

When giving ABM for medical reasons, there are alternative methods for feeding that can help avoid nipple confusion. See Chapter 13, "Making Up for a Poor Start," if you think this has already happened.

If you want to ensure continued breastfeeding but are not sure if you want to exclusively breastfeed multiples, wait several weeks before introducing partial breastfeeding if possible. (For more on partial breastfeeding, see Chapter 17, "Full and Partial Breastfeeding.")

Breastfeeding after Surgical Birth and Maternal Conditions

Many mothers have breastfed multiples after a surgical birth. Generally, mothers say the first 24 to 36 hours after surgery are the most uncomfortable. Incisional tenderness or soreness persists, but decreases, over the first several weeks. (Post-surgical pain medication is discussed below.)

You probably will feel more comfortable breastfeeding after a surgical birth if you use the feeding positions discussed in the first section of this chapter on beginning breastfeeding soon after surgical delivery. If two babies seem ready to breastfeed simultaneously, most mothers recommend the double football (double clutch) position as the most comfortable, since it avoids pressure on the incision. This position is described in Chapter 12, "Coordinating Feedings."

Mothers of multiples are more likely to experience various pregnancy-related conditions. However, such conditions rarely require postponing breastfeeding initiation. Surgical birth should not interfere with early breastfeeding unless a mother was given a general anesthetic; still breastfeeding often can be initiated within several hours of birth. Pregnancy-induced hypertension (PIH) (preeclampsia) usually resolves within day(s) after delivery. Occasionally a mother must continue to take medication for several days to weeks, but most related medications are compatible with breastfeeding. Diabetic conditions, whether gestational in nature or chronic, are not a reason for delaying breastfeeding initiation.

The effects of surgical delivery and some other pregnancy or birth-related conditions may leave a new mother feeling weak or exhausted and unable to assume full care of her babies immediately after birth. Most mothers experience more discomfort with movement after a surgical birth and many are less mobile during the early recovery phase of many conditions. A few older studies reported delays in adequate milk production of a week or more in mothers having surgical births or diabetic conditions. More recent research indicates that such delays tend to be associated with postponed first breastfeeding(s), infrequent breastfeedings, and too frequent supplementation with artificial baby milk (ABM or infant formula).

Recovery from surgical birth and other conditions do not affect the basic mechanics of breastfeeding or the number of times each baby needs to eat. Each baby still needs eight to twelve effective breastfeedings in 24 hours. If you arrange for someone to stay and help you physically manage multiple newborns during your hospital stay, you can have the babies with you (or go to the NICU to be with babies) as much as possible. This helper may be dad, a relative, or a friend, but you'll probably gain confidence more easily if it is someone who supports breastfeeding. A postpartum doula also is a good option. (See "Resources.") If unable to arrange for such help, ask that the babies still be brought to you for all feedings. Ask that they be brought one at a time if a health care worker, such as a nurse, cannot stay in your room to help you with all the babies.

Should your condition interfere with direct breastfeeding for some or all feedings, you can **compensate** by expressing your milk for all missed feedings. Occasionally a mother must focus all her energy on physical recovery for several hours to several days. In those rare instances, a nurse can apply an electric breast pump to express a mother's milk every two to three hours or she may teach a family member or friend to do it. See "Milk Expression" later in this chapter for more information.

Pain Medication

You may find a mild analgesic, or pain reliever, helps relieve any perineal tenderness if you received an episiotomy. Medication may also be helpful if "afterpains" become unusually severe or are long lasting. Generally nonnarcotic analgesics compatible with breastfeeding are prescribed. Local analgesic or anesthetic sprays and creams prescribed for episiotomy discomfort should not affect breast milk. However, your obstetric care provider or a lactation consultant should have references if there is a question about any given medication.

Mothers are more likely to be given narcotic analgesics for a day or two after surgical deliveries. Most narcotic analgesics are considered to be compatible with breastfeeding, and you may be better able to care for and breastfeed your babies when you are more comfortable. Many mothers and health professionals advise taking pain medication at regular intervals, which vary depending on the medication, rather than wait until pain or discomfort become severe during the first few days after the surgery. This helps maintain blood levels of the particular medication. Often less medication is taken overall when taking smaller maintenance dosages.

Some mothers receive a narcotic analgesic through a patient-controlled analgesia (PCA) pump. The medication is "piggy-backed" into the IV tubing already in place, and it is attached to an automatic timing device. When a new mother becomes uncomfortable, she presses a button to receive more medication. The timing device will not allow overdosing. It generally is used for about 12 to 24 hours and then a less strong analgesic will be offered instead.

Another method of delivering a narcotic analgesic is through an epidural while in the delivery suite. This medication usually lasts for about 24 hours. Most women find a milder analgesic provides enough pain relief once it wears off. Mothers tend to say they felt more alert and able to care for their babies when they received narcotic medication through the epidural; however, nausea and extreme itching are reactions associated with receiving medication via this route.

Some mothers find they are more comfortable and much more alert after a surgical birth when they are given intra-muscular (IM) injections of nonnarcotic analgesics, such as the nonsteroidal antiinflammatory drug ketorolac (toradol, acular)—a medication that is commonly prescribed for pain after surgical deliveries. (See Chapter 6, "Getting Ready: Birth Preparations," for information on preparing for birth.)

When One (or More) Cannot Breastfeed

There are many pregnancy- and birth-related reasons that may interfere with breastfeeding for only one (or more) multiple for several hours to several weeks after delivery when other(s) can. Each multiple was not necessarily subjected to the same degree of stress during pregnancy, labor, and birth, so their readiness and ability to feed may vary. Also, exposure to analgesics and anesthetics during labor may make one multiple too groggy or sleepy to breastfeed effectively for several hours to several days after birth while another seems unaffected. (See Chapter 8, "Happy Birthday.") As a result one is ready and eager to breastfeed, another is eager but can't quite get the hang of latching on or staying on long enough, and another simply falls asleep within seconds of coming to the breast. Each multiple is an individual, so each one's responses to life outside the womb will be unique from the start.

Breastfeed any of the babies who are able to go directly to the breast. To increase milk production and provide your milk for any babies who will not or cannot breastfeed directly, you will also want to express your milk. You can use a pump to express milk from one breast as a baby feeds on the other. If this requires more coordination than you and a baby are yet ready for, express milk after feeding any babies who are able to breastfeed directly.

You will want to ensure that any multiple not yet able to breastfeed receives whatever colostrum or milk you express, unless that baby is on IV feeds only. Your colostrum and milk are beneficial in whatever amounts you produce. See the following section and Chapter 11, "Newborns in the NICU," for more specific information about milk expression and alternative methods of feeding that help avoid nipple confusion.

Milk Expression

If your or any baby's physical condition interferes for any reason with the eight to twelve daily breastfeedings that each baby needs, you will want to compensate by using some technique of milk expression within 12 to 24 hours of the babies' births. Although most women will still produce adequate milk if milk expression is not initiated the first day or two, the earlier milk expression begins the earlier a mother should expect to produce an increased volume of milk. There are no benefits to be gained by waiting to begin expressing milk.

Delaying frequent milk expression beyond the first days after birth can lead to a permanent reduction in milk production following birth. Because there are many factors that influence milk production, the degree of reduction may vary widely for different women. If even one baby cannot breastfeed or is not breastfeeding effectively, it never hurts to begin milk expression.

There are a variety of techniques that allow for effective milk expression. The most important aspect of any method is that you are able to use it frequently and effectively. In many areas of the world, hand-expression is the only method available and mothers have used it for weeks or months to provide milk for preterm or sick newborns. Mothers have also used a variety of small pumps to provide their milk for their babies. However, many mothers now prefer to use an automatic self-cycling, electric breast pump with a double collection kit that enables them to pump both breasts at once. It saves time so they feel able to pump more often. Some research indicates that double pumping results in higher volumes of milk.

The idea of milk expression is to simulate the typical routine of eight to twelve daily feedings for each newborn. How much time should be dedicated to milk expression will depend on the number of multiples that can breastfeed directly and the number that cannot. You may produce only drops the first day or two of milk expression. Don't let that discourage you. If you do not see any increase in milk production within 36 to 48 hours, ask an obstetrical health care provider, a lactation consultant, or a La Leche League Leader to review your pumping technique and routine. They will have suggestions for increasing milk production.

Refer to the earlier section that discussed milk expression for situations when at least one baby is able to breastfeed effectively. Pumping when all multiples are unable to breastfeed initially is addressed in Chapter 11, "Newborns in the NICU."

Early, frequent, effective breastfeeding or pumping is the best way to ensure double, triple, or quadruple milk production. When you are not certain if one or more babies are breastfeeding often enough or effectively, get help. And don't expect to be an expert immediately. It takes time to get to know two or more babies and differentiate their individual approaches to breastfeeding.

Chapter 10
Effective Breastfeeding

It takes time to learn to recognize and adapt to the different, yet normal, approaches of two, three, four, or more babies. Many of the questions LLL Leaders get from worried mothers of multiples are about perceived rather than actual breastfeeding problems. Understanding how enough milk is produced, what infant behaviors and feeding patterns are considered normal, and how to coordinate multiples' multiple breastfeedings may increase your confidence during the early learning period with your newborns.

Establishing and Maintaining Lactation
Making Enough Milk for Two, Three, or More
When you are lactating, or producing milk, demand for the product (your milk) determines the amount made. Milk is produced within each breast in cells that cluster to form numerous balloon-shaped alveoli. One such cluster is called an alveolus. Milk is made in these cells from nutrients taken from your blood and then secreted into the lumen of the alveoli, which may be likened to the inside of a balloon. The milk stored in these lumen empties into small milk ducts, which in turn empty into larger ducts that transport milk to even larger mammary ducts before widening into what are called the lactiferous, or milk, sinuses lying just beneath the areola.

There are about 15 to 25 lactiferous sinuses that open at the nipple tip. It is through these openings, or nipple pores, that milk is released during the milk-ejection, or let-down, reflex. This occurs when the hormone oxytocin causes muscle cells around alveoli to contract, forcing milk stored in alveolar lumen into the ducts and eventually out through nipple pores.

When a baby breastfeeds effectively, the breasts are "told" to produce more milk in two different ways. First the hormone prolactin is released, which stimulates the alveolar cells to make milk. Also, the removal of available milk from the alveolar lumen signals the milk-making cells of that alveolus to increase production.

An alveolus is essentially a milk-making factory and the lumen its warehouse. When the milk is removed from this "warehouse" through breastfeeding, biochemical messengers inform the "factory" that the product is in demand and to step up production. On the other hand if milk builds up in the warehouse because of infrequent breastfeedings or from a baby's ineffective sucking, messengers let the factory know that demand for the product is down and the factory slows production. If no milk is removed for several days, the alveoli "factory" begins to close down.

When multiple newborns breastfeed effectively, they kick the factory into high gear. The more often multiple babies breastfeed, the more milk the "factory" makes. The "factory" usually can produce enough for all multiples as long as their mother trusts her babies by putting them to breast whenever they "ask" to feed, or she expresses her milk frequently when one or more is not yet feeding effectively or is not yet able to breastfeed.

Feeding Behaviors
Getting It "Right"

A baby breastfeeds effectively by using the lower jaw and tongue to draw the entire nipple and a mouthful of areola into its mouth. To do this correctly, a baby's mouth must gape wide open. Tickle the baby's lips with your nipple or a finger to stimulate a reflex that will cause him to open wide and stick his tongue over his lower gum. Once this occurs, bring the baby deeply onto the breast in one motion. When latched on properly, the baby will look as if he has a mouth full of areola, and the tip of his nose and chin will touch your breast.

As the baby sucks, his lower jaw and tongue compress the areola up against his palate. His tongue continues to work with a wave-like motion to move the milk from the lactiferous sinuses beneath the areola toward and out of the milk pores in the nipple tip. When properly latched, the baby's tongue and palate do not come into contact with the nipple tip, so effective breastfeeding should not hurt your nipples.

Typical Feeding Patterns

There is a range of "normal" feeding behaviors within each feeding itself, and within a 24-hour period, for an individual baby, yet certain behaviors almost always are present during effective breastfeeding. Since you will be working with two or more new learners, you must look for these behaviors when breastfeeding each multiple yet also recognize normal variations in their individual patterns. Babies who are breastfeeding effectively generally:

- Wake and cue for at least eight, up to about twelve, daily breastfeedings by the second day after birth. (Each baby should cue and breastfeed several times during the first 24 hours after birth. Feeding cues are described in Chapter 9, "Beginning Breastfeeding.")
- Initiate each feeding with a brief period, or burst, of rapid **non-nutritive** sucking that may be followed by a pause of about 30 to 90 seconds.
- Resume with **nutritive** sucking (with let-down) in a rhythm of about one suck per second, pausing for a breath every several sucks.
- Remain awake and sustain almost continuous sucking for at least five to ten minutes and for up to about 30 minutes.
- Detach from the breast without mother's help after 10 to 30 minutes of feeding at the first breast.
- Demonstrate satisfaction (a full tummy) by relaxing as the feeding progresses, until they are sleepy or asleep by the time of self-detachment from the breast.

Typical variations for each multiple occur in the total number of eight to twelve feedings each baby desires in each 24 hour period and in the total time taken for an individual feeding. Some babies cue for and do well with eight feedings a day; others require 10 to 12, and occasionally up to 14, feedings daily.

Most newborns breastfeed for at least 20 to 30 minutes on the first breast, others feed a little longer, and some are satisfied after 10 to 15 minutes. A baby sometimes might "ask" for more after the first breast for some feedings yet act satisfied after feeding on one breast for others. He might take 30 minutes to feed for some feedings and self-detach after 10 minutes for others.

A few newborns, and many older, more efficient breastfeeders, act as though they are going through a fast-food, drive-through window and gobble all they want in one five to ten minute cycle of sucking. Most newborns feed for several minutes, pause and perhaps snooze for several minutes while still latched on, and then resume feeding through another cycle or two (or even more) within a 20 to 30 minute feeding before self-detaching from the first breast. These "gourmet" babies seem to enjoy the ambiance of the "restaurant" and space enthusiastic suckling so their meal arrives like different courses.

The challenge of multiples is that one may be a gobbler and another a gourmet. One may be happy with seven to nine daily breastfeedings, but another may need at least 12 feedings every day. One may breastfeed at regular two to three hour intervals; another "crowds" several feedings into a couple of hours here, then spaces a feeding three to five hours apart there.

The feeding styles of the multiples described above are within the "normal" range, but a mother may wonder if any baby is breastfeeding as he should when keeping track of two or more babies having different styles. Both styles, and anything in between, may be considered a normal variation of the feeding cycle as long as each baby breastfeeds effectively and continues to grow and develop. However, it may be reassuring to know how to measure if babies are getting enough when breastfeeding.

Measuring Breastfeeding

Diaper Count

Less experienced mothers often lament that they cannot measure how much their babies are getting when breastfeeding. Yet mothers have breastfed for thousands of years without worrying that their breasts weren't equipped with ounce (oz) or ml markers. They simply watched what came out a baby's other end. Any baby producing enough daily wet diapers (voids) and bowel movements (stools) generally is getting enough breast milk.

In the first few days after birth a baby may wet only two to four diapers in a 24-hour period. These early wet diapers may be barely damp and the urine may look darker and more concentrated. As your milk "comes in," you will notice wet diapers increasing in number and in the degree of saturation throughout the first week. By the end of that week you should count at least **six to eight heavy wet diapers** for each multiple. Each also should pass at least **three stools** every day by their third or fourth day.

If the babies latch on and breastfeed well, but you still feel concerned about their intakes of breast milk, weigh each baby nude once a week. Always use the same scale so you can be certain that the weight gains are accurate for the individual babies. When their diaper counts are appropriate, you should see each baby gain **at least one-half to one ounce (15 to 30 gm) a day**, or **four to seven ounces (120 to 210 gm) a week**, by 24 hours of when your milk "comes in" at two to four days after their birth. You may need to take daily weights, or weigh one or more before and after some feedings, if any are having difficulty breastfeeding or are not gaining appropriate weight. A more sensitive scale is available for rent in these situations. (See Chapter 14, "Breastfeeding Difficulties in Young Babies.")

Keeping Track

Making sure that two or more new learners are breastfeeding often enough and having appropriate diaper counts in the first weeks can be confusing. To feel reassured and begin to get a sense of each baby's breastfeeding pattern, monitor each baby's feedings, wet diapers, and stools on a simple, checklist style 24-hour chart. (Ask a hospital nurse or midwife, a lactation consultant, or an LLL Leader for a copy of such a chart.) Most charts also include columns to note times for breast milk expression/pumping and alternative feedings—those not directly at the breast.

Make enough copies of the chart to last for several days to several weeks. (This is a good task for Daddy to handle.) Writing babies' names on charts is one way to identify each one's chart, but printing the chart on different-colored papers and then assigning each multiple a specific color can make life simpler. When things get hectic—an everyday occurrence when young multiples are around—it is easier to identify a color than search for a name. Date each chart and note the babies' weekly (or daily) weights when taken.

If charting interferes with what you had considered the ease of breastfeeding, toss the charts in the trash once a weight gain is established for each baby and you feel confident that each is breastfeeding effectively. At times it may be necessary to maintain a chart for one but not for another. Some mothers continue to monitor their multiples' daily feedings and urine and stool output. They find that charting helps them recognize their babies' emerging daily feeding patterns or wake-sleep routines. The charts provide a visible reminder that the babies' feeding styles and daily routines are improving from week to week.

Growth Spurts and Frequency Days: Sudden "Demand" for Extra Feedings

Just when you thought a little bit of order was emerging from the chaos, your babies suddenly demand several extra breastfeedings a day. They may also seem fussier. Any semblance of a daily routine flies right out the window. You may worry that you are losing your milk and wonder if your body can really make enough milk for multiples.

Never fear. If your babies have been breastfeeding well and suddenly want to breastfeed several more times in a day, the most likely cause for the increased feedings is a growth spurt. To keep pace with their increased growth needs, your babies must "ask" to eat more often for several days. This is the best way to let your body know they need more milk.

The additional breastfeedings result in increased milk production, although it will take several days to happen. Once milk production increases, most babies return to fewer daily feedings. It's not unusual for one or more to actually feed a little less often than she did prior to the growth spurt.

Anticipating Growth Spurts

Babies generally experience about three growth spurts before four months. The first one occurs at about 10 to 14 days, another one at some time between four to six weeks after birth, and again at about three months. Preterm babies may not experience signs of a growth spurt on this schedule, but they can be expected to have several growth spurts in the early months.

Multiples' growth spurts tend to last longer than the two to three day period that is common for a single infant. When two or more multiples go through a growth spurt simultaneously, the time may stretch to four to seven days. The breasts cannot respond instantaneously when two or more babies need extra calories. Multiples' longer growth spurt periods may reflect a need for additional time to meet the extra demands two or more babies place on a mother's system to produce milk.

Multiples also may "piggy-back" growth spurts. Only one multiple experiences the typical two to three day increase in feedings while the other(s) feed as usual. As the growth spurt ends for one baby, who now is ready to resume a routine of fewer feedings, another multiple enters a growth spurt and increases the number of feedings for a few more days.

In addition to growth spurts, babies have occasional frequency days from time to time. Most adults vary the number of times and the amount they eat from day to day. Babies are the same. It may help to think that today's breastfeeding tells your body to make tomorrow's milk. If there is not quite enough today, one or more babies will breastfeed more often to ensure more milk for tomorrow.

Getting through Growth Spurts and Frequency Days

Growth spurts can be quite confusing. They often take mothers of multiples by surprise. Mothers become so busy accommodating two or more babies who suddenly want to eat more often that they don't have time to realize they are in the midst of a growth spurt or frequency day until it is over. If a growth spurt isn't recognized for what it is, a mother may think she's "losing" her milk and consider supplementing her babies' diet. However, this is not the time to supplement or offer solid food.

You cannot go wrong, whether you know why the babies are asking to eat more often or not, when you respect each baby's requests for more frequent breastfeedings. **Let each baby be your guide.** Breastfeed each baby when each baby cues to feed. Do not try to impose an inflexible feeding schedule, especially before the second growth spurt between four to six weeks, since this can interfere with increasing milk production.

Stop and examine your situation any time a baby suddenly wants to breastfeed more frequently or whenever you find yourself wondering whether you are making enough milk. Mothers often say that just the realization that one is in the midst of a growth spurt or frequency day can help to weather this temporary challenge.

Even when a mother recognizes that her babies are in the midst of a growth spurt, she may wonder after several days if she will get through it. "Survival" seems less of an issue if someone is available to help hold babies or to take over household tasks when any multiple demands extra feedings beyond a day or two. Since the timing of growth spurts can be anticipated to some extent, plan for help in advance. That way all you have to do is shout "growth spurt" into the phone when one hits, and help will come running.

Thus far, every mother of multiples **has** survived her babies' growth spurts, although few mothers ever forget them. Fortunately, most growth spurts are followed by a period of relative calm for mother and babies.

Most women can make enough milk for several babies, since milk production is based on milk removal. Multiple babies breastfeeding multiple times each day results in milk production for that number of multiples. Although normal babies' feeding patterns vary, most babies breastfeed about eight to twelve times a day. When they breastfeed effectively, it is reflected in their diapers. Charting the number of feedings and the diaper count for each baby can help assure that all babies are getting enough breast milk. If you are ever not certain whether one or more babies is breastfeeding correctly, read Chapter 14, "Breastfeeding Difficulties in Young Babies," and call an LLL Leader or a lactation consultant for help and encouragement.

Chapter 11
Multiples in the Newborn Intensive Care Unit

Multiple-birth newborns are several times more likely to spend their first several hours, days, or weeks in a newborn intensive care unit, or NICU, (often pronounced "nick-you"). Higher-order multiples are more likely to be born at, or transferred to, regional care centers. These hospitals have the most advanced care and equipment available to handle high-risk pregnancies and extremely preterm or sick babies.

Most multiples requiring a stay in the NICU are there because of their physical conditions after preterm birth. There are other reasons that multiples are more likely than single newborns to be cared for in a NICU. Multiples, including those born at full or almost full-term, are more often affected by low birth weight, stress during labor or birth, or the effects of pregnancy-related complications. (For information on pregnancy and birth factors associated with NICU stays for multiples, see Chapter 2, "Multiple Pregnancy as High Risk: Fact or Fiction," Chapter 4, "What to Do If...," Chapter 6, "Getting Ready: Birth Preparation," and Chapter 8, "Happy Birthday.")

Not every multiple in a set may need special care or have to remain in a NICU as long as the other(s), since babies don't mature or recover from physical stress at exactly the same rates. Sometimes only one baby requires special care, especially when the multiples are close to full term at birth. The length of time a baby stays in a NICU varies depending on the reason for special care.

Babies may be discharged once they can maintain a stable body temperature and steady heart and breathing rates in room air. They should also be able to take food well by mouth. Usually a baby must be gaining weight first, but few care providers still insist that all babies reach a certain weight, such as 2200 grams (five pounds) before discharge.

In the NICU

First Impressions

Entering a NICU for the first time can be an overwhelming and intimidating experience. Scary-looking and scary-sounding, high-tech equipment takes up space everywhere. And much of it may be attached to one or more of your babies. Since you probably already are concerned about your multiples' conditions, their little bodies may look particularly vulnerable with wires and tubes taped or inserted at several spots. The alarms triggered by changes in the babies' physical conditions may only add to anxiety levels.

Babies in a NICU need their parents' help to get well and grow, so parents must adapt to this foreign territory in a hurry. It may take courage to transform worry into a working relationship with a NICU staff, but your role is as important as theirs. Most staff members are happy to help you feel more comfortable. Some of these ideas may help.

- Ask for explanations. Learn the names of the equipment and how each item works. Find out what the tubes and wires are for and why each is being used for a particular baby.
- Learn the NICU language to help you understand the technology and what certain measurements mean in terms of a baby's condition. Words like "oxygen saturation" and "CPAP" aren't intimidating once they are explained.
- Ask for descriptions of the physical signs that may indicate either improvement or a problem for a baby.
- Keep a pad of paper and a pen handy. Write down questions as you think of them. Ask staff members to write down pertinent points when they are explaining something about a baby's condition, so you can go over the notes again at a later time.

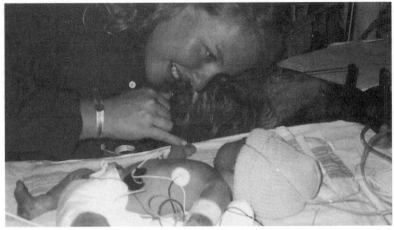

Machines may be monitoring a baby's condition but parents
still can provide a loving touch.

Your vulnerable-looking babies may be "tougher" or in less serious condition than they appear. You may be surprised to learn that some of the fancy-looking equipment and the wires running from them are routinely applied to all babies, such as the probes that are taped to skin to monitor a baby's temperature or pulse.

The machines that monitor a baby's breathing and heart rates can be noisy. Alarms frequently sound, but sometimes they are false alarms. For example, a baby's movement may disrupt the message to a machine monitoring breathing, causing an alarm to sound. Most NICU staff members would rather reset machines for false alarms than cut down on the noise and possibly miss a true emergency. Once familiar with the different equipment, you may begin to tune out unimportant sounds.

Parents' Role

Parents can feel left out or unimportant when a baby's life depends on the technical skills of highly trained neonatologists, neonatal nurses, and other members of the health care team. Don't underestimate your role in your babies' care. Your actions can have a profound influence on their physical and emotional progress.

You can provide the human milk and the kangaroo-style cuddling that positively affect the babies' physical conditions. When everyone else is using technical terms to refer to bits and pieces of the babies' physical systems, you can help the staff look at each baby as a person.

There are many things parents do better than staff members for the babies. Only you can provide the human milk that protects your tiny or sick multiples from many diseases and health conditions. The components of human milk are adaptive. Preterm milk is different from full-term milk; it is uniquely suited to preterm babies' immature body systems.

Because your milk is made for your babies—no matter when they are born—it is more digestible, and therefore, easier on their cardiac (heart), respiratory (lungs, breathing), gastrointestinal (digestive tract), and urinary (kidneys) systems. This means the babies don't have to use as much energy to digest their food, which saves their energy for other functions—such as getting well and growing.

Preterm babies who receive breast milk have fewer infections, and they are much less likely to develop an intestinal condition called "necrotizing enterocolitis" (NEC).

Spend as much time as possible with your babies. If your condition doesn't allow for long visits yet, limit yourself to frequent but brief trips to the NICU. Spend whatever time you can with them now, but leave the NICU when you begin to tire. Initially, a 30 to 60 minute visit may demand all of your energy. Taking care of yourself will speed your recovery, and you will be able to increase the length of your visits with your babies sooner.

If you are recovering in a different hospital, call the NICU frequently for updates on the babies' conditions. Ask a staff member or a family member to take a photograph of each baby. Some family members may hesitate to bring photographs if any baby is in poor condition. You may have to tell others that seeing a photo and understanding the reality are less frightening than what your imagination can come up with.

Multiples are often discharged from a NICU at different times. This staggered, or phased, discharge may complicate visits to any baby still in a NICU, since you now will be busy with at least one newborn at home. Sometimes a mother can continue to make daily or several visits a week to the NICU if she can bring the baby who was already discharged with her.

Often a family member watches this baby in a private waiting room, so mother can leave the NICU briefly when this baby wants to breastfeed. This plan may be especially helpful if she lives a distance from the NICU or if she plans to spend several hours with any baby still in the NICU. Mothers living close to the NICU often plan more frequent, but brief visits to any baby in the NICU. They usually visit the NICU between breastfeeding times for the baby or babies at home, so any baby already discharged can stay with a sitter.

In the high-tech NICU world, a parent's unofficial task may be to remind everyone that each baby is a complete person. Ask that everyone call each baby by name; post the babies' names on their incubators or cribs. Share your observations with the staff about each baby's unique behaviors and responses. When you call during the day or night for a report, ask how each baby is responding to the NICU environment or any change in routine.

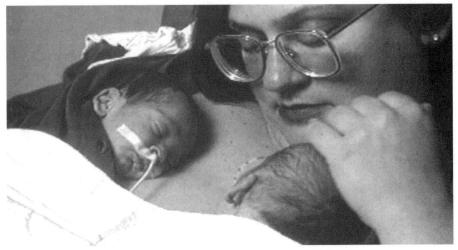

This mother lovingly holds her premature twins in kangaroo care.

Ask staff members to describe the unique behaviors they see when each baby is fed, bathed, or undergoes some procedure. If any procedure seems to upset a particular baby, work with staff members to find a less stressful way to do the procedure.

Talk to your babies when you are with them, even if they can't yet be handled or held. Tell each that you love him or her. Staff members talk to babies too, but it is your voice each baby heard during the pregnancy. It is your voice each baby recognizes now. Your voice can provide some continuity in a confusing new world.

You can't be with your babies 24 hours a day, but you can make audio-tape recordings of your voice for them. It doesn't matter what you talk about on tape. Your babies will be able to hear you even when you can't be with them.

Touch each baby as soon as conditions allow. Whether you can only stroke a baby's arm or hold a tiny hand, let them know you are there through touch. As each baby's condition improves, handle and hold your babies as much as possible.

If their sizes or conditions make you hesitate, share your concerns with staff members. They can show you how to pick up a baby without disturbing crucial equipment. They also know the kind of touching that is more soothing for preterm babies.

Ask if the NICU encourages "kangaroo care" once any baby is considered to be in stable condition. During kangaroo care a baby is dressed only in a diaper and placed on the mother's (or father's) bare chest for skin-to-skin contact. Mother's clothing or a blanket is then placed over both. Often one parent can provide kangaroo care for two multiples at once.

Babies become more relaxed during kangaroo care. The skin-to-skin contact with a parent's body helps a preterm baby regulate body temperature as well as cardiac (heart) and respiratory (lungs, breathing) systems. Kangaroo care also enhances babies' brain development, so ask to initiate kangaroo care if it isn't routine procedure.

Some NICUs begin kangaroo care with very low birth weight babies that still are on respirators. They have found it helps these babies relax and stabilize their body temperatures, and their heart and breathing rates, too. Some find it is easier to hold these very tiny babies in a modified clutch position, with the baby's head against a parent's breast and the body "wrapped" skin-to-skin around a parent's ribcage, rather than on a parent's bare chest.

It is often during kangaroo care that a baby first begins to root for or nuzzle at the breast. (Described later in this chapter.) Kangaroo care seems to have positive benefits for mothers' milk production, too. Mothers have noticed greater amounts of milk available when they pump after beginning kangaroo care for their babies.

You also might ask about co-bedding physically stable, hospitalized multiples. There is some evidence that placing two multiples in the same incubator or crib is comforting to the babies and helps both regulate body temperature, and heart and breathing rates. It also appears to help multiples develop more similar sleep-wake routines—a situation most parents prefer. When co-bedding is not yet possible because of any baby's condition, ask that your multiples' incubators or cribs be placed side-by-side.

When Babies Are Sick

Emotional Ride

Don't be surprised if you find yourself on an emotional roller coaster with peaks and valleys based on daily changes in the babies' conditions. Of course, parents of multiples may find themselves simultaneously riding two, three, or more roller coasters that are traveling at different speeds and peaking at different times. It may be difficult to celebrate the progress one baby makes when another is still sick. Or you may begin to celebrate one baby's progress but find yourself feeling guilty, as if you shouldn't feel happy that one is making progress when another is sick.

A feeling isn't good or bad. It simply is. It is possible to feel both happy about one baby's progress and sad about another's condition. Accept all your feelings as valid.

Share your feelings and concerns with staff members. Ask if there is a support group in your area for parents who have had babies in a NICU. Most of these groups will include many parents of multiples. Talking to someone who has "been there" is often the most helpful thing you can do for yourself.

Parent-Infants Attachment

The attachment you begin to form with each newborn multiple creates the foundation for your later relationship with each. Certain infant behaviors, such as the ability to make eye contact with a parent, encourage the interaction that helps the attachment process along. Parents tend to respond to a responsive baby, which encourages the baby and the parent to interact even more.

A premature or sick baby may not be ready for such interaction. This baby may need all her energy to get well. Because each multiple progresses at her/his own pace, one may begin to interact before the other(s). It may help to recognize that the sicker baby is not avoiding interaction; the baby simply doesn't have the energy to interact. Do spend time with a sicker baby. Talking, touching, and cuddling will help both of you feel closer as you wait for the baby to get well.

Many mothers have said they felt more deeply attached, and felt it sooner, to any multiple(s) they handled and interacted with before they felt an attachment to the other(s). Mothers have expressed similar feelings when one multiple requires a stay in a NICU while she cares for the other(s) in the hospital or at home.

It isn't surprising that a parent might develop a close feeling more quickly for a more responsive baby. However, every baby depends on the development of a deep attachment with his or her parents. If you find you consistently respond more quickly to one than to the other(s), don't feel guilty for your natural response and don't panic. Do take immediate action. You may have to work harder on developing a relationship with a less responsive or sicker baby. (For specific ideas, see Chapter 18, "Enhancing Individuality.")

Breastfeeding

Initiating breastfeeding often must be postponed when multiples are preterm or sick at birth. A baby's maturity and general health help determine readiness for oral, or "by mouth," feedings. One multiple may be ready to begin breastfeeding days or weeks before the other(s). Just as full-term babies differ in their approaches and abilities to breastfeed initially, preterm babies do, too. While she waits for each baby to begin breastfeeding, a new mother must depend on other means to establish and maintain milk production.

Milk Expression

To provide your babies with antibody-rich colostrum and to tell your body to release the hormones that will help it gear up for a high rate of milk production, begin to express your milk as soon after the babies' births as possible. Ideally, you can begin the same day your multiples are born—within six to twelve hours of birth. If your physical condition makes it difficult to express milk initially, a nurse can apply the breast pump or teach a family member to do it.

Most mothers prefer to use a **hospital-grade, automatic-cycling electric breast pump** with a **double collection kit** to build, and then maintain, adequate milk production for preterm or sick multiples. The automatic-cycling feature automatically creates and releases suction the way a baby does during breastfeeding, which is gentler on a mother's nipples. The "double kit" allows you to pump both breasts at once, so it saves time. In addition, simultaneous pumping is associated with producing greater amounts, or volume, of breast milk.

If you do not begin to pump until the second or third postpartum day, it might take longer for your milk volume to increase or "come in." Usually frequent pumping allows mothers to make up for any time lost during brief delays.

Failing to initiate milk expression for several days after birth may have a negative long-term effect on the amount of milk produced, as this may send a false message to some of the breasts' milk-making cells that they will not be needed. Once a cell responds to this message, it can't reverse the process. The impact that a longer delay may have on milk production varies, since not all cells get the message or respond at the same time. Even when production is affected significantly, mothers can partially breastfeed. So don't panic if your circumstances result in a longer delay, but do start pumping as soon as possible.

Developing a Pumping Routine

The best breast pumping routine is one that simulates a newborn baby's typical breastfeeding routine. Most newborns breastfeed at least eight, and as often as 12 to 14, times in 24 hours. Most breastfeedings last about 10 to 40 minutes, so the total amount of time a baby breastfeeds usually ranges from 120 to 160 minutes over the course of a day. Few newborns have more than one span of four to five hours between feedings in 24 hours.

To imitate a single newborn's breastfeeding routine, pump your breasts at least eight to nine times each 24 hours, for a minimum daily total of 100 to 120 minutes. The milk-making hormones and your breasts need frequent reminders that you are serious about producing milk for all your babies, so pump every two to three hours for most of each 24-hour period. The length of each pumping session will vary depending on the amount of milk that continues to flow into the collection bottle. For most women each session takes about 10 to 20 minutes, but when possible, continue to pump if milk continues to flow steadily beyond this time.

One span of four to six hours to sleep without pumping may help you recover from birth, particularly a surgical birth. Avoid taking more than one such "break" each day, especially during the first two weeks when establishing milk production. Less frequent pumping may "tell" some of the breasts' milk-making cells to stop producing milk, which can make it difficult to increase production later when babies are ready to take more.

Of course, you have multiple newborns, so you need to produce more milk than is needed by one full-term baby. You probably can "get by" with eight to nine pumping sessions initially, since the babies are small and will only be eating limited amounts at first. Also, your condition may make it difficult to pump more often than eight to nine times a day at first.

Many mothers produce plenty of milk for multiples as long as they use a hospital-grade, automatic-cycling pump with a double collection kit, and they continue to pump eight to nine times a day for a total of 100 to 120 minutes. Some mothers are able to drop a pumping session after the first couple of weeks if they are consistently producing a lot more milk than their babies need. However, it is often necessary to add an extra pumping session or two as babies require more calories. Within a day or two, the additional minutes spent pumping will translate into increased milk production.

Some mothers add a pumping session to "stay ahead" of babies' caloric requirements or to achieve the plentiful milk production needed for hindmilk feedings of one or more. (Hindmilk feedings are discussed later in the chapter.) Also, settling in with multiples once all are home is easier when a mother doesn't have to work to increase milk production significantly.

The postpartum staff, a lactation consultant, or a local La Leche League Leader should know where to rent or purchase hospital-grade, automatic-cycling electric breast pumps in your area. Renting this type of breast pump may seem to be a major expense when the family budget already is stretched with the arrival of multiples. And frequent pumping sessions may seem like a lot of time spent collecting milk. There are ways to make pumping more affordable and convenient.

- The cost to rent a hospital-grade, automatic-cycling breast pump and the kit purchase are less per month than the cost of infant formula for multiples. Mini-electric or battery-operated pumps may appear to be a less expensive alternative, but they were not designed for the eight to twelve daily pumping sessions needed to establish and maintain full milk production for days, much less weeks. Pumping sessions also take longer

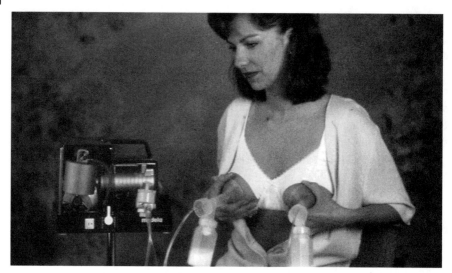

Using a double-pump to express milk.

with most of the smaller pumps, because single-breast pumping is the only option with many of them. Mothers complain more often of sore nipples when using pumps that don't automatically cycle.

Fortunately, health insurance companies often reimburse for this equipment when used to produce milk for preterm or sick babies. You may need to ask a neonatologist to write a note "prescribing" human milk for the babies, which can be attached to your reimbursement request to the insurance company.

• Develop a **regular pumping routine,** but one that fits your particular situation. Pumping at regular two to three hour intervals works best for some mothers. Other mothers prefer to "cluster" several sessions— pumping every one to two hours for part of the day and then less frequently at another part of the day. For instance, it is possible to take a four to six hour break from pumping at night if a mother pumps more frequently during the day.

Although it isn't necessary to rigidly follow a schedule when pumping, mothers report they often produce more milk, and produce it faster, when they pump at approximately the same times each day. They say once their body clock adapts to the routine, their milk lets down more quickly and more efficiently.

If you miss a scheduled pumping session, pump as soon as you are able. Pump again at the next regularly scheduled time.

• **A pumping session ritual** may also speed sessions. For instance, find a convenient and comfortable spot and use that location to pump as often as possible. Then assemble the pump equipment. Follow this by getting your breasts ready for the session through breast massage. Even for sessions when you can take only one or two minutes for massage, do it before centering the pump's flanges on your nipples and areolae.

- **Breast massage** is easy and quick, and many attest to its benefits when pumping. One breast massage technique is to place both hands on either side of one breast, starting at the chest wall or rib cage, and then compress or "squeeze" the breast gently but firmly, while moving hands down the breast toward the areola. Move the location of your hands slightly and repeat until all areas of one breast, and then the other, have been massaged. A different massage technique is to make one hand into a fist and, starting at the chest wall or rib cage, roll the fist down over the breast toward the areola. Again the movement is repeated until all areas of each breast have been massaged. Use the technique that works best and feels more comfortable.

  Some mothers find it helps to apply warm compresses to the breasts prior to massage as part of their ritual. They may drop the compresses and only massage, however, if time is short.

- Many mothers like to look at a **photo of the babies,** listen to a tape of them crying or making other baby noises, smell a blanket or cap that one of the babies has used, or call to talk to the staff in the NICU as they pump.

- Mothers often find they produce more milk when they **pump twice during each session.** This does not take more time.

  1. When you first apply the pump, expect to wait a minute or two for milk to begin to spray or drip steadily. Then pump until the steady flow slows to a drip only once every few seconds.
  2. Turn the pump "off" and take a two to three minute break. Massage your breast again.
  3. Reapply the pump, expect to wait before seeing a steady flow, and continue to pump until you see no more milk dripping into the container for a minute or two.

- Some mothers develop **sore nipples** while pumping. If you become sore, review your technique. Make sure you are centering nipples within the flanges, so there is no friction on nipple tips during the suction phase of the cycle. Be sure you are not inadvertently shifting the flanges when you become distracted during pumping. Apply a small amount of modified lanolin, such as Lansinoh® for Breastfeeding Mothers, to nipples and areola after each pumping session.

- **Set a timer** or an alarm clock to remind you of when to pump, including during the night. You may need a watch with an alarm feature to remind you to pump during visits to the NICU. Reset the alarm to remind you of the next session as soon as you turn it off for the current one. Life with multiples is complicated enough without having to remember when to pump.

- **Record pumping sessions on paper** by placing a check mark next to the hour you pump and note the amount pumped from each breast on a single-sheet, daily checklist chart. Mothers often think they are pumping much more frequently than they actually are, and a chart is a concrete reminder of whether you are pumping enough to establish and maintain milk production.

- Buy a **second collection kit** or purchase extra flanges, which are the pieces that are placed directly on the breasts during pumping. It may save time if you can clean several flanges at once. For easier cleaning later, rinse any residual milk from pump parts with cool water after each use.

- Nighttime pumping sessions disturb sleep less when you **assemble the pump pieces before going to bed.** Then the only thing to do during the night is place the flanges over the breasts and turn the machine to "on." You can avoid getting out of bed entirely if you place the pump near your bed. (Hospital-grade electric pumps are very quiet to operate, so the pump probably won't disturb your husband or any baby in the room with you.)

  To refrigerate bottles of milk without getting up, place them in an insulated cooler with adequately sized freezer cold/ice pack(s). Cover the cooler with a tight-fitting lid to maintain the temperature, and place the cooler next to the pump. Milk can be transferred to the refrigerator when you, or a family member, get up. You also can use this cooler to keep milk refrigerated when you transport it to the hospital.

- **If you have another child,** you probably will need someone in your home to help with her care. Otherwise, it will be difficult to pump frequently enough and also visit the babies in the NICU.

- **Take your collection kit to the NICU** so you are prepared to pump during visits with the babies. Breast pumps may be available in the NICU, but mothers are expected to go to a designated "pumping room" in many hospitals. Since mothers don't like to take time away from the babies to go to another room, pumping sessions may be missed unnecessarily.

  Ask to have a breast pump moved from the pumping room to the NICU. If pumps are fastened in place and cannot be moved, bring the pump you are using at home to the hospital with you so you don't have to leave the babies. (Put a label with your name on this pump.) Actually, being able to see the babies during pumping sessions can have a positive effect on the let-down, or milk-ejection, reflex.

- Ask the staff to inform you when they anticipate a change in any of the babies' feeding routines. As one baby's condition improves, an increase in breast milk intake for that multiple may be planned in advance. You can adapt your pumping routine when needed if you are aware of their plans. On the other hand, you may be able to drop a pumping session if you have been producing well above what the babies are expected to take for awhile.

How Much Milk?

Mothers often want to know how much breast milk they should expect to collect at each pumping session. The amount produced varies from mother to mother and from session to session, which is one reason some mothers must pump more, and some less, than others.

- Only small amounts of colostrum are produced for the first few days. However, colostrum is especially high in illness-fighting antibodies, so save every drop of this liquid "gold." No matter how little there is from a single pumping session, it still can be drawn up easily in a syringe to be fed to the babies.

- Once the milk "comes in," most mothers pump from one to several ounces each session. Generally, they are able to keep up with their multiples' caloric requirements if they pump slightly more than the babies take each day. They usually do this by adding a pumping session when the babies increase the amount they are taking and consume all the milk pumped in a day.

- A mother's physical condition may delay the increased milk volume associated with milk "coming in" in some situations. Don't worry if you have been pumping regularly for several days, but you are not yet seeing large volumes of milk. It may be related to your prenatal or postpartum health. Usually milk production will improve by seven to ten days postpartum as long as you pump at least eight times every 24 hours.

- **Milk production tends to fluctuate** when a mother is pumping for several weeks. A baby's condition may influence production briefly, and you are being influenced by the conditions of two or more babies. Production also will dip after a couple of days if you inadvertently drop a pumping session, so review your routine. Add a session or two to increase production.

- **Check breast pump equipment** if you suspect a mechanical problem or when you have increased the amount of pumping for several days without seeing an increase in milk volume. Machine parts do break down or wear out. Also, some breast pumps seem to work better than others for an individual mother. The agency that rented the pump, NICU staff, or a certified lactation consultant (IBCLC) should be able to help you find a pump that works well for you.

- A **galactogogue,** a medication that appears to aid milk production, may be prescribed for a short time when production is not improving after several days of increased pumping. Most known galactogogues generally are used for other physical conditions and have side-effects, so they are not prescribed routinely. Several herbs are believed to be galactogogues, but the amounts needed usually are high. Herbs in large doses are medications. Speak to your health care provider, a dietitian, or a certified lactation consultant (IBCLC) before taking anything that is considered a galactogogue.

- If a **delay or a drop in plentiful milk production** interferes with pumping sessions, continue to pump frequently but avoid looking at the milk as it drips into the bottles. Place paper or foil around the bottles if necessary. Some mothers phone the NICU staff or a friend to distract them while pumping.

- **Visualization** is a tool that can be relaxing and improve milk flow. For one scenario, close your eyes after applying the pump and "see" yourself sitting next to a babbling brook. Not far upstream you notice a waterfall. Watch the water tumble over the falls. As you become more relaxed, you can watch the water going over the falls turn to milk. (Mother sometimes report their milk lets down as the waterfall becomes white. If you prefer, substitute a fountain or the waves on a beach that roll in and then back out for the waterfall.)

- If you sit down to pump and feel as if **you are going to cry,** do it. Don't hold tears inside. The increased tension can give you a headache you don't need. It's okay to cry. When tears start falling, milk sometimes lets down, or starts falling too.

- Sometimes mothers are unable to produce enough milk to meet all of the babies' caloric requirements each day. Perhaps a family situation does not lend itself to the frequent daily pumping sessions usually needed to keep up with multiples' growing appetites. Occasionally, a mother pumps frequently, the equipment is working well, but milk production does not appear to respond.

When milk production is low, or lower than the babies' combined intakes, **the sickest baby is often given the most human milk.** The other(s) receive the remaining breast milk and then are supplemented with infant formula. Occasionally, banked human milk is available for a sick baby. Banked human milk is scarce because of the low number of milk banks in most countries. (See "Resources" for a list of milk banks in the USA and Canada.)

Storing and Handling Expressed Breast Milk

Most NICUs have a procedure for pumping and storing the breast milk you collect for your babies. **Follow the hospital's instructions.** Ask the staff if the hospital can provide sterile glass or hard plastic **storage containers.** Often you will be given bottles that can be attached to the breast pump, so milk can be expressed directly into the containers.

Your hands and the pieces of the breast pump **collection kit** that come in contact with your milk should be clean before you begin a pumping session. Follow the NICU guidelines for cleaning collection kit pieces that are in contact with milk. Most recommend washing these pieces in hot soapy water and then rinsing thoroughly after each session. Once a day, the pieces in contact with the milk should be sterilized by boiling them in water for at least 15 minutes.

Label containers before placing the milk in the refrigerator. Most NICUs want a baby's name and admission number on the labels. Ask the staff how they want you to include this information when bringing milk in for multiple babies. Always add the date and the time of day that milk was pumped. If you are taking any **medication,** write that on labels as well. Many NICUs have a system for marking containers so that colostrum can be distinguished from mature breast milk and fresh breast milk from any that previously was frozen.

Generally, mothers are instructed to **refrigerate** the colostrum or mature breast milk that will be fed to the babies within 48 hours and then freeze the remaining milk. If babies are not yet being fed milk, you probably will be told to freeze the expressed colostrum or mature milk immediately. Once thawed, breast milk must be fed to the babies within 24 hours. It should not be refrozen. The NICU staff may have you use a thermometer to check your refrigerator (it should be approximately 4 degrees C/39 degrees F) and freezer (less than -19 degrees C/0 degrees F) at home to ensure that the milk is kept at an appropriate temperature.

Because of increased antibody activity, fresh refrigerated breast milk usually is preferred to frozen when it's available. However, frozen breast milk retains most of its antibody action after thawing, and it still is nutritionally superior and more digestible than any other food available for preterm or sick babies.

You will want to keep milk cold as you transport it from your home to the hospital. Any type of **insulated cooler** lined with adequately sized freezer cold/ice pack(s) is perfect. Usually, frozen milk does not begin to thaw unless you are traveling a great distance. NICU staff should show you where to refrigerate or freeze your labeled milk at the hospital.

Feeding Expressed Breast Milk

Colostrum was designed to be babies' first food, and many NICUs choose to follow Nature's sequence by offering colostrum as preterm or sick babies' first milk feedings. Colostrum is valuable in any amount. Do not pour even a drop down a drain thinking you have expressed too little. Those few drops are extremely valuable because the antibodies are present in high amounts in colostrum. Whether fresh or frozen, it is the perfect first food for your babies. Although only a small quantity may be expressed during a pumping session, any amount can be drawn up in a syringe and fed to babies.

The NICU neonatologists, nurses, and dietitians will determine when each baby is ready for milk feedings and how much each should be given. If there is not enough milk for each baby at every feeding, you should be involved in any discussion of how to "divide" your milk. As noted earlier, a sicker multiple often is given more breast milk than the other(s).

Preterm human milk is not the same as human milk produced for full-term babies. Nature adapted human milk to suit the needs of babies who arrive early. However, tremendous advances have occurred in NICU care of the very early (less than 30 weeks gestation) and very low birthweight (VLBW) (less than 3.3 lb, 1500 gm) preterm babies. The small stomachs of VLBW babies may not be able handle the volume of breast milk required for their rapid growth needs when they first begin milk feedings. Because of this, a **human milk fortifier** may be added to a mother's milk to provide extra calories and more of certain vitamins and minerals. A powdered fortifier generally is used when a mother's milk is in plentiful supply. When smaller amounts of breast milk are available, a liquid fortifier may be used to add volume to feedings.

Some NICUs are decreasing and, in some cases, eliminating the use of a commercial fortifier by offering several daily **hindmilk feedings** to very early and VLBW babies to boost their weights. Hindmilk is the breast milk that is obtained later, or toward the end of, a breastfeeding or pumping. Hindmilk is higher in fat, so it has more calories than the foremilk—the breast milk available at the beginning of a feeding/pumping.

Hindmilk feedings usually are used for only a week or two until a baby shows a steady weight gain. Then "regular" breast milk can provide the appropriate calories to meet a baby's growth requirements. If your babies are growing at different rates, you may be asked to separate milk for hindmilk feeding of only one multiple.

Save all the foremilk you collect. The NICU staff will tell you whether to freeze some or all of it. They eventually use the foremilk for some, or part, of the babies' feedings. Most mothers of multiples are happy to have some foremilk still frozen when babies are discharged from the NICU. It can come in handy later at home.

Plentiful milk production often is necessary in order to separate expressed milk into foremilk and hindmilk portions. If you are keeping pace with or exceeding the amount of milk your babies need, here are the basics for obtaining hindmilk for feedings:

- Prior to pumping, attach milk collection containers labeled "foremilk."
- Begin to pump and continue for about one to two minutes beyond the time when you notice milk spraying/dripping steadily with "let down."
- Stop pumping and change to milk collection containers labeled "hindmilk."
- Continue to pump until a minute or two beyond the time when no drops of milk can be seen dripping from your breasts.
- Save both foremilk and hindmilk by refrigerating or freezing it according to the instructions from the NICU.
- **If pumping hindmilk for one baby** but not for the other(s), it is probably easiest to pump at each session as if providing hindmilk for all. As long as collection containers are properly labeled, the NICU staff will use the foremilk to make up the difference for any multiple on regular breast milk.

If you are interested in providing hindmilk feedings for one or more of your multiples but the NICU staff is unfamiliar with the concept, they may contact one of the several NICU lactation programs listed in the "Resources" section.

Feeding Methods

How each baby receives food depends on a baby's condition and maturity. Some preterm babies, usually those more than 34 weeks gestation, are ready to go directly to the breast soon after birth at least for "practice" sessions. When babies are born before 30-32 weeks gestation, they are more likely to first receive fluids **intravenously (IV).**

Milk feedings often are initiated before a baby is able to take food by mouth. Milk is then **gavage fed** via a thin tube (catheter) inserted through the baby's mouth (orogastric) or nose (nasogastric) to its stomach. Based on each multiple's condition and responses, the NICU staff will decide whether a baby is fed a "bolus" of milk intermittently or receives milk more slowly with the help of a syringe infusion pump system. A baby may be offered a pacifier, or "dummy," during gavage feedings. If a baby is ready for a pacifier during gavage feeding, it's likely that this baby could breastfeed on an "empty" breast for at least some feedings instead. Generally, a baby ready to take liquid by mouth is ready to begin breastfeeding.

Beginning Breastfeeding

Making the transition from IV or gavage feeding to direct breastfeeding will go more smoothly for you and each multiple when the transition is planned. Ideally, each baby's first experience of sucking will be at your breast. Be sure the NICU staff understands that you want to avoid, or at least minimize, infant feeding practices that might interfere with breastfeeding.

Working with NICU staff. Some NICUs have specific procedures for helping babies transition to breastfeeding. Staff members at these NICUs are trained to support mothers and babies as they learn to work together to breastfeed. Even when a NICU does not have well-established procedures, most NICU staff members will be willing to support you as you begin to breastfeed your babies.

Different NICU staff member teams may be coordinating the medical care for each multiple. The teams may vary somewhat in their approaches— in part due to the babies' differing conditions and in part because there can be more than one way to address a health issue. If different NICU teams care for your babies, you will have to get to know and work with each. This may get a little confusing at times.

You will want to be certain that each staff team is aware of your goal to form a long-term breastfeeding relationship with each baby. Let them know that you want your breast to provide each multiple's first sucking, or oral feeding, experiences. You might write a reminder and attach it to a strategic spot on each multiple's incubator or crib that reads, "No pacifiers or bottles before mother's breast." To add emphasis, draw a pacifier or bottle within a slashed red circle—the universal sign for "no."

Non-nutritive breastfeeding. For a baby to effectively breastfeed, or transfer milk from your breast into his mouth, a baby must rhythmically coordinate sucking and swallowing with breathing. Babies begin to suck and swallow amniotic fluid during the second trimester of pregnancy, but they cannot coordinate these actions with breathing until they are about 32 weeks gestation. Then it may be weeks before a preterm baby consistently and effortlessly coordinates **sucking-swallowing-breathing** to take in enough calories at each feeding.

Preterm, VLBW babies often show an interest in sucking before they actually are ready for oral feedings. Some studies found preterm babies relaxed, their breathing became more stable, and they gained weight more quickly when given a pacifier to suck on during gavage feedings. When a baby sucks without ingesting any liquid it is called **non-nutritive sucking.**

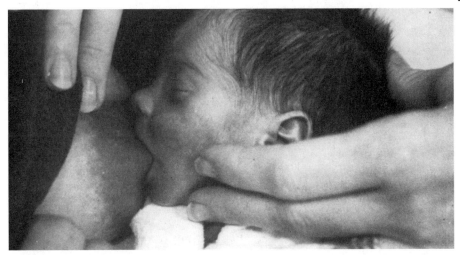

A premature baby can latch on and breastfeed sooner than you might think possible.

Sucking on your **emptied breast** is an excellent way to introduce each multiple to non-nutritive sucking during a gavage feeding. Once the NICU staff determines that one of the multiples is ready for non-nutritive sucking, it shouldn't be difficult to arrange for that first experience to be timed with one of your visits to the unit. Then try to be available as much as possible so your multiples can take advantage of numerous "at breast" non-nutritive sucking sessions. During these "practice" breastfeedings, your babies will begin to associate the taste and smell of breast milk with your breast.

A preterm baby's first experience with non-nutritive sucking often occurs spontaneously during a **kangaroo care** session. This may surprise the mother, the baby, and even the NICU staff! During kangaroo care babies sometimes "seek" the breast, and if close enough they may begin to nuzzle and lick. Occasionally, a baby takes advantage of the opportunity and latches on. For this reason you may want to empty your breasts before you and a baby begin to enjoy a kangaroo care session.

To offer an emptied breast, pump your breasts completely immediately before a (potential) non-nutritive sucking session. The fresh breast milk you pump can be used for the gavage feeding. Of course, your breasts are never totally empty, but the amount of milk will be slight and it will flow much more slowly if you pump first. Plus, any remaining droplets the baby tastes will be higher-calorie hindmilk droplets.

Nutritive breastfeeding. The NICU staff will watch for the signs that indicate each multiple is developing an ability to coordinate sucking and swallowing. Each baby's first nutritive sucking experience ideally will occur at the breast. Babies who are ready for oral feedings of liquid food are ready to begin drinking, rather than just tasting, during breastfeeding.

It used to be thought that breastfeeding was more difficult or stressful for a preterm baby than bottle-feeding. Several studies have shown that the opposite is true. Actually, preterm babies had fewer episodes of cardiopulmonary (heart or breathing pattern) distress during breastfeeding. Some newer research also indicates that breastfeeding may help preterm babies develop rhythmic suck-swallow-breathe coordination more quickly.

You may find that during early breastfeedings one baby latches on as if she has been doing it forever; it may be days or weeks before another multiple can breastfeed as well. This can be frustrating, but it may help you maintain perspective if you consider all early feedings as practice sessions. Then you can applaud the "know-it-all," without becoming discouraged or developing unrealistic expectations about a multiple that needs more time to learn.

Preterm babies often have difficulty controlling a fast flow when milk lets down, so some mothers pump their breasts for a few minutes before feeding these early learners. Pumping through the initial let-down slows the flow of milk. It also means milk is readily available to a baby as soon as he goes to breast. As each baby learns to coordinate the actions of suck-swallow-breathe, a mother can begin to breastfeed without pumping first. Some babies still may have difficulty controlling the initial forceful flow of the let-down and need to be taken off the breast until the flow slows. That is all right. Each baby will learn to handle the flow with let-down as he matures.

A few babies balk later when they are expected to trigger a let-down without the help of the breast pump. Most babies get the idea of what is expected of them after a day or two if mother consistently breastfeeds without offering another alternative. The reluctant baby may figure out what to do more quickly if breastfed simultaneously with another multiple. One can stimulate a let-down for both. After a few such simultaneous feedings most babies get used to a pause between going to the breast and the increased flow with the let-down.

Getting Ready for Discharge

Parents often feel ambivalent about taking preterm babies home. They worry that they won't be able to care for such tiny or vulnerable babies. Also, babies are being discharged earlier than in the past. They often are less than five pounds (2200 gm), and many still require monitoring devices, oxygen, medications, and so on.

You will feel more comfortable taking the babies home if you have spent lots of time in the NICU learning to use any equipment or give any medication that a baby will be discharged with. You also will want to

These parents are providing kangaroo care for their premature triplets.

discuss with staff members what to expect as typical feeding routines and how to know if each baby is getting enough. If you are asked to weigh a baby before (pre) and after (post) breastfeeding at home, be sure you understand how to use an electronic scale and how to interpret the results. Also, ask the staff to show you alternative methods for feeding additional milk to any baby who is not ready for full breastfeeding at discharge. (See "Alternative feeding methods," in Chapter 13, "Making Up for a Poor Start.")

Some NICUs have rooms where parents can spend the night with one or more babies prior to discharge. If this is available where your babies are hospitalized, try to take advantage of this practice before bringing home the first baby to be discharged. It can really boost confidence.

Homecoming marks a transition for each multiple and for his or her parents. You may have just gotten used to the NICU routine and now you are faced again with establishing a new routine. After discharge, babies sometimes continue to follow the NICU routine, but some begin to wake more often. This may be due in part to the transition to home, to attentive parents, and to normal infant development.

In case any baby needs to ease into being home, you may ask to take a blanket, t-shirt, or some other item that has the scent of the NICU home with each baby. Make an audio-tape of the sounds your babies have become accustomed to hearing in the NICU. Listening to the tape may help soothe one or more fretful babies when first home.

Arrange to have help at home after each baby's discharge. If babies are discharged one by one, you will want to be free to breastfeed any baby now at home, pump your milk as necessary, and visit any multiple(s) still in the NICU. Once all babies are home, it may take a while before everyone learns what to do at breast and before a new routine emerges. You will need extra hands for babies and for other household tasks.

Staggered/Phased Discharge

Multiples rarely mature or recover at exactly the same rates, so one or two may be discharged from the NICU before the other(s). In some ways it may be easier to bring babies home and learn to care for them one or two at a time. However, many mothers find the period between the discharge of the first multiple and the discharge of the last is the most hectic. Each time a baby is discharged, the household routine is disrupted again. Mothers often feel torn between the needs of all the babies—those at home and those in the hospital.

When busy with a baby or two at home, it may become difficult to find time to pump for any multiple(s) in the hospital. Visits to the NICU to see the other multiple(s) become more complicated, which may mean the hospitalized multiple(s) will miss some "practice" breastfeedings. Staggered, or phased, discharge can affect the attachment process. Many say they feel close to a baby who is at home and in their care sooner than the multiple(s) requiring a longer hospital stay.

- Make it a priority to provide your milk for any baby still in the hospital, as this can help you feel closer to that baby. If any baby at home is breastfeeding well, you and that baby can work together to provide milk for the hospitalized multiple. **Pump one breast while you breastfeed a baby on the other.** This method also may save you time yet keep you linked with the baby separated from you at the hospital. (Alternate breasts each feeding if only one baby is breastfeeding well.)

   When the baby at the breast is still learning to breastfeed, a mother may find it too difficult to pump while breastfeeding. In this case, **pump after breastfeeding or between breastfeedings.** Some mothers prefer this routine even when a baby breastfeeds well, as it allows them to focus on the multiple(s) in the hospital during the pumping sessions. Some place a photo of the hospitalized multiple(s) near the breast pump, or they hold and smell an item, such as a blanket, cap, shirt, etc., that has been worn by the hospitalized baby during pumping sessions.

- Another priority is to continue to visit any multiple(s) still in the NICU. You and the multiple(s) in the NICU need to have physical contact. Whether you leave the multiple(s) already discharged at home or you take one or more babies with you to the hospital during visits, it will require arranging for some type of child care.

If you live nearby, it may be easiest to leave any baby already discharged at home with a sitter and visit a baby in the NICU between two breastfeedings for the multiple(s) at home. You may want a sitter to accompany you and the already discharged multiple(s) to the hospital when you are increasing "practice" breastfeedings with a baby in the NICU or if you live some distance from the NICU. The sitter can care for the discharged multiple(s) in a private waiting area where you can go to breastfeed as needed.

- When the NICU is far from home or care of the discharged multiple(s) limits visits to any baby still in the hospital, maintain close telephone contact with the NICU. Mothers sometimes use a speaker-phone so they can talk to hospital staff while pumping. Some believe milk production improves when they are able to discuss the multiples in the hospital as they pump breast milk for those babies.

Take advantage of available technology to help you keep in touch with the hospitalized multiple(s). With your permission, staff members may be able to fax or email reports on a baby to you at home. As computer technology improves, it soon may become a standard practice to turn on the computer or TV and "watch" a baby in the NICU on the screen at home.

It is a red-letter day when you bring the last of multiples home. Of course, it usually takes time for a regular routine to develop. And you may rely on outside help for weeks, months, and even years. Still, most parents find it is less stressful to finally have everyone in one place.

Increasing breastfeeding. Preterm or sick babies rarely are fully breastfed when they are discharged from the NICU. You probably will find it takes patience and persistence to work on improving breastfeeding with two or more babies. Allow time to gain confidence in your ability to produce enough milk and in each baby's ability to breastfeed correctly.

When preterm or sick babies first come home, a mother usually wants concrete evidence that each baby is getting enough milk. There are ways of "measuring breastfeeding" as noted in Chapter 10, "Effective Breastfeeding." You also may be reassured if you test-weigh the babies on an electronic scale before and after some or all breastfeedings. By using an electronic scale to weigh a baby before and after a breastfeeding and then subtracting to find the difference between the two weights, you can determine exactly how much milk a baby received during a feeding. **Test-weights** are an indication of how well each baby breastfeeds, which should help you know when you can safely begin to decrease the number of supplementary feedings.

Once a baby is gaining weight steadily, a mother may still want to weigh babies daily and then weekly. Before long, you will find weight checks during routine pediatric examinations are all that are necessary. (Information about renting an electronic scale is in "Resources.")

Juggling breastfeedings, pumping sessions, and alternative feedings can leave a mother feeling overwhelmed and exhausted. You will feel more in charge if you have someone help with babies' supplementary feedings or hold babies while you use a breast pump. See Chapter 13, "Making Up for a Poor Start," for a discussion of alternative feeding methods and ideas for coping until babies make the transition to being mainly or fully breastfed.

Multiples' ability to breastfeed will vary—from baby to baby and from day to day. Don't be discouraged. Do what you can do to keep breastfeeding. It may take time, but if you and the babies keep practicing, eventually each will figure out how to breastfeed well. A couple of true stories illustrate how this can work.

Case A: A set of quadruplets was born at 31 weeks gestation and they were discharged one or two at a time between what would have been their 34th to 36th week of gestation. All four had significant difficulty breastfeeding at the time of discharge. Although their mother had help much of each day, she still found it hard to care for four babies, give them "practice" breastfeedings, and pump her breasts often. However, she remembered the breastfeeding relationship she had with her older child, so she kept putting each to breast two to three times a day. Usually she pumped at least once or twice a day, but some days she had no time to pump at all. About three months after the quads' births she began to breastfeed one baby almost fully because infant formula was upsetting his system. Milk production increased, so she began breastfeeding the other three babies more often. At a year one quad weaned, but the other three continued to breastfeed beyond their second birthday.

Case B: Both babies of a set of twins born at 36 weeks required a stay in the NICU because of breathing difficulties at birth. One baby was discharged at one week and the other came home at two weeks. Their mother pumped and for the next two weeks both twins were fully fed with breast milk. Both babies were put to breast several times a day, and one or both would seem to make progress one day only to slide backwards the next. By four weeks the mother was discouraged and exhausted. She did not think she could continue to pump, work at breastfeeding, and handle double bottle-feedings for much longer. After paying a lactation consultant to observe each baby at breast and make suggestions to improve technique, she decided to delete all bottles for one baby at a time closely watching baby's wet diapers and stools. (Both babies were gaining weight appropriately.)

She started with the baby having the most difficulty. Over one weekend that baby was offered only the breast. Between feedings the mother increased skin contact with this baby, and by Monday morning this twin was fully breastfed. Dad meanwhile had been caring for the other twin. He now took over the care of the fully breastfeeding baby, except for the baby's feedings, so the mother could continue the progress made with the first baby yet concentrate on the twin who had been under dad's care for the weekend. Both babies were fully breastfed by the next morning, and they continued to be fully breastfed until they started taking solid foods after six to seven months.

Full and Partial Breastfeeding

Many breastfeeding "teams" have made the transition to full breastfeeding after a stay of days or weeks in a NICU. Sometimes full breastfeeding may not be possible or desired because of an ongoing feeding difficulty for one or more babies or due to a family situation. Any breastfeeding, or the bottle-feeding of breast milk, still is valuable. (For a more complete discussion of these options, read Chapter 17, "Full and Partial Breastfeeding.")

One of the greatest challenges of breastfeeding multiples is that a high percentage of these babies initially require a stay in a hospital NICU. Nonetheless, many mothers and their multiples have gone on to breastfeed, fully or partially, for months or years. Mothers succeed by expressing their milk frequently to establish lactation, practicing breastfeeding until each baby gets it "right," and persisting even when difficulties last days or weeks.

Chapter 12
Coordinating Feedings

The breastfeeding "learning period" lasts longer with multiples for both babies and mother. It takes about four to six weeks for a mother with a single newborn to learn how she and her baby work best together as a breastfeeding couple. Don't be concerned if it feels as though you and your babies still need learner permits at four to six months! When you have double, triple, or quadruple the number of babies, it only makes sense that it may take at least double, triple, or quadruple the time to learn to work as two or more breastfeeding couples.

Coordinating breastfeedings for multiples is easy—virtually anything will work. You will be amazed at the adaptability of your fantastic female body! As long as each baby latches on and sucks well, all you have to do is respond to each one's feeding cues by offering a breast on cue.

Feeding Rotation

Mothers of multiples tend to use some variation of three different feeding rotations. Some initiate and continue breastfeeding and never change how they rotate their multiples at the breast. Many begin using one "plan" but try a different one as babies grow and milk production adapts. Since almost anything works, work out a rotation plan that suits you and meets your babies' needs.

Alternate babies and breasts every feeding. For instance, Baby A (and C) begins feeding on the right breast, and Baby B (and D) begins on the left. The opposite, or second, breast is offered when any baby indicates interest after self-detaching from the first even when another multiple will or already has fed on the opposite side. For the next feeding, Baby A (and C) begins on the left breast and Baby B (and D) begins on the right. If Baby A fed from both breasts before Baby B fed at all, Baby B probably will cue to feed first at the subsequent feeding. Likewise, quads C and D are likely to wake first for the next feeding.

A variation of this plan is to offer the fullest breast to the first to wake or cue for a feeding. Mothers of odd-numbered multiples, such as triplets or quintuplets often continue to use some variation of this plan until their babies wean.

Many mothers use a variation of this plan for the first few weeks after birth, especially if one or all babies do not breastfeed effectively and when one or more usually wants to feed at both breasts. Once lactation (milk production) is well established, multiples sometimes overfeed when offered both breasts during a single feeding. When this occurs, mothers often change rotation plans to make it easier to keep track of who ate where and when.

Alternate babies and breasts every 24 hours. Feed Baby A (and C) on the right breast and Baby B (and D) on the left today, and switch who feeds on which breast tomorrow. Most mothers like this plan because each baby affects milk production in both breasts, yet it is easy to keep track of who ate where and when. Mothers with triplets sometimes adapt the plan by rotating breasts and babies every eight to twelve hours.

Assign a specific breast to each of even-numbered multiples. Each breast then adapts to that multiple's intake. Although this plan may sound the least complicated, and it has worked well for many mothers, it can have drawbacks. You could end up with a lop-sided chest measurement for a few months if the babies' food intakes greatly differ! This problem is merely cosmetic when both babies are gaining weight adequately, but it may reflect decreased milk production in one breast if any multiple breastfeeds ineffectively. And once used to a particular breast, some babies later refused to feed from both breasts when another was unable or unwilling to breastfeed for a period of time, such as when one multiple had a nursing strike.

If assigning each baby a breast works best for you, alternate feeding positions occasionally so that your babies' eyes receive stimulation similar to feeding from both breasts.

Feeding Routine vs. Schedule

Unrestricted, "on cue," or "demand" breastfeeding is best during the early weeks after birth. Always responding to the babies' feeding cues by offering the breast helps establish sufficient milk production for multiples. Respecting multiples' cues can help you develop a sense of each baby as an individual with a distinct feeding pattern and sleep-wake cycle. Also, putting babies off in an effort to lengthen the time between feedings and develop a schedule can result in insufficient milk production and fussy babies who may not gain weight.

Mothers of identical multiples are more likely to report that their babies fall into the same or very similar feeding routines without their help. This makes sense since body clocks have a genetic component. When body clocks have babies awake and hungry at about the same times, simultaneous feedings really help out. (See next section.)

Fraternal multiples may develop very similar or very different routines, since they may share as much as 75 percent of the same genetic material or as little as 25 percent. If your babies fall into the "different" category, you may find it saves time if you can wake one and feed him along with the other. Or you might want to breastfeed one alone, then wake and feed another. Some mothers combine unrestricted, or demand, feeding with these more "scheduled" feedings. One mother may feed "on cue" during the night, but wake one to feed with or after another during the day. Another mother might feed on demand during the day and wake both at once during the night. The part of the day when babies are fed on cue and the part that is more scheduled are optional depending on what works best for an individual mother and her babies.*

There are pros and cons when possibly disrupting a baby's body clock. On one hand feeding babies together or one after another may give you some time for yourself and other family members, but it also means you are always dealing with at least two babies at once—which can seem overwhelming. And on the other hand, opportunities to hold one baby and look into his face are luxuries to be enjoyed, yet it means you are caring constantly for a baby because one wakes just after another falls asleep. You may also miss the baby ready to lengthen time between feedings during the day or at night.

Some babies seem perfectly willing to be awakened to eat with or just after another. Others will have nothing to do with manipulation of their

---

*Scheduling higher-order multiples' feedings. Mothers of triplets, quadruplets, or more sometimes have to breastfeed on a schedule. Their babies usually are fed every three hours for part or all of the day and night. (Some feed babies "on cue" for part of the day or night.) If one baby is not content to wait three hours, a mother may breastfeed that baby earlier when she is able, or she may complement a feeding with expressed breast milk or infant formula. (See Chapter 17, "Full and Partial Breastfeeding.")

natural routines. Some may be willing during early infancy yet balk as they get older. And of course, others cannot tolerate "scheduled" feedings when tiny but several weeks or months later they think it's a grand idea.

Give yourself and the babies a break when trying to manipulate feeding routines isn't working. You only create extra work and feel more frustration when you persist. You can always try again later.

Simultaneous–"Twogether"–Feedings

Feeding two multiples at once saves time and often tears when two are hungry or need attention at once. A few mothers simultaneously breastfeed for every feeding to save time or because babies want to feed at about the same time. Some mothers always feed multiples separately. They may enjoy the individual time with each baby, find it easier to manage, or have babies with very different routines. Most mothers combine simultaneous and separate feedings. As with other aspects of breastfeeding, the beauty of feeding multiples simultaneously is in the adaptability to meet your babies' changing needs.

There is some evidence that mothers make more milk when multiples breastfeed simultaneously. However, many mothers have breastfed multiples individually for all, or most, feedings and made more than enough milk to completely feed all of them. The important issue in feeding multiples is to allow unrestricted breastfeeding by responding to each baby's cues to breastfeed at least eight to twelve times daily.

Your babies will have as much to "say" about any decision to breastfeed two of them together as you do. Some babies latch on quite well from birth. Others continue to need help for several weeks or months, which makes it more difficult to physically manage simultaneous feedings. Some babies seem to resist simultaneous feedings, yet other multiples have refused to breastfeed unless they could hear or touch another feeding on the opposite breast. You may need time to feel comfortable and able to coordinate one alone before feeding two at once. If simultaneous feeding is not practical during one period of infancy, try it again when the babies can latch on with little or no extra help and have gained more head control.

Simultaneous feedings are very helpful if you have multiples that are awake and hungry at about the same time. It is difficult to enjoy feeding Baby A if Baby B is breaking your heart with cries of hunger. Of course, you then may feel guilty as you feed Baby B because you rushed poor Baby A through her feeding. When simultaneous breastfeeding isn't yet possible but two (or more) are hungry at the same time, mothers usually rotate babies onto and off the breast every few minutes until everyone is satisfied. Also, it often helps to at least touch a crying baby while feeding another. (See Chapter 18, "Enhancing Individuality," for ideas.)

Whether you choose to breastfeed multiples simultaneously because two are hungry or because it makes life easier to wake one with another, don't worry that you aren't spending individual time with each baby. You can interact with only one baby at a time, anyway. Make eye contact with one and spend a few minutes talking to that baby. Then do the same with the other. Actually simultaneous feedings can help you get to know each baby because you don't feel as though you are rushing one to get to another. And it probably will be months before the babies realize or care that someone else is around the bend and feeding on the other breast.

Getting Comfortable

It can take time to learn to manage simultaneous feedings. Experiment with different chairs (or a sofa), pillows, and different feeding positions until you find an arrangement that works best. If you are feeding triplets or more, you may find that particular baby pair combinations feed together better than others.

Most mothers recommend a roomy sofa or chair with a stool for propping your feet. An upholstered recliner may be ideal. Gravity can help hold the babies in place and a footrest is built in when you adjust the chair to a semi-reclining position.

Experiment with different sized pillows, placing them across your lap and under your arms. Pillows can help you relax during feedings by supporting your head, back, or legs to relieve muscle tension. They also become "extra arms" that prop, support, and hold the babies in position. Some mothers prefer using bed pillows that "cradle" the babies. They also can put one off to the side on a pillow and then pull him over once the first baby is latched on. Other mothers swear by the breastfeeding pillows that wrap around the waist. They report these firmer pillows support babies' heads better. And there are mothers who combined a breastfeeding pillow to "hold" the babies in place with bed pillows under their arms or at their backs to relieve tension. A few mothers say they felt "trapped" and didn't like using a breastfeeding pillow. If you are unsure which might work best for you, try using pillows you have available at home before investing in a commercial pillow.

Ask someone to help when you and the babies are learning. An extra pair of hands can hold Baby A in place after latch-on so you can concentrate on helping Baby B get started. If one or both has difficulty latching on, you may find it helps for someone to continue to hold one or both baby's head(s) in place for a few minutes or for the entire feeding.

Simultaneous Feeding Positions

There are three basic simultaneous positions used when sitting. Most other position descriptions are variations of these.

Double cradle or crisscross hold.

1. **Double-cradle** or **crisscross hold.** Place one baby in the crook of each arm in the traditional cradle hold. Crisscross their bodies along your abdomen or in your lap.

A variation of this is the **V hold.** Sit with your knees flexed and your legs slightly propped. Place each baby in the cradle hold with one of their bodies lying along each of your thighs—their knees or feet meet to form a V. You can use a modified V hold to breastfeed in bed by using pillows to lie nearly flat or in a semi-reclining position. Another variation used for night feedings in bed or a recliner is a **side-lying position** in which the babies' bodies are shifted off to the sides of your body with each supported by and along one of your arms. Your elbows would bend less to form less of a crook when using this position.

Mothers like that the double-cradle is a "hands on" position. This position is more difficult to manage initially, especially when either baby has difficulty latching, since a mother has no free hands in this position. This position becomes easier as babies gain head control or can latch on easily, so mothers tend to use it more often as babies get older.

Double football or clutch hold.

2. **Double football** or **double-clutch hold.** Hold each baby in the football, sometimes called the clutch hold, position with a baby's body tucked under each of your arms supported on a pillow. You can hold a baby's head in each of your hands or support their heads on a firm pillow.

A variation of this position is to hold each baby's head as for the football hold, but position each of their bodies on a pillow almost at a right (90°) angle, or perpendicular, from yours. Check the babies' ear-arm alignment to make sure both are in a good position to suck, swallow, and breathe.

This position often is used initially by mothers who've had a surgical birth to avoid pressure on the incision. It may be easier to manage babies having difficulty latching on in this position because your hands are free to help the babies latch on. Once home you can read a story to older children, eat a snack, or look something up in this book because your hands are free.

However, this is the least "hands on" position. You literally can prop your breasts and ignore the babies. If that happens often, it defeats one of the main advantages of breastfeeding multiples.

Combination cradle-football hold.

3. **Combination cradle-football hold.**
Position the first baby in the crook of your arm in the cradle hold. The second baby is held in the football position. It may help to place the second baby in the football hold on whichever side leaves your dominant hand free. (For right-handed mothers this means holding the first baby in the cradle of the left arm and positioning the second baby in the football hold at the right breast. Left-handed mothers would simply reverse this.)

A common variation of this hold is called the parallel, or layered, hold, in which the first baby begins feeding in the traditional

Babies in a V-hold.

cradle hold. The second baby is positioned with her head resting "gently" on the first baby's abdomen or legs and her body tucked under your arm or supported on a pillow at a right angle.

Many mothers cite this as their favorite position. They like the fact that they have skin contact with the babies yet still have a free hand. It is more easily mastered than other positions even when one or more babies had difficulty latching. They also say they can feed most discreetly using this position.

Additional Positions

There are several other simultaneous feeding positions that tend to be used less often. However, you might find one is more comfortable for you and your babies.

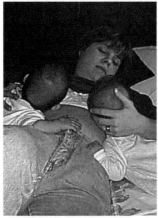

Double prone position.

Double saddle or **double straddle position.** Seat a baby on each of your thighs facing you. Hold the back of each one's head in each of your hands and support their backs/torso areas with your forearms. Each baby's legs straddle one of your thighs as if sitting on a saddle. If you lean back, the babies would lean forward during the feeding. Or you can lean forward while supporting the babies in a more upright position. This position is used more often with older babies; however, a few mothers have found it helpful with babies less than three months.

Double prone position. Lean back in a recliner or on pillows until you feel well supported in a semi-sitting or supine (flat, or almost so, on your back) position. Lay the babies on their tummies/abdomens so they face your breasts. Their abdomens and legs lie parallel along and facing your abdomen.

Mothers with larger breasts sometimes find a baby can latch on more easily in this position, as some of the breast may "disappear" when lying back. This position or a prone/side-lying variation in which one baby is more prone and one is held in a side-lying position has been used by mothers at night for feeding babies in bed or in a recliner.

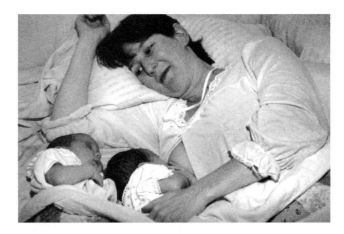

Side-lying position, nursing babies one at a time.

Double or **single kneel position.** As babies grow in length and gain more head and torso control, some mothers manage simultaneous night feedings by placing one or both babies in a kneeling position at the side(s) of the body. Help a baby to "kneel" on the bed facing the side of your body. The baby then leans forward to latch on and is supported by your chest wall. Both babies can be placed in this position or it can be used in combination with one baby in a prone or side-lying position. If one baby is in a more exaggerated side-lying position, so that you also are rolled to the side to face that baby, the kneeling baby may become more of a "standing" baby!

Older babies develop their own variations of nursing positions.

Elbow-prop position. In this position you are prone—lying on your abdomen—propped up by your elbows. The babies lie on their backs underneath you. (Their feet could point in any direction that works!) This probably is the least-used simultaneous feeding position; however, some mothers set up a mattress on the floor and use this position so that babies can remain where they are if they drift off to sleep. Other mothers report they found this position beneficial when treating a plugged duct.

Other Hints

Who latches on first? Most mothers find it is easier while learning to breastfeed simultaneously if they put the more proficient "latcher" to breast first. The mother then uses her free hand(s) to work with the baby needing more help. Yet some mothers report the opposite; they say it is easier to help the less-skilled baby latch on when they have two free hands and an empty lap. When the more proficient baby knows what to do, all they really have to do is pull that baby over and help it get into position. In other words, different methods work for different mother-babies trios, so experiment until you find what works best for you and your babies.

Burping

Burping often is less of a concern for breastfed babies. The newborn that feeds smoothly, taking in very little air during feedings, may not need to burp. A gulper, however, may be happier after a good belch.

Wait for a baby to self-detach from the breast. Positioning for burping then depends on which simultaneous feeding position is used. When using the double-cradle position, move your arm to help Baby A lean forward and cup that baby's chin in the hand of the arm still cradling Baby B. This frees the arm and hand that had been cradling Baby A so you can pat his back. Moving one up onto your shoulder to burp may be easier from the combination, double-football, -straddle, or -prone positions. Some mothers quickly figure out how to move one after the other onto their shoulders to burp two at once, but it generally is easier to burp one at a time, especially with very young babies.

Discreet Feeding

It may take time to achieve discreet simultaneous breastfeedings. The combination and double-football positions usually lend themselves more to discreet feeding with very young babies, but many mothers can feed older multiples discreetly using the double-cradle.

Once you are able to feed two discreetly, you still may feel rather conspicuous. It's fairly easy to feed one baby "invisibly," but two create more of a show—some mothers would call it a circus! So feed the babies separately or together—whichever is more comfortable for all concerned—when at the homes of others or in a public place.

Chapter 13

Making Up for a Poor Start

Newborn multiples often get off to a poor breastfeeding start because of pregnancy or birth-related complications. Even full-term, healthy multiples sometimes get off to a poor breastfeeding start if early feedings are delayed or only one baby is brought to breastfeed at each feeding while the other(s) is given a bottle in order to "let mother rest." If this has already happened to you, it's too late to go backward. But mothers and babies can usually make up for lost time.

Babies do learn to breastfeed better. Mothers can increase milk production. Believe in your body's ability to make milk for your multiples, and believe in their ability to learn to breastfeed well. It takes motivation for any mother to improve milk production for a single baby, much less for multiples. But you and your babies can do it together.

Keeping Babies Healthy

When you are working to increase milk production because of a slow breastfeeding start, babies' hydration and weight gain may be a concern whether each baby breastfeeds well or there is one or more having difficulty. Read the section in Chapter 9, "Beginning Breastfeeding," so you will know the signs that the babies are doing well.

- When babies breastfeed well and diaper counts are within the normal number, you may find it reassuring to weigh each baby once or twice a week until you feel confident that each is gaining weight appropriately. To make sure you are getting accurate weights, use the same scale, weigh each baby in the nude, and check weights at about the same time of day.
- You may want to check weight more frequently for any baby who is having difficulty breastfeeding. There are more sensitive electronic scales available that record how much a baby receives during a single feeding. To use this type of scale, you weigh a baby before a feeding, "lock" in the weight, and weigh the baby again after feeding. The scale subtracts the "before" from the "after" weight and lists the difference, the amount that the baby took in during the feeding, in ounces or grams. Using this type of scale provides more reliable information about day-to-day weight differences for any baby who must be weighed daily for a period of time.

Although frequent weighing is not necessary for most babies, parents often appreciate having this type of scale available when a baby's nutritional intake or a baby's weight is in question. The results may help guide decisions about the need to supplement any baby and whether breast pumping is needed. These scales can be rented. See "Resources" at the end of this book.

For Effective Breastfeeders

For babies able to latch on and breastfeed correctly, the best treatment for a poor breastfeeding beginning is to take the babies to bed with you for several days of almost round-the-clock breastfeeding. As long as each baby can breastfeed when she cues, usually about eight to twelve times in 24 hours, you probably will find you are bursting with milk within a few days. If milk production needs a boost but you can't go to bed for a few days, try these suggestions.

- Breastfeed each baby 10 to 12 times a day, simultaneously or separately. Because babies may become hungrier sooner when milk production is not yet what it needs to be, babies usually are happy to go along with this many feedings.
- You could also increase "feedings" by expressing or pumping your breasts. Some mothers save time by pumping one breast while feeding a baby on the other; other mothers pump immediately after a feeding or between feedings.

- Keeping track of each baby's wet and dirty diaper count and each one's weight gives you an idea whether any baby needs additional milk in the form of expressed breast milk or infant formula and about how much to offer. Develop a plan with your babies' pediatric care provider so that you are offering a baby no more of the supplement than is necessary to produce a good diaper count and an adequate weight gain. (See Chapter 10, "Effective Breastfeeding.")
- If any baby does need additional milk, rarely is it necessary to offer it with every breastfeeding. Offering a little extra once or twice a day is often enough. Offering other milk, especially infant formula, too often interferes with breast milk production. Babies digest artificial baby milk/infant formula differently, so babies usually "request" fewer breastfeedings. This lowers milk production even more. It also leads to juggling breastfeedings and other feedings—with a few pumping sessions thrown in for good measure. It's easy to become overwhelmed and lose confidence when trying to do it all.
- Gradually decrease any additional milk the babies are receiving by decreasing the amount given at each feeding by one to two ounces (30 to 60 ml) every few days. Expect the babies to breastfeed an extra time or two. Their diaper counts might dip or their rates of weight gain might plateau for a few days each time you do this. When babies fall back into their usual routines, their diaper counts pick up again and they are gaining at least a half ounce (28 gm) a day, you are ready to subtract another ounce or two (30 to 60 ml) from each feeding.

When One (Or More) Has a Feeding Difficulty

Newborn babies do not all have the same level of breastfeeding proficiency. The ability to latch on and breastfeed well may vary a little or lot among multiples. If you think any baby is not breastfeeding correctly, read the section on "difficulty latching or sucking" in Chapter 14, "Breastfeeding Difficulties in Young Babies."

When one or more newborns has difficulty breastfeeding correctly, it can be doubly or triply (or more) frustrating to work through a problem with that multiple(s) while also caring for the other(s). The sheer number of babies may mean it takes longer to work with an individual baby experiencing difficulty, which may add to everyone's frustration level.

Relax. Do what you can for today. Take it one day at a time, and expect some days to go better than others. With patience and persistence the magic moment will come when each multiple figures out what must be done to get that good milk from your warm breast.

- As often as possible, work at breastfeeding with the one having difficulty for five to thirty minutes before offering expressed milk or some infant formula. (Depending on family circumstances, "as often as possible" may vary from every feeding to only a few feedings a day.)

  Move on to an alternative method if either you or the baby becomes extremely frustrated. When you and the baby have been "working" at breastfeeding for about 30 minutes and it still doesn't feel right, you may need to offer that baby something else.

- When a baby who has been having difficulty demonstrates early feeding cues, such as rooting, licking, or putting hands to face or mouth, put that baby to breast immediately when possible, even if that baby appears to be sleeping.

- Increase skin-to-skin contact with this baby as much as possible. Take the baby's shirt off and yours too. Lie down with the baby on your chest. Put a sheet or blanket over both of you if necessary. The baby will get to know the comfortable feel and smell of the breast without the "pressure to perform."

- Some babies begin to breastfeed better when on mother's chest in a tub of water maintained at skin-temperature (98.6°F, 34 to 35°C). Place the baby chest-to-chest and allow him to seek the breast without much assistance from you. **Warning:** Ask the babies' health care provider before taking a preterm baby in the tub with you, and take only one baby in the tub at a time.

- Breastfeed the multiple having difficulty simultaneously with another multiple that is breastfeeding well. The baby with effective sucking will stimulate a good let-down (milk-ejection) reflex, which sometimes forces a "weaker" multiple to move his mouth correctly to swallow milk. You could also use an electric breast pump at one breast while simultaneously feeding the baby having difficulty. At best, the baby may finally figure out what he must do to handle the flow of milk. At worst, he will sputter and let go of the breast.

- Sometimes a baby having difficulty latching on to or feeding directly from the breast will be able to latch on and breastfeed when the mother covers her nipple with a thin, silicone **nipple shield.** This type of shield also has been used as a transitional device for some babies who seem to be confused when at the breast. Many of these "confused" babies have gotten used to receiving their meals from another feeding method, such as bottles with artificial nipples (teats). Ideally, the nipple shield is removed at some point during the feeding. However, some babies will breastfeed only when the shield is in place for a while.

When a baby who has had difficulty begins to breastfeed through a nipple shield, a mother often allows herself to feel hopeful about long-term breastfeeding for this baby-and she should. It is a big step forward. However, nipple shield use has its drawbacks. The use of a nipple shield is associated with a decrease in milk production. Also, some babies appear to become dependent on them for feedings and refuse to breastfeed without the shield. Therefore, it is best to remain in contact with an LLL Leader or a lactation consultant when considering the use of a nipple shield for any baby. The goal is to breastfeed this baby without the nipple shield.

Compensatory Milk Expression

Milk production is affected when any baby cannot suck correctly, since this baby is not removing milk well. Nipple shield use also is associated with reduced milk production. Therefore, continue to express your milk as needed, until all babies are breastfeeding well. (See the first section "For Effective Breastfeeders" above.) You also will want to continue to pump if milk production is low because of your own need to recover from a pregnancy or birth condition.

- To save time, **consider renting a hospital-grade, automatic, self-cycling electric breast pump.*** Using this type of pump with a double collection breast pump kit allows you to pump both breasts at once, which is associated with improved milk production. Because this type of electric pump is easy to use and pumping sessions take less time, many mothers find they express milk more often than they would by hand or with other kinds of breast pumps.

- Many mothers pump one breast while breastfeeding one multiple on the other side. (A double collection kit can be adjusted so you can pump only one side when breastfeeding on the other breast.) This may save a lot of time. It also may result in better milk production, so there is more breast milk available if another multiple is still having difficulty breastfeeding.

---

* Any rental fee is quickly made up by what it would cost to purchase infant formula for multiples. In addition, many insurance companies reimburse for breast pump rental if an explanatory letter from the pediatric care provider accompanies the reimbursement claim. (See Chapter 11, "Multiples in the Newborn Intensive Care Unit," for general guidelines about using a breast pump.)

Some mothers would rather pump immediately after all, or several, daily feedings. Other mothers pump between feedings. Almost any milk expression routine will work as long as a mother is consistent about it.

- How often you pump probably will depend on each baby's ability to get nourishment at the breast, your family situation, and whether your goal is full or partial breastfeeding. If your goal is to fully nourish your babies with your milk for several weeks or months, your babies and a pump will need to remove milk from your breasts at least 10 times and up to 16 times a day. This translates to a total of at least 140 to 160 minutes spent with a baby breastfeeding (correctly) or for pumping sessions. To establish or maintain adequate milk production for partial breastfeeding, milk should be removed from your breasts **at least** eight times a day or for a total of about 100 to 120 minutes.

  Perhaps your goal is to fully breastfeed your babies, but for now you can only meet the feeding/pumping quota for partial breastfeeding. Give yourself a break and meet the goal for partial breastfeeding today, tomorrow, and maybe the day after that. When you are able, increase the number sessions or the total time spent breastfeeding or pumping. Most mothers find milk production increases within days of adding extra breastfeedings or pumping sessions.

- When one or more babies breastfeed well, you may find you can reduce the number of pumping sessions or spend less total time pumping. However, you will want to pump every day as long as any baby continues to have difficulty breastfeeding. Your body still can use the reminder that it is making milk for multiple babies.

Alternative Feeding Methods

Any baby that is not yet able to get all the nourishment he needs at the breast can be fed your milk, or an infant formula, by some other means for some or all feedings. Ideally, your milk is available for alternative feedings, but it is not always possible to achieve the ideal when providing for multiple babies. When plentiful milk production is delayed for any reason, your multiples will require nutrition from another source until production improves. Once an initial breastfeeding difficulty is resolved, it may still take extra time to increase milk production enough for multiples.

There are many alternative methods for feeding your expressed milk or some formula to the babies. However, some methods are less likely to interfere with the physical behaviors babies use during correct breast-

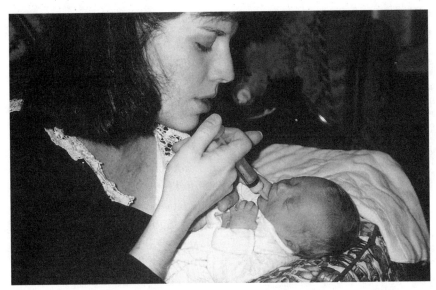

Feeding a newborn with a syringe.

feeding. Most mothers would rather not use a feeding method that might compound a difficulty a baby already is having or one that could create a new problem. Ideally, you can avoid feeding methods that may confuse a baby still learning to breastfeed correctly.

There are **exceptions.** You must use whatever method works best if you have to get nourishment into a baby who is in danger of becoming dehydrated or one whose weight gain is severely compromised. You can try a different feeding method later when the baby is hydrated and gaining weight.

Work with a La Leche League Leader or a lactation consultant when choosing and learning to use an alternative feeding method. Many mothers are unfamiliar with all the alternatives; they may not realize how many options are available. Several methods require a demonstration to ensure that they are used correctly. The Leader or lactation consultant can show you how to use an alternative feeding device and explain how other mothers have used it. Most alternative feeding methods are easy to learn. Incorrect usage of any method, including bottle-feeding, creates physical stress for a baby.

The following is a discussion of some of the options that might work when one or more multiples is not yet breastfeeding well.

- A couple of methods deliver nourishment to a baby through a tube. For instance, a thin feeding tube may be taped to a mother's breast. As the baby breastfeeds, he also receives milk through the tube. For the baby

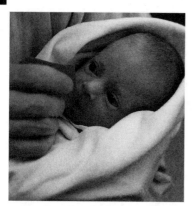

Cup feeding

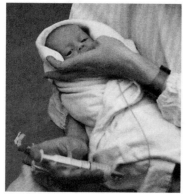

Finger feeding with a syringe and tubing

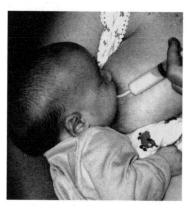

Using a feeding syringe at the breast

who breastfeeds correctly, or one who seems to have the basic idea, this may be an excellent way to offer supplementary food. Baby gets extra calories, and at the same time he "tells" the breast to boost milk production.

To feed a baby who isn't yet breastfeeding well but one who is able to suck adequately, a parent may tape a feeding tube to a (very clean) finger. As the baby sucks on the finger, milk is drawn through the tube and swallowed. This is called "finger-feeding."

Commercial feeding tube systems have been designed for alternative feedings. One system comes with two tubes so that a tube can be taped to each breast, which is ideal when two multiples need supplementary fluids. Of course, one of these tubes could be taped to a parent's finger instead. An infant feeding tube, such as the catheter used in the NICU for gavage feedings may also be used; one end is attached to a syringe, or placed in a bottle, of milk.

• Other methods deliver milk directly into a baby's mouth. Devices used for direct feeding include the use of a spoon, medicine dropper, syringe, or cup. Although most of these devices are readily available, it's important to let a baby set the pace of feedings when using any of these devices.

1. Spoons and medicine droppers are items available in most households, but neither holds much liquid. Both work well but some mothers find that using them can become tedious. Some mothers use a hollow

medicine spoon that will hold more or they fill several droppers and line them up before beginning a feeding. Another problem is that the bulb end of a medicine dropper can be difficult to keep clean.

2. Syringes come in various sizes-from less than 1 cc (1 ml) to 30 cc (30 ml, 1 oz). Adjusting the syringe barrel size as a baby takes more reduces the need to refill syringes during a feeding. Syringes that come without needles are available in hospital supply shops. If you cannot buy them over the counter in your area, your baby's pediatric care provider may be able to "prescribe" them for you.

When using a dropper, medicine spoon, or syringe, fluids are "dripped" into the buccal space, the space between the gum and the lip/cheek, of the lower jaw. Only a drop or two are offered at first. The pace of the feeding should be adapted to the baby's responses. Parents quickly learn how much to offer at a time.

3. Cup-feeding newborns may be unfamiliar to many living in Western cultures. However, it has been used to get liquids into larger preterm or sick newborns in many countries. A small glass or flexible plastic cup, such as a medicine cup or shot glass is used for cup feedings. (Check the rim of the cup for rough edges before offering liquids to a baby.)

Only awake, alert babies should be cup-fed, since the idea is for the baby to sip or lap the fluid in the cup with its tongue. Studies show that spillage may be a problem, especially if the amount a baby is taking is supposed to be measured.

- Feeding with bottles using **artificial nipples** (teats), especially in the first several weeks after birth, is associated with a greater number of breastfeeding problems and early weaning. The design of most bottle nipples (teats) causes babies to use very different tongue, jaw, and mouth movements than for breastfeeding.

The main reason a baby uses its mouth differently during bottle-feeding is that a fast flow of liquid forces baby to hold her tongue behind her lower gum. She then presses her tongue up against the roof of the mouth in order to stop the flow of liquid so she can take a breath. This movement is counterproductive to correct breastfeeding behavior, since the breastfed baby must stick her tongue out beyond the lower gum if she is to latch on deeply and suck correctly. No wonder babies get confused.

If **using bottles** is the only way you can cope or the only way to get food into a baby (and sometimes it is), using a slow-flow brand of nipples (teats) may help minimize the interference with breastfeeding behaviors.

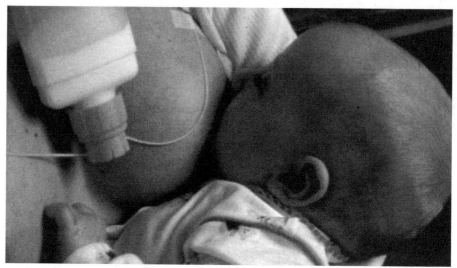
Using a nursing supplementer at the breast to provide additional calories.

A slow-flow nipple (teat) may avoid, or at least minimize, the need for a baby to hold her tongue behind the lower gum. Test the flow of all nipples (teats) by holding them at the angle used for feeding. You should be able to count several seconds between drops of milk. If the flow rate is too rapid, you may want to try another one or a different brand.

No Method Is Perfect

There is no "best" alternative feeding method. Some methods work better in one situation, or for one baby, than another. Paradoxically, all may prolong a feeding problem or create a new problem, while at the same time they enable you and a baby to work through a breastfeeding difficulty.

Besides the different mouth movements a baby uses with alternative methods, alternative methods may prolong or create a problem in a couple of ways. The breastfed baby must wait for the let-down reflex; every other feeding method offers a baby instant gratification. The breastfed baby must stick out her tongue and open wide if she is to latch on and feed correctly; babies barely have to open their mouths when fed by most other methods.

- When putting the baby to the breast, pump for a minute or two just prior to breastfeeding to hasten the let-down reflex. This may avoid or lessen the issue of instant gratification. It also may be helpful when any multiple has difficulty controlling the initial flow with let-down or for one who could use more hindmilk than foremilk.

- Encourage breastfeeding behaviors when using an alternative feeding method. Stroke a baby's cheek or the center of her lip to stimulate the rooting reflex. Wait for her to extend, or stick out, her tongue and open her mouth wide before offering the spoon, syringe, bottle, etc.

Additional Tips

Unless you are supplementing with a feeding-tube device taped to your breast, let family and friends help manage babies for other types of feedings. Their assistance will free you to focus on working with the babies at the breast and pumping your breasts to maintain adequate milk production. When one multiple is fed by a helper more often than the other(s), make time for other kinds of skin-to-skin contact with that baby.

Offer available human milk before offering an artificial infant formula. When there is not enough expressed milk for every baby who needs it, mothers of multiples sometimes have to make hard decisions about which baby will get how much. A baby who has been sick or one who has more difficulty digesting infant formula may need more of the expressed human milk than the other(s).

Don't mix expressed milk with infant formula. You'll want to keep the ingredients, the tastes, and the odors separate. Whether you have a little or a lot, offer your milk first and then follow it when necessary by some artificial formula. (See Chapter 17, "Full and Partial Breastfeeding.")

It seems unfair that the mother of multiples, the mother most in need of a good breastfeeding beginning, is the least likely to get a good start. Although life is not always fair, it is almost always possible to make up for lost time when multiples or their mother get off to a slow start. When is not possible to completely make up for a slow start, it is possible to combine feeding methods. Contact a La Leche League Leader or a lactation consultant to help you. She will have ideas to help you save time and maintain perspective.

Chapter 14
Breastfeeding Difficulties in Young Babies

Odds are high that at least one baby of a multiple set will experience some difficulty breastfeeding. Sheer numbers account for some of the odds. The more babies one has the greater likelihood that one or two will need more time to get the hang of it. Sometimes there is no real difficulty, but one or two may not be as adept as the other(s). However, multiple-birth babies are more likely to be affected by the pregnancy and birth complications, procedures, or medications associated with breastfeeding difficulties.

Multiples are more likely to be born early, which means their nervous systems may not yet be mature enough to coordinate the behaviors needed for feedings. Pregnancy, labor, and birth complications, procedures, or medications may affect temporarily a part of a baby's nervous system or the physical structures involved in breastfeeding. The effects of pregnancy, labor, or birth may delay early, frequent breastfeedings. They have also been implicated in the introduction of alternative feedings, which means that other objects, such as artificial nipples (teats), pacifiers, and other feeding devices may be put in a baby's mouth. These oral objects seem to confuse some babies, causing difficulty when a baby goes to latch on or breastfeed.

Many so-called breastfeeding difficulties actually are "having multiples" difficulties. Often an aspect of adjustment is labeled a breastfeeding difficulty when the breastfeeding itself is going well. For instance, a mother may consider it a problem when trying to figure out the breastfeeding styles of two or more unique individuals when the real issue is related to differentiating and caring for two or more babies. Since each breastfed multiple can be expected to eat eight to twelve times in 24 hours, it's easy to understand when issues about multiples in general become thought of as breastfeeding problems in particular.

Many problems can be avoided when a mother understands a few basics of breastfeeding, such as how milk is made, the mechanics of infant latch-on, and typical infant breastfeeding patterns. (See Chapter 10, "Effective Breastfeeding.") If a problem should arise, ask yourself if it's a true breastfeeding problem or whether breastfeeding somehow has gotten caught up in an "adjusting to multiples" issue.

A difficulty with one baby can upset the entire breastfeeding "team" if a mother, and those helping her, indulge in "unit" thinking. Don't lump all the babies together. When faced with the care of multiple babies, it is easy to think the entire "team" has a problem when more likely it is just one baby who needs some help.

Try to figure out where a problem truly lies. Is it your problem, a problem with one (or more) of the babies, or is it related to someone/something outside of your breastfeeding team? Ask yourself how you would feel, and how you would approach the problem, if it had occurred when you were coping with only a single baby.

Most baby-related breastfeeding difficulties are related to the "mechanics" a baby uses at the breast or his feeding pattern. Often only one multiple has a particular difficulty; however, it's possible for two babies to have the same difficulty. Just to cloud the picture, two babies could have a difficulty, yet each baby's difficulty could be with a different aspect of breastfeeding. No wonder mothers of multiples feel confused.

Common baby-related difficulties are addressed in this chapter. Most baby problems are related to either a problem with basic breastfeeding management or to a baby who is having some difficulty latching on or sucking well. In either case, the baby is not able to obtain as much of your milk as he needs.

Work with your babies' health care provider. Also call an experienced La Leche League (LLL) Leader or a lactation consultant today. She can help you look at the babies' individual breastfeeding behaviors and patterns to see where a difficulty might lie. She also can help you develop a realistic plan to begin to deal with a problem. Most importantly, she will listen when you need to express concerns or vent frustration. While others may ask why

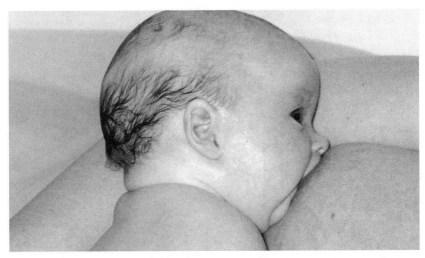

This older baby shows a good latch-on with lips flanged and chin against the breast; mother's nipple is far back into baby's mouth.

you want to continue breastfeeding multiples, she will provide the praise and moral support you deserve.

It may take both patience and some persistence to work with a baby who is experiencing difficulty breastfeeding when you have multiples to care for. However, if you do persist, most babies learn to breastfeed in time.

Difficulty Latching On or Sucking

Mothers usually know when any multiple is not yet breastfeeding "right." Some signs that a baby is not breastfeeding effectively are obvious, but others are more subtle. For instance, it is possible for a baby to latch on to the breast correctly yet not be able to suck well. A baby must also suck well, remove the milk in the breast, if that baby is to get sufficient food. Review the following list, but if your baby's difficulty isn't on this list and you still are concerned, trust your instincts too. A baby **may** be having difficulty if he **consistently** exhibits any of the following behaviors:

1. Breastfeeds fewer than eight times, or more than 12 times, in 24 hours;
2. Has difficulty latching on to the breast, which may include clamping or "biting" down during latch-on, attempting but being unable to grasp the breast, or "pushing away" from the breast;
3. Rarely continues with uninterrupted sucking for at least five to ten minutes on the first breast—may easily "fall" off of or seem to drift to sleep at the breast within a few minutes of latching on;

4. Continues to make rapid, non-nutritive sucking movements of two or more sucks a second beyond the first minute or two at the breast (See Chapter 10, "Effective Breastfeeding.");

5. Dimples his cheeks, makes clicking sounds, or purses his lips feedings;

6. Continues to feed on the first breast longer than 30 to 40 minutes without self-detaching and does the same when offered the other breast, so that feedings last longer than 45 to 60 minutes, and may act hungry again within minutes of some feedings;

7. Has fewer than two or three bowel movements a day;

8. Does not experience a daily increase in the number of wet diapers or an increase in the degree of saturation during the first few days after birth, or is not producing at least six sopping wet diapers by five to seven days after birth.

A mother is more likely to experience sore or cracked nipples when a baby has difficulty latching on or actually breastfeeding. Severe engorgement, a plugged duct, or mastitis may also be a result of a baby's inability to breastfeed well. Any nipple or breast problem is a sign that a baby's behaviors during breastfeedings should be more closely examined. (See Chapter 15, "When Mother Has a Breastfeeding Difficulty.")

Extreme difficulty with latching on, "weak" or uncoordinated sucking, and drifting to sleep soon after beginning to breastfeed may be related to preterm birth, complications that affected a baby's oxygen supply during labor or delivery, and medications or procedures used during labor or birth. There may also be differences in the maturity of each multiple's brain and nervous system. One baby may not yet be able to coordinate the mouth movements used for breastfeeding as well as the other(s). A baby might have a physical problem that interferes with the ability to latch on or suck, such as a short frenulum or tongue-tie.

Problem-Solving Ideas

Get help if you think any baby is not breastfeeding correctly even if you were told earlier that this baby appeared to be breastfeeding well. No one can see into a baby's mouth and watch a baby breastfeed. You know what you are feeling.

To pinpoint the problem, you may want an experienced pediatric care provider, an LLL Leader, or a lactation consultant to examine the structures in the baby's mouth and to watch that baby breastfeed. Sometimes they can detect a minor problem with breastfeeding mechanics, so that a simple change in technique makes all the difference. Someone experienced in helping mothers and babies breastfeed also is more likely to figure out and have ideas to resolve a situation that is more than a matter of mechanics.

If a baby's maturity, pregnancy, or birth complications, or labor and birth medications have affected his ability to suck, it may take several days or several weeks for the baby to learn to breastfeed correctly. The baby will learn, but in the meantime you can:

- Offer the breast as soon as the baby demonstrates feeding cues. When a baby is having difficulty at the breast, feeding behaviors tend to become more disorganized as his cues escalate to hard crying.

Tickle baby's lips.

- If a baby "resists" or seems to push away, alternate breastfeeding positions until you find one that seems more comfortable for the baby. Support only the back of the baby's head and neck so that the baby still can turn or adjust his head.

- A sleepy baby may cue to breastfeed fewer than eight times a day. If you notice this baby moving arms or legs or making facial and eye movements, stimulate the baby by unwrapping blankets that might be keeping him too warm. Change the baby's diaper if he drifts to sleep within a couple of minutes

Wait for baby to open wide.

of beginning to breastfeed. The sleepy baby may breastfeed better if you massage and then "squeeze" your breast when the baby pauses during a breastfeeding.

Getting enough food into a sleepy newborn can be a challenge. (See Chapter 13, "Making Up for a Poor Start.") Be certain the pediatric care provider is aware of the daily number of feedings and both the wet and soiled diaper counts for this baby. Contact the provider if there is ever a decrease in feedings or diapers. You may have to monitor this baby's weight for a while.

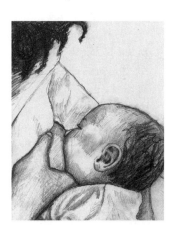

When baby is latched on well, his nose and chin should touch your breast.

- If a baby can latch on but the let-down, or milk-ejection, reflex overwhelms him, take the baby off the breast until the flow of milk slows. You also could offer an "emptier" breast by pumping through the let-down or by feeding this baby after the other multiple(s) breastfeed.
- Feed one having difficulty simultaneously with a multiple that breastfeeds well. Sometimes the one having difficulty figures out what to do in response to the flow of milk triggered by the better breastfeeder. (The worst that may happen is the one having difficulty will sputter and release the breast.)
- Place a silicone nipple shield over your nipple to see if it helps the baby latch on to the breast and breastfeed. **Warning:** The use of a nipple shield may interfere with a baby learning to latch directly onto the breast and it is associated with a decrease in milk production. Stay in touch with an LLL Leader or a lactation consultant when using a nipple shield. (See Chapter 13, "Making Up for a Poor Start.").
- Continue to offer the breast but stop if you or the baby becomes extremely frustrated. Neither you nor the baby has to feel under "pressure to perform." Try again in an hour or two when you are calmer and the baby again demonstrates feeding cues.
- Use an alternative feeding method to offer some expressed breast milk or infant formula when a baby experiences an ongoing difficulty or when either of you becomes really frustrated. Discuss the pros and cons of the different methods with someone experienced in helping women breastfeed, so you can decide which one may encourage a baby to learn to breastfeed better and also which may be more practical when caring for multiple babies.
- When any multiple has a difficulty, place that baby skin-to-skin on your chest as often as you can. Let the baby learn that your breast is a pleasant place to be. If the baby acts interested, offer the breast but don't worry if he doesn't take it this time—or the next, or the time after that. Almost all babies eventually learn to breastfeed when a mother continues to offer the breast.
- Try bathing with a baby born at or near full term or whose adjusted age is nearing full term. Some full-term babies begin to breastfeed better when chest-to-chest with mother in a tub of water heated to about skin-temperature (98.6 degrees F, 34 to 35 degrees C).
- Continue to pump your milk until all babies are breastfeeding well. How often you pump may depend on the baby's problem, how well the other(s) breastfeed, and the amount of help you have at home. The more help you have, the more time you will have to work with a baby still

learning to breastfeed and the more time you will have to pump milk for alternative feedings.

- If anyone suspects that incorrect breastfeeding mechanics are associated with a physical structure in a baby's mouth, have that baby examined as soon as possible by an appropriate health care provider. A pediatrician, ear-nose-throat specialist, oral surgeon, or dentist may all be trained to handle a problem such as tongue-tie. Tongue-tie can be treated very quickly by a trained care provider. If treatment is delayed, it may take longer for a baby's breastfeeding mechanics to improve.

- On days when you think a particular multiple will never breastfeed, call the LLL Leader or a lactation consultant. She'll give you a pep talk that can help you maintain perspective. (For more detail and additional ideas, read Chapter 10, "Effective Breastfeeding," Chapter 13, "Making Up for a Poor Start," and Chapter 17, "Full and Partial Breastfeeding.")

Minor Feeding Difficulties

Some babies experience difficulty for the first week or two whenever they first latch on or begin to feed, yet after a few minutes they do latch on and breastfeed correctly. Mothers of these babies often say they feel nipple soreness or pain when the baby first goes to the breast, but their discomfort eases after the first few minutes of feeding. These babies usually have diaper counts and weight gains that are within normal limits.

If you experience this type of problem with one or more multiples, it probably is related to breastfeeding mechanics. Often a simple fine-tuning of positioning or latch-on technique will "cure" the problem. See the illustrations earlier in this chapter. Call an LLL Leader or a lactation consultant if you still have difficulty correcting the mechanics after looking at the illustrations. She may be able to offer advice over the phone or you and the baby may need to be seen in person to work on technique.

Growth Spurts and Frequency Days: Sudden "Demand" for Extra Feedings

It may not seem so at the time, but newborns' sudden demand for more frequent breastfeeding usually is not a problem. When any baby who has been breastfeeding correctly suddenly asks to eat several additional times in a day, suspect a growth spurt or frequency day. Growth spurts and frequency days are discussed in greater detail in Chapter 10, "Effective Breastfeeding," since they appear to be a normal aspect of breastfeeding.

Weight Gain Issues

New mothers often express concern about their babies' weight gains, especially when breastfeeding for the first time. It may take a while for new mothers to gain the confidence that their bodies will produce plenty of milk so babies will be able to get enough breast milk to grow. Confidence may take even longer to acquire when breastfeeding multiples. However, each baby will let you know how she is doing through her breastfeeding pattern and her diaper count. (See Chapter 10, "Effective Breastfeeding.")

Babies with typical feeding patterns and adequate diaper counts usually gain **at least** one-half ounce (15 gm) a day, or four ounces (112 gm) a week, and most gain about an ounce (28 to 30 gm) a day (six to eight ounces/200 gm a week) for the first three or four months. (Count from the babies' due date if they were born early, and measure weight gains from each baby's lowest weight after birth—not a baby's birth weight.) Weight gain often tapers off after several months. Babies still continue to gain but at a slower rate.

A few babies gain less than four ounces some weeks. However, their diaper counts are appropriate and they maintain a steady, albeit slower, rate of gain. Although this baby may need to be monitored more closely, a slow but steady pattern may be normal for some babies. It is important to identify the difference between a normal, slow-gaining baby and one with a true weight gain problem.

It can be fascinating to watch the growth patterns of fraternal multiples. Although they are getting the same milk, they often grow and develop at very different rates. Sometimes one gains several pounds a month, yet another barely falls within the normal range. However, both may be perfectly healthy; they simply have different genes for body build.

There are times, though, when one (or more) truly is not gaining the weight he should. A problem with weight gain may occur during the newborn period or it may arise later. When any baby is not gaining adequate weight, review the information above about "difficulty latching on or sucking" and examine the baby's breastfeeding routine. Sometimes a lack of breastfeeding know-how results in inadequate weight gain.

- Is the baby truly breastfeeding at least eight times a day? If so, is that often enough for this particular baby? Are you trying to develop a schedule by stretching the time between feedings, or might one baby often get "put off" because you have to care for the other(s)?

- When a baby is unable to suck correctly, she may be unable to take in enough milk for growth. Are you certain that this baby's breastfeeding technique is correct? Does latch-on seem to take a lot of time or does this baby frequently have difficulty latching on? Does she have trouble staying latched on? Does she quickly fall asleep after latching on?

Or do many of her feedings take longer than 35 to 40 minutes? Does she often fuss or act hungry again within minutes of "finishing" a feeding? Does she typically breastfeed more than 12 times a day? (Many babies feed more often during the occasional growth spurts or a frequency day.)

- Count wet and soiled diapers. Frequently, a decrease or an inadequate number of daily soiled diapers is one of the first signs that a baby isn't getting the calories needed to gain weight. When the number of wet diapers decreases, it may be a sign that a baby is not getting enough fluid as well.

- Does the baby use a pacifier? Pacifier use can interfere with the daily number of breastfeedings, and it may affect the baby's ability to suck correctly when at the breast.

- Is this baby receiving supplementary water? Water alone has no calories. It may help hydrate a baby, but it does not contribute to weight gain. Plus, it can confuse your ability to interpret the wet diaper count. Human milk, or complementary infant formula, contains calories and enough water to keep babies well hydrated.

- Are you taking care of yourself? True, a baby's feeding pattern or his incorrect breastfeeding behavior is at the heart of most infant weight gain problems. However, milk production in a mother of multiples may be somewhat more sensitive to that mother's poor diet, extreme fatigue, minor illnesses, etc. These things may also affect your fatigue level and subsequent ability to respond to your babies' cues.

Problem-Solving Ideas

You will want to work closely with the babies' health care provider when any multiple's weight gain is inadequate. Read Chapter 13, "Making Up for a Poor Start," and the ideas for "difficulty latching on or sucking" above. These suggestions also help when coping with a baby who breastfeeds well but is not gaining adequate weight.

- Breastfeed this baby more often when possible—about every two to three hours during the day for about 10 to 12 feedings daily. Put this baby to breast whenever the baby demonstrates feeding cues. (These cues are described in Chapter 9, "Beginning Breastfeeding.") Watch for the baby to begin to move his extremities and make facial grimaces. These are signs that he has reached a light sleep state and can be awakened more easily to breastfeed. Do not give this baby a pacifier.

- Monitor this baby's daily feedings and diaper counts on a chart. (See Chapter 10, "Effective Breastfeeding.")

- Weigh the baby as often as the pediatric care provider suggests. Different types of scales and their usefulness are discussed in Chapter 11,

"Multiples in the Newborn Intensive Care Unit," and Chapter 13, "Making Up for a Poor Start." You may be expected to bring the baby to the provider's office more often until an adequate weight gain is established. Let the provider know if it will be a hardship to make frequent office visits for weight checks. Accurate electronic scales are available for rent and some pediatric care providers or community lactation consultants are able to make home visits to monitor a baby's weight. (See "Resources.")

- Supplement this baby's feedings with your pumped milk or an infant formula as needed. A feeding tube system may be the best method to supplement a baby who is able to breastfeed well. This method provides a baby with the extra nutrition while breastfeeding, which may increase milk production and may avoid other breastfeeding difficulties.
- Pump your breasts as needed to increase (or maintain) milk production, especially when a weight gain problem may be related to a sucking difficulty or the baby who has not been breastfeeding often enough.
- As the weight improves, ask the baby's care provider and an LLL Leader or a lactation consultant about a plan to decrease or eliminate supplemental feedings.

Many breastfeeding problems can be resolved quickly and some take more time. The information in this chapter may help you identify and begin working on a problem, but you may need help to sort through it. Do yourself a favor; get help as soon as a breastfeeding difficulty develops. Contact the babies' health care provider, but don't wait to reach the end of your particular rope before you call an experienced LLL Leader or a lactation consultant. Having her help may save you and your babies a lot of time and trouble.

Chapter 15
When Mother Has a Breastfeeding Difficulty

A new mother is not more prone to breastfeeding difficulties simply because she has multiple babies to feed. However, the presence of two or more babies with differing breastfeeding abilities or styles multiplies the likelihood that a baby will experience some difficulty. A mother and her babies work together when they are breastfeeding. If breastfeeding isn't quite "right" yet for a baby, the mother often experiences a problem too.

This chapter deals with difficulties that can affect you—the mother. Baby-related difficulties are discussed in the previous chapter. The information in this chapter is meant to complement, not take the place of, the support of an experienced LLL Leader or a lactation consultant. She can help you get to the root of the problem, individualize a plan for solving it, and help you decide if it is something that should be reported to your care provider.

Sore Nipples

Sore or cracked nipples usually tell a mother that there is a "mechanical" problem with some aspect of breastfeeding. When any baby does not latch on correctly or cannot suck well, the action of the baby's mouth can irritate the skin at the nipple tip or "bruise" breast tissue. Slight irritation may produce some redness and a feeling of soreness; greater irritation can lead to nipple cracks or fissures. If dealt with immediately, most nipple soreness is short-lived.

The best way to prevent sore nipples is to get off to a good breastfeeding start when your babies are born. (See Chapter 9, "Beginning Breastfeeding, and Chapter 10, "Effective Breastfeeding.") Ask a nurse or a lactation consultant to help you initially, as each baby latches on and begins to breastfeed. A little nipple tenderness when a baby first latches on is not unusual during the first week. (If you've experienced tenderness at certain times in the menstrual cycle, it may feel similar to that.) However, it should not be so painful you want to "bite a bullet" during any part of a feeding, and you should not see any redness, scraped nipple or areolar skin, or nipple cracking.

Although it may sound contradictory, frequent feedings are beneficial when nipples are tender or sore. Babies are usually more willing to work at fine-tuning their latch-on and feeding technique when they are not ravenously hungry. Waiting to put hungry babies to the breast can lead to nipple damage, as it may be more difficult for them to latch on to overfull breasts. Also, extremely hungry babies may be less gentle when they latch on.

A baby's mouth must open/gape wide to latch on to the breast. Failing to open wide may cause a baby to "inch" his way onto your breast, which may damage nipple and areolar skin. Try to avoid giving babies pacifiers or bottles during their first weeks. Babies barely have to open their mouths to take a pacifier or bottle nipple (teat). Also, damage to nipple or breast tissue may occur if a baby uses bottle or pacifier sucking behaviors when breastfeeding.

If your nipples become sore, you develop any redness or cracking, or nipple tenderness persists beyond two weeks, something is not quite right. You don't have to grin and bear it. Now is the time to take a closer look at breastfeeding mechanics with each multiple. (Look again at the illustrations in Chapter 14, "Breastfeeding Difficulties in Young Babies.")

1. Is any baby having difficulty latching on to the breast or do you think that one is not breastfeeding well once latched? A nurse or a lactation consultant can tell you how the latch or feeding behaviors appear, but only you know whether it feels "right."

2. Is each baby positioned so that she is in good alignment to coordinate sucking, swallowing, and breathing? When a baby is in good alignment, you can draw an imaginary straight line from a baby's ear through the upper arm to the hip.

3. Could the "hold" you are using to support your breast during latch-on interfere with a baby's ability to latch on correctly? For example, your fingers might cover part of the areola on the underside of the breast— where it is difficult for you to see—making it impossible for a baby to latch on deeply.

4. Is any baby latching on before he opens his mouth wide in a gape or yawn? All babies, including preterm babies, can open wide. Some babies go through a series of mouth movements, gradually opening wider and wider, before they open wide enough for a deep latch-on.

5. Does the baby get deeply on the breast in one motion, or is he "nibbling" his way up the areola, until he finally achieves a correct, deep latch? You want to help a baby latch on deeply in one smooth motion. Nibbling onto the breast usually is a sign that the baby's mouth wasn't opened wide enough.

6. Are you trying to help two babies latch on so you can feed them simultaneously? This may take a little more skill on both mother's and at least one baby's part. Incorrect latch-on techniques may be reinforced when distracted by two hungry babies at once.

Often a minor "mechanical" issue is the root of the problem, which means many, or most, sore nipple problems are easy to resolve. Once someone figures out where the problem lies and the mechanics are corrected, you'll probably be amazed at how quickly sore nipples heal. While you and your babies are working on correcting the mechanics, you may want to try some coping ideas that have worked for other mothers.

• Some mothers find it helps to express a little milk before a baby latches on to "soften" the areola and hasten the let-down (milk-ejection) reflex.

• Avoid simultaneous feedings until at least one of the babies participating in the feeding consistently latches on correctly.

• Let a baby with correct mechanics breastfeed more often on the sorer side. (Or alternate babies and breasts each feeding, rather than every 24 hours, if you are worried that poor technique will create a similar problem on a less sore side.)

• Do not shorten feeding time, since this usually has little impact on soreness. Limiting feeding time can interfere with a baby's nutritional and caloric intake, since milk with higher fat content is "delivered" later in each feeding. If soreness persists throughout a feeding, it is a signal to get help from someone qualified in breastfeeding problem management.

- Express a little milk onto the nipples and then apply a small portion of an ultra pure modified lanolin, such as Lansinoh® for Breastfeeding Mothers to the nipples after every feeding. Lansinoh® has been found to both soothe and help heal irritated tissue. Avoid other creams, oils, or lotions. Do not air- or blow-dry nipples or expose nipples to a heat lamp. These treatments have been found to dry the skin, causing further damage and unnecessary scabbing. (Modified lanolin should not cause a reaction for those with an allergy to sheep or wool. However, you can test for a reaction by applying a small amount of modified lanolin to an area at the inside bend of your elbow before using it on your nipples.)
- Nipple soreness may persist for a few days or weeks when a baby's sucking is affected by labor or birth complications, medications, or procedures. Until the baby "outgrows" the behavior contributing to sore nipples, nipples will still be less sore when babies are well positioned at the breast and correct breastfeeding mechanics are encouraged. (See Chapter 14, "Breastfeeding Difficulties in Young Babies," for a discussion of baby-related problems.)

Suspect a **thrush** (fungal/yeast) infection when each baby is using correct breastfeeding "mechanics," yet sore, red nipples persist. Thrush infection may also be the cause of sore, cracked nipples that develop in later months of breastfeeding. Nipples may feel "itchy" and have a shiny or flaky appearance with thrush. These infections may be associated with a burning pain of the nipple, or a burning sensation that is felt deep into the breasts, which may last throughout and even after feedings. Some mothers complain of cracking on the side of the nipple or at the base of the nipple, where the nipple meets the areola.

One or more babies may also have symptoms. Babies infected with thrush often develop cheesy-white patches in the mouth. A fiery-red diaper rash can also be a sign of a yeast/fungal infection.

Nipple soreness caused by thrush is not related to breastfeeding mechanics. Both you and (all) your babies will require treatment with an anti-fungal medication to eliminate it. Be scrupulous about continuing treatment through the recommended period. An LLL Leader or a lactation consultant will be able to give you more in-depth information.

Engorgement

Milk production markedly increases in the amount (volume) produced by the second to sixth day after birth. (Delays in plentiful production occasionally are seen for up to 10 to 14 days in mothers affected by certain health or birth-related conditions.) With the fairly rapid increase in milk volume, a new mother's breasts may feel fuller, heavier, and the skin may be more taut. These pronounced breast changes cause some to say their breast milk has "come in," but this statement is not completely accurate.

The breast changes do signal an increase in the volume of milk being produced and a change in the proportion of the nutrients in breast milk. However, breast milk has been available to the babies since birth. They have been receiving important nutrients and high levels of antibodies in colostrum for several days.

The breast fullness many women experience is not due simply to an increased volume of breast milk. When hormonal changes after birth tell a mother's body that the time has come to make milk, extra blood and lymph fluids are sent to the breasts to provide the materials that will become breast milk. When the flow of these fluids gets ahead of milk production or the removal of "stored" milk via breastfeeding or pumping, the breasts become congested with blood and lymph. This causes swelling in the breasts.

A combination of the rapid increase in milk production and the swelling due to blood and lymph congestion is referred to as breast engorgement. The degree to which women experience the signs of engorgement varies widely. The breast changes associated with engorgement are very dramatic in some women and are hardly noticed by others.

Labeling the normal breast fullness that often accompanies plentiful milk production in the first week postpartum as "engorgement" is controversial. How to treat it is not.

Full breasts should be "emptied" frequently and completely by babies who breastfeed correctly.* The idea is to keep milk moving out of the breasts and into the babies, so the extra blood and lymph can be used to make more milk or it can move back into the mother's circulation. This is also the best way to avoid severe engorgement.

Healthy newborn multiples that are able to breastfeed well may help a mother avoid severe engorgement. Blood and lymph don't have a chance to become congested when multiples breastfeed frequently. If any multiple is not yet able to breastfeed or any baby is not removing milk effectively, a hospital-grade, automatic, electric breast pump can be used every one to three hours to "empty" full breasts. **Keep the milk moving—one way or another.**

---

* During lactation, the breasts never are truly "empty," since milk production is an ongoing process.

Severe Engorgement

If a mother becomes severely engorged, her breasts become hard and "lumpy"; she may feel as if they are filled with small rocks as far up as the collarbone and under the armpit. Engorged breasts usually feel sore or painful and may look red. The areola may become so "tight" that a mother's nipples flatten, which can make it difficult for a baby to latch on. The signs of severe engorgement are caused as much, or more, by swollen, congested breast tissue as by the rapid increase in milk volume.

When severe engorgement occurs, it usually appears some time between three to seven days after birth. The most common cause is infrequent or ineffective milk removal by any baby during breastfeedings, especially once milk volume has increased. A few women seem to be prone to severe engorgement. No matter what they do or don't do, their breasts become extremely engorged within several days of giving birth. It may develop with or without a mother first noticing the breast fullness that marks an increase in milk volume.

Fortunately, severe engorgement usually responds to treatment within a few hours. It is important to begin treating severe engorgement as soon as the symptoms develop. For one thing, you will feel comfortable sooner. More importantly, quick treatment may help avoid a long-term milk production problem.

To understand how prolonged severe engorgement can affect long-term milk production, it first helps to know how milk is made, which is explained in Chapter 10, "Effective Breastfeeding." When milk builds up too long in the lumen of a milk-making alveolus, chemical signals are sent back into the cells of that alveolus that "tell" it to slow milk production. These chemical signals eventually tell the alveolus to stop making milk, to "dry up" altogether, unless the process is reversed within a certain amount of time by removing the stored milk from the lumen. (The alveoli can regenerate during a subsequent pregnancy.)

This is the process that will occur if severe engorgement goes untreated for more than a day or two; it's how the milk "dries up" when a woman doesn't breastfeed. Not all alveoli "quit" at the same time, so even when severe engorgement is not reversed quickly, most mothers will continue to produce a lot of milk for their babies. Unresolved severe engorgement can also lead to other problems, such as plugged milk ducts or mastitis—a breast tissue inflammation or infection.

- The most important thing to do if you become severely engorged is **remove the milk** by breastfeeding or pumping your breasts frequently. Until engorgement resolves, breastfeed or pump every one to three hours.

1. Massage your breasts before you breastfeed or pump. Use both hands on one breast, and apply firm but gentle inward pressure as you move your hands from your chest wall over the breast and downward to the areola.
2. Some mothers say it helps to apply a warm compress briefly before breastfeeding or pumping. This may encourage a let-down especially if combined with breast massage. However, do not use heat for longer than one to two minutes because it can increase the amount of swelling if milk does not start to flow.
3. If any baby has difficulty latching on to engorged breasts, hand-express or pump enough milk to soften the areola and then try again. Reapply the pump to "empty" your breasts if a baby continues to have difficulty.
4. If you cannot feel a marked softening of the breasts after breastfeeding any baby, pump your breasts with a hospital-grade, electric breast pump or breastfeed another multiple at that breast. (When you've run out of babies to breastfeed, use the pump if your breasts still don't feel a lot softer.)

- Occasionally, it takes 20 to 30 minutes for the milk to begin to flow the first time a mother applies a hospital-grade, electric breast pump to severely engorged breasts. The let-down (milk-ejection) reflex may not be able to respond as well due to the swelling.

  1. Make certain you are using a hospital-grade, automatic electric breast pump. These pumps are more effective, and they also are more gentle because they automatically cycle and release the suction.
  2. Pump for at least 20 minutes even if you are not seeing milk droplets. It may help to take a break and massage your breasts again if you pump several minutes but see very little flow. Then reapply the pump for another 10 to 20 minutes.
  3. Adjust the suction to a lower rate or stop and take a break if pumping becomes uncomfortable, but pump again in an hour.
  4. Pump every one to two hours until milk begins to flow within minutes of beginning to pump.
  5. If you don't begin to get a good flow within five minutes of beginning to pump by the third pumping session (and third hour), get help from an LLL Leader, a lactation consultant, or another health care provider. There may be a problem with the equipment, pumping technique, etc.

6. Continue to pump for a minute or two beyond the time you last see a drop being expressed. Pumping usually takes 10 to 30 minutes. Some mothers find that a pumping session takes less time overall when they break for a minute or two after the initial flow noticeably slows. These mothers massage their breasts a second time, reapply the pump, and then continue to pump for a minute or two beyond the time they last see drops expressed.

- Apply cold cloth compresses or ice packs to engorged breasts for at least 30 minutes after breastfeeding or pumping. (It may help to do 30 minutes on, 30 off, 30 on, etc.) Cold helps reduce swelling in the breasts just as it is helpful for reducing swelling in any other part of the body. When swelling decreases, a mother feel more comfortable and her milk often flows better during the next breastfeeding or pumping session. Continue to apply cold packs between breastfeedings or pumping sessions for 24 hours or until swelling is no longer a concern.
- Some mothers find frozen peas, beans, corn, etc., in sealed, plastic bags create compresses that "mold" more easily to breasts.
- Some mothers find engorgement resolves more quickly when they apply **cabbage leaf compresses** after a breastfeeding or pumping session. (Apparently, ordinary, fresh, uncooked cabbage leaves contain a substance that reduces swelling, so it will work as well on a sprained ankle as on engorged breasts.)

  1. First wash fresh cabbage leaves in cool water, some recommend adding a little soap to the water, rinse, and refrigerate. Washing removes any chemicals used to grow the cabbage; cool water is recommended to avoid "cooking" the cabbage, which may decrease the helpful substance in the leaves; and refrigerated leaves usually feel more soothing for hot, engorged breasts.
  2. Apply cooled, uncooked cabbage leaves directly to all areas of the breasts except the nipples. You can hold the compresses in place by wearing them inside your bra.
  3. Remove the cabbage once the leaves have "cooked"/wilted, which usually is between 20 to 60 minutes. You may want to apply cold compresses immediately following a cabbage compress or wait and apply after "resting" breasts for 30 minutes.

- Contact an LLL Leader, a lactation consultant, or your health care provider if severe engorgement **does not begin to respond** to treatment within 12 to 18 hours. Certainly, call her before this if you have questions or need encouragement.

Later Engorgement

Engorgement can occur whenever any baby or a mother abruptly "drops" a breastfeeding or when a breastfeeding is "put off" in an attempt to lengthen the time between feedings. A mother of multiples already is producing significantly more milk than the average breastfeeding mother, so she will have more milk building up if a feeding is missed, especially if two (or more) babies suddenly drop a feeding or are encouraged to wait longer between feeds. Because of the greater milk volume, a mother of multiples may be more prone to developing a plugged duct or mastitis following such engorgement.

The treatment for this type of engorgement is the same as for engorgement during the first week. **Remove the milk.** Put a willing baby to the breast. If you are trying deliberately to decrease production, do it slowly so the breasts can adapt to the change gradually. You could hand-express or pump milk briefly—only to the point of relieving fullness—if you become engorged. **Warning:** Delaying feedings to lengthen the time between feedings may also result in poor infant weight gains and one or more unhappy babies.

Insufficient Milk Production

In several surveys of mothers of multiples, the fear of not producing enough breast milk was one of the biggest reasons for weaning the babies. Almost every mother wonders at some time or another whether she is making enough milk. Although many mothers fully, or exclusively, breastfeed twins, triplets, and even quadruplets, multiples' needs for breast milk could push mothers' milk-making ability to the limit—or beyond—at times, especially for higher-order multiples. If you ever feel concerned about the amount of milk you are producing for your babies, you may want a La Leche League Leader or a lactation consultant to help you figure out whether there is a problem or not.

Perceived Milk Insufficiency

Normal breastfed babies tend to eat more often than artificially fed babies. The total number of breastfeedings for multiple babies' adds up to a lot of feedings each day. Turn back to Chapter 10, "Effective Breastfeeding," to read about normal feeding patterns and the signs that each baby is getting enough milk. If each baby usually is satisfied with eight to twelve daily feedings, and all have diaper counts and weight gains that are within the normal range, you can feel assured that you are making plenty of milk.

Sometimes mothers express concern that they are "losing" their milk once the initial breast fullness or engorgement subsides. The breasts feel soft much of the time. This is not indicative of a production problem as long as babies' diaper counts and weight gains are normal. It usually means the breasts have adapted to each baby's demands and are producing that daily quantity of milk.

Friends, relatives, and even some health professionals may question whether a mother can produce enough milk for multiples. They may point to babies' requests for frequent feedings as a sign that one or more babies isn't getting enough milk. Don't allow pressure from others cause you to lose confidence in your body's ability to meet the demands placed upon it. Instead look at your babies' feeding patterns, diaper counts, and weight gains.

True Milk Insufficiency

It is thought that about one percent of mothers worldwide are physically unable to produce enough milk for one baby. That figure could be as high as five percent in the USA, perhaps because cosmetic breast surgery is more common. Breast size is not related to a woman's ability to produce milk. Mothers with breasts of all different sizes and shapes have fully breastfed twins and triplets for several months.

Although no one has yet studied large numbers of women breastfeeding multiples, especially those with triplets or more, insufficient breast milk production usually is related to infrequent or inadequate removal of breast milk rather than a mother's physical inability to produce enough milk. Increasing the number of breastfeedings or pumping sessions almost always results in increased milk production within several days. If you truly are concerned about adequate milk production, first look at the babies' feeding patterns, diaper counts, and weight gains.

- Typically, breastfed babies are satisfied with about eight to twelve daily breastfeedings. If any baby is breastfeeding fewer than eight times in 24 hours, he may not be removing milk often enough to generate adequate production. Beware of the "good" baby who is sleepy or undemanding. A baby who rarely seems satisfied and consistently "demands" to breastfeed 14 or more times in 24 hours may not be sucking correctly, so the baby breastfeeds more but milk removal is less effective. This can also have a negative effect on milk production.

- A baby who is not getting enough milk often has fewer than two to three dirty diapers a day. A decrease in a baby's daily number of stools (bowel movements) often is the first sign that a baby is not getting enough milk.

- A baby who consistently gains less than one-half ounce (14 to 15 gm) a day, or less than four ounces (112 to 120 gm) a week, during the first three months, is probably not getting enough breast milk.

What do you do if any baby's diaper count or weight gain indicates you are not making enough breast milk? First, stay calm. Then figure out whether the problem belongs to the baby or to you.

1. Most problems with insufficient breast milk are baby issues. If at least one baby is gaining weight normally and the other(s) is not, the problem most likely is with the multiple(s) that isn't gaining. A diaper count and weight gain problem for two or more babies, however, does not automatically mean that the mother is the one with the problem. It is not unusual for all multiples to experience some sucking difficulty in the first weeks, especially when babies are preterm or all experienced some complication. Most baby problems can be "fixed." See the previous chapter for ideas to cope when a baby isn't getting enough to eat because he can't remove milk well or isn't waking often enough to eat.

2. Be sure you are not managing breastfeeding in a way that interferes with any baby getting enough to eat. Sometimes mothers try to lengthen the time between feedings for one or more multiples in order to develop a household routine. Eight daily feedings may be an adequate number of feedings for some babies, but it isn't enough for the baby who needs to breastfeed 12 times a day to get enough calories. Imposing rigid feeding restrictions or inflexible schedules on any baby could lead to inadequate weight gain and reduced milk production.

3. Occasionally, there is a structural problem with a mother's breasts that leads to insufficient milk production. A few women do not develop enough glandular tissue to support full milk production. These women often report that they noticed little, or no, breast change during pregnancy or soon after birth. Rarely, both nipples are severely inverted and neither can be drawn out for feedings. Another rare occurrence is when breasts or nipples don't mature during puberty. Women with a history of breast surgery, especially certain breast reduction procedures, or severe breast injury may have suffered damage to some of the breast tissue involved in milk production.

A woman should report such "warning flags" to her health care provider, and she and her babies should be monitored closely, but she can still feel cautiously optimistic about breastfeeding. Many women with these histories produce plenty of milk. Sometimes "plenty" would apply for a single baby but this mother may need help with multiple babies. However, usually only time will tell whether milk production will be affected.

4. To increase milk production, there need to be more effective breastfeedings or an increase in the number of pumping sessions— no matter what the reason that production is currently lowered. That is the only way to learn whether your body can make more milk.

If you have been maintaining milk production only by pumping your breasts or by combining breastfeeding with pumping, look at your pumping routine. A pumping session may have been dropped inadvertently as you became more involved with babies' care. It also is possible that babies' nutritional requirements have increased, and an extra session or two is needed for a while to boost milk production.

Alternatives

If you are not producing the quantity of milk needed for your multiples, it does not mean you must wean your babies. Consider partial breastfeeding if milk production does not improve significantly after more frequent breastfeedings or pumping sessions or if time constraints interfere with your ability to work on improving production. Partially breastfed babies still receive many of the nutrients and the antibodies to illnesses that are not found in artificial baby milks/infant formulas. Partial breastfeeding still allows you to enjoy the special closeness that comes with breastfeeding each baby. (See Chapter 17, "Full and Partial Breastfeeding.")

Flat or Inverted Nipple(s)

Flat or inverted nipples are fairly common structural variations of the breast. Often only one nipple is affected or one may be flatter or more inverted than the other. Many women report that flat or inverted nipples improve during pregnancy.

Many alert, full-term babies have no difficulty drawing out and latching on to an affected nipple, since babies actually latch on to the areola of the breast—not to the nipple. Some babies initially have difficulty grasping one or both inverted or flat nipple, but with a little time and patience they learn to latch on well.

Mothers of multiples sometimes find that one baby has little or no trouble latching on to the same flat or inverted nipple that causes difficulty for another baby. If only one nipple is causing any baby difficulty, a baby more adept at latch-on could be assigned the affected breast until the other(s) becomes more proficient.

Breast shells are hard, lightweight plastic domes that are worn inside the bra for short periods of time. They are often recommended for treating flat or inverted nipples, because the shell exerts a slight, steady pressure on the areola to help draw the nipple out. Some mothers begin to wear them during the last trimester of pregnancy, although the effectiveness of wearing shells is debatable. **Warning:** This type of nipple stimulation may be considered an unnecessary risk for preterm labor during a multiple pregnancy. **Do not wear breast shells during multiple pregnancy** unless your obstetric care provider approves their use. If you decide to try breast shells after giving birth, begin to wear them for about 30 minutes before each breastfeeding.

Exposing the nipple to cold air or a cold cloth briefly, or using a breast pump for a few minutes immediately before breastfeeding, often helps draw out a flat or inverted nipple. LLL Leaders and lactation consultants will be aware of other devices that some mothers have found helpful, such as a suction device that draws out a flat or inverted nipple. Because inappropriate use of devices can hurt nipple tissue or affect milk production, it is best to get an LLL Leader's or lactation consultant's guidance before using any of them.

Plugged Ducts and Mastitis (Breast Inflammation or Infection)

Plugged ducts and mastitis seem to be no more a problem for the mother of multiples than for the mother of a single infant. However, factors that contribute to plugged milk ducts and mastitis are more common, and they may have a greater effect on someone producing double, triple, or quadruple amounts of milk.

- When making so much milk, the body cannot adapt as quickly to a delayed, dropped, or missed feeding. Milk "build-up" may then contribute to a plugged duct or mastitis.
- Inadequate milk removal caused by poor breastfeeding technique or ineffective sucking is associated with plugged ducts and mastitis just as it is for sore nipples. Therefore, be more aware of the signs of a plugged duct or mastitis in a breast where the nipple is sore, red, or cracked.
- Some mothers of multiples find they are more prone to develop a plugged duct or mastitis if they become extremely fatigued. Poor nutrition also appears to be a factor in some cases. All of these factors tend to lower a mother's resistance to illness.
- A number of mothers have developed a plugged duct or mastitis within days of preparing for and hosting a special event, such as hosting a party to celebrate a holiday or the multiples' christening. They almost always reported that such events were "stressful." Most of these mothers lost additional sleep in the days before the event, and a breastfeeding or two was delayed or missed while they were trying to get ready or entertain

guests. Trying to accomplish too much at home or at work are other sources of stress that appear to be associated with an occurrence of a plugged duct or mastitis. Both may be related to a mother's fatigue level and with inadvertent delays/missing of breastfeedings or pumping sessions.

- Poorly fitting nursing bras and the bunching of a shirt under the armpit during feedings may contribute to a plugged duct. Either can put pressure on the breast's glandular (milk-making) tissue or milk ducts.

A plugged duct feels like a lump or knot in the breast and it usually is tender to the touch. Mastitis is associated with a red, swollen, tender area on the breast. It differs from engorgement in that mastitis usually occurs in only one breast and any swelling tends to be in a particular area rather than of the entire breast. The first sign of mastitis may be the flu-like symptoms associated with it.

If you develop a plugged duct or mastitis, you can use heat or cold on the area for comfort. (If the entire breast is swollen, you may also be engorged so applying cold is a better idea.) Heat may be applied to the affected area in the form of warm compresses or a heating pad. A mother may shower and let the warm water run over the area or immerse her breasts in a basin of warm water. Many women prefer a cold compress or an ice bag on the affected area. Massage the area after applying heat or cold. Let babies breastfeed frequently on the affected side to ensure that the breast remains as empty as possible. Some mothers find it helpful to take extra vitamin C.

For a plugged duct without mastitis, try massaging the plug during feedings. Move your hand above the plug and massage downward toward the areola and nipple. Repeat several times.

Many mothers have used a rather unusual breastfeeding position to help resolve a plugged duct: Place one of the babies on her back on the floor (on a blanket or pad) or on a sofa. Then lean over, bending at the waist, to feed the baby. Use this position for several feedings a day. Perhaps it's the gravity that works, but mothers often say a plug resolved or it was much smaller within a day. Contact your obstetric care provider if there is no change in a plugged duct or it has grown in size after treating it for several days.

You will want to call your obstetric care provider immediately if your **temperature is above 100.4°F (38°C)** with mastitis. The increased temperature indicates infection, so an antibiotic may be prescribed for 10 to 14 days. Although most of these antibiotics are compatible with continued breastfeeding, be sure to ask your care provider about the one being prescribed. Ask to be given a different medication if there is a question about compatibility. Since inflammation of the affected breast tissue is an aspect of mastitis, you also might want to ask your care provider about taking a compatible nonsteroidal anti-inflammatory medication at regular intervals.

Overabundant Milk Production and Forceful Let-Down/Milk-Ejection Reflex

Mothers of multiples tend to worry that they will not produce enough breast milk, but many mothers find themselves coping with the opposite problem. Producing milk for multiple babies sometimes leads to "oversupply" or rapid "refilling" with milk. Generally, this is a good problem to have, but some babies quickly become overfull which may cause them to spit up or develop stomachache symptoms.

If babies frequently choke, sputter, or break off crying within a minute or two after beginning a feeding, it may be due to a forceful let-down, or milk-ejection reflex. Forceful let-down may occur alone, but frequently it occurs in conjunction with overabundant production. Your babies will learn to handle a forceful let-down as they mature. In the meantime, the following ideas may help.

- Offer each baby only one breast at a feeding (if you have not already begun to do this). If overproduction continues to be an issue, assign each baby a specific breast and see if production in each breast adapts more to each multiple's nutritional needs. (You may want babies to switch sides for an evening feeding a few times a week so that each baby remains willing to feed from both breasts.)

- Do not limit feeding time on the one breast unless absolutely necessary. If you must limit feeding time to 10 to 20 minutes, you may find babies "ask" to breastfeed more frequently but for the shorter period.

- Offer the breast when you notice any baby's early feeding cues. This can help in two ways. The let-down often is more gentle and you may avoid overfull breasts.

- Breastfeed in an "uphill" position to slow both a forceful let-down and the rate of milk delivery. Let-down may be more manageable for babies, and they can often breastfeed for a longer period. To breastfeed uphill, lean back in a semi-reclining position or lie down, and place one or two babies in the clutch, prone, or kneeling positions. (See "Simultaneous feeding positions," in Chapter 12, "Coordinating Feedings.")

- Some babies are very good about knowing when to stop. These babies will refuse to take the breast again until their tummies are less full, yet they still act interested in sucking after they have finished feeding. Some mothers find that babies are more content if offered a pacifier at these times.

Avoid offering a pacifier to any baby who is not consistently breastfeeding correctly or one who is not gaining weight appropriately. (See Chapter 14, "Breastfeeding Difficulties in Young Babies.") Be aware of the potential for overuse of pacifiers, which is associated with early weaning. As much as possible hold and cuddle babies when offering a pacifier.

Many multiples find a thumb or a finger more pleasant to suck.

• Overabundant production may put you at more risk for developing a plugged duct or mastitis. For some mothers overuse of a breast pump increases milk production well beyond the babies' need for milk, which may contribute to the problem. Contact an LLL Leader or a lactation consultant if overabundant production causes discomfort for you.

Milk Leakage

Milk leakage is not truly a breastfeeding problem, but it can seem a nuisance. It is more common during the early weeks or months of breastfeeding. Leakage usually diminishes as a mother's body "gets used" to babies' breastfeeding patterns, and by several weeks or months it often stops altogether. There are ways to minimize leaking in the meantime.

• Often you can halt leakage by immediately applying firm, direct pressure over the nipple with the heel of your hand. If at first that doesn't succeed, keep trying. Sometimes it takes a while for your body to figure out what you are telling it to do.

To discreetly apply pressure to both breasts at once, lace your fingers, spread your hands over your chest so that the heel of each palm is over a nipple, and then press inward firmly.

• Turn milk leakage to your advantage. When feeding only one baby, hold a clean cup under the other breast and collect the leaking milk. Pour it into a bottle or a milk-storage bag, and refrigerate or freeze it for later use. (See the Appendix, "Guidelines for Storing Human Milk.")

• There are alternatives to the expensive nursing pads on the market. Large white cotton handkerchiefs work, but washing all those handkerchiefs may be one thing you can live without when caring for multiples. White paper towels are another option. Fold one paper towel (or double it) in half lengthwise and then into thirds to make a disposable, inexpensive nursing pad. Many paper towels come in bulk packs, but be sure to choose a brand that is soft yet absorbent. Mothers also have cut disposable diapers (minus the outer plastic lining) or sanitary napkins for disposable nursing pads; however, some contain perfumes or deodorants that may be irritating to nipple or areola tissue.

Maternal Illness, Disability, or Health-Related Conditions

Mothers have breastfed multiples when coping with many different kinds of short- or long-term illnesses, physical disabilities, or other health-related conditions. Many of these mothers have said that family, friends, and health care providers expressed concern that breastfeeding two or more babies might be "too much" for them, yet they found breastfeeding actually simplified caring for more than one baby.

Physicians' greatest concern may be about the medications recommended to treat various illnesses and conditions. They may question whether a medication will get into breast milk and affect the babies. If a doctor is unsure about the effect of any medication for the babies, contact an LLL Leader, a lactation consultant, or the babies' pediatric care provider. They often have scientific references about a medication's effects on breast milk. A few medications are not compatible with breastfeeding, but in most cases, there are almost always alternative medications that can be taken instead.

Sometimes a mother's illness or health condition requires medical or surgical treatment in a hospital. (See Chapter 16, "Avoiding Problems during a Hospitalization," for more information.) Some mothers find that milk production decreases temporarily after surgery or with an infectious illness. It may be related to the mother's recuperative needs or she may not have been able to breastfeed or pump her breasts as often as necessary. However, a return to frequent breastfeedings or pumping sessions quickly reverses any reduction in production.

Breastfeeding multiple babies can be confusing enough without developing sore nipples, severe engorgement, or a plugged duct. Since most mother problems are related to a minor snag in breastfeeding management or one multiple's mechanics at the breast, the majority of these problems go away once the management or mechanical issue resolves. Get help immediately when a problem develops. No mother caring for multiple babies needs to devote extra time to handle these kinds of problems for any longer than necessary.

Chapter 16
Avoiding Problems During a Hospitalization

Occasionally, a mother or one of her multiples has a health problem that requires hospitalization. Sometimes a close family member must be hospitalized, and the mother's presence is needed for that relative. No matter who is hospitalized, the mother often feels torn.

If a mother faces hospitalization, she may feel concerned about separation from her babies and a possible drop in milk production in order to meet her health needs. Knowing that each multiple needs her presence intensely, a mother feels pulled when she must weigh the hospitalized baby's need for comforting against those of any other(s) that remain at home. When a close family member is the patient, a mother often feels she should be in two places at once—at home with the babies and at the hospital to support the family member.

It doesn't matter who is hospitalized, the ideal is for a mother and her breastfeeding multiples to stay together for the duration of a hospital stay. This ideal often is attainable, but it will be up to you, and possibly your husband, to pursue it. As a parent, you not only have the right, you also have the responsibility to see that the needs of your babies are met in the best possible way.

Exploring Options

If you find you, one of your babies, or someone close faces a hospitalization, there usually are options that can help you meet the needs of all involved.

- Explore with the physician whether there are alternatives to actual hospital admission. Often diagnostic tests, treatment interventions, and even surgery can be done on an outpatient basis. Ask whether elective procedures could be postponed safely for a period of time.

  If you ever feel uncomfortable with a physician's explanation of a health problem, or the reason for a particular treatment and the need for immediate intervention, continue to ask questions until you are completely satisfied. Ultimately, you are responsible for your health care and that of your family, so never feel inhibited about seeking adequate information. It is your right.

- When hospitalization is unavoidable, arrange to take the babies to the hospital—especially if the hospital is many miles from home. Some parents have changed physicians or hospitals to keep the breastfeeding family intact. Taking multiples has worked well for many mothers of twins, although it gets more complicated when higher numbers are involved.

  It may be less complicated to rotate babies. Some mothers of higher-order multiples keep two babies with them much of the time. A helper picks up one baby and drops off another every few hours. (If you or another family member is the patient, you might prefer to use this plan with twins and keep only one baby with you at a time.)

  Most mothers recruit extra helping hands. It is too difficult to care for multiples alone in this situation. Having someone to help is crucial when you are the patient, but it is also very important if you must be available to a hospitalized baby or family member.

- The second-best arrangement is to have babies brought to the hospital several times a day. In many areas babies may be brought directly to a patient's hospital room. When this is not possible, there is always some area on a hospital unit or on another floor where you and the babies can be together for a while. (Insist that the babies be brought to the unit or same floor if you are the one hospitalized and babies are not allowed in patient rooms. If you continue to ask, a place to visit will usually be found.)

If a baby or family member is the patient and bringing babies in is forbidden, you could leave the hospital to go to the babies. However, you may become exhausted if you constantly run between hospital and home (or hotel). Parents have changed physicians or hospitals when a multiple required a hospital stay, so that the other(s) may be brought to the mother at the hospital. When a baby or another family member is hospitalized in an intensive care unit, there is usually a family lounge or waiting area nearby. It is reasonable to expect that the hospital staff can help you find some way to accommodate your babies' need for close contact with you during the hospitalization.

- When a brief hospitalization is anticipated, you can express milk over time and freeze it for any baby that is to remain at home. For example, a surgical procedure that required an overnight hospital stay was planned for one of twins. The well twin stayed home with family members rather than being taken back and forth to the hospital for breastfeedings. The mother left enough expressed breast milk in the refrigerator and freezer to last the 18 to 24 hours she would be at the hospital with the other baby.

- Whether the babies are with you throughout a stay or are brought to you every few hours, you will want to have certain items available. Some items may be available at a hospital, but others will have to be brought from home. You probably will want a rocking chair (a folding lawn-chair type will do), a baby carrier or sling, a lightweight single or double stroller, and disposable diapers. If any baby enjoys playtime in an infant seat, be sure one is available. You will want to take extra changes of clothing for babies, unless each can wear hospital-issued gowns.

Emergency Situations

Sometimes hospitalization is necessary for a sudden health need or an actual emergency. Immediacy may be unavoidable for some surgical or medical treatments. In these situations, there may be little, or no, time to explore alternatives for keeping the breastfeeding "team" together. Yet mothers have continued to breastfeed multiples during or after such unanticipated events.

To maintain breastfeeding with an unanticipated hospitalization, begin by maintaining milk production. Express milk as soon as possible—soon after you get to the hospital or as soon as you think of it. Whichever comes first! You will also want to express milk as often as possible—at regular two to three hour intervals during the day and about every four to six hours at night. If you are the one who is ill or had surgery, you may need your husband, a nurse, or a close relative or friend to help you use a breast pump for the first 12 to 24 hours. After 12 to 36 hours of treatment for an illness, or post-operatively, many mothers find they are ready to have babies brought to them in the hospital.

Be sure the hospital staff understands the consequences of delayed or missed breastfeedings for a mother of multiples. Frequent breastfeeding or pumping will help prevent severe engorgement or the development of a plugged duct or mastitis, which can complicate recovery if you are the one who is ill or had surgery. If contact with the babies must be limited due to your situation, ask whether a breast pump is available on the hospital unit where you are staying. If necessary, the unit where you are staying may be able to borrow a breast pump from the postpartum unit.

If it's accessible, take your double collection kit with you; it may be the same brand as the hospital pump. Sometimes mothers rent a pump to take into the hospital. If you take in a rental pump, be sure it is compatible with any collection kit you already have. Some mothers chain a rented breast pump to the frame of the hospital bed with the type of chain and lock used for securing a bicycle.

Don't panic if it seems milk production diminishes during a hospitalization. It isn't unusual. If you have been ill or had surgery, your body may have needed some of the fluids usually used to make milk for other functions, so you will heal more quickly. Also, it can be difficult to breastfeed or express milk often enough when you or someone close to you is in the hospital. Plus, a high level of stress probably doesn't help.

To get milk production back on track, do what you would do any time milk production isn't up to the babies' needs. Breastfeed each baby more frequently, eat a balanced diet, drink adequate fluids, and let other things go so you get enough rest. If you and the babies have been separated, they may cling to you when you return. On the other hand some babies ignore their mother for a while after being reunited, which may include resisting breastfeeding for several days. Increasing skin contact with them usually helps in either case. (Consider taking a "babies' vacation"—a few days of round-the-clock breastfeeding in bed, with few clothes on anyone, and room service for all meals. [Picture yourself in the tropics!])

When Breastfeeding Is Contraindicated

There are few health-related situations in which breastfeeding is contraindicated. Weaning is rarely necessary for health care problems or because of medications you must take. A health care provider may know a great deal about a specialized area of health care yet know little about breastfeeding and lactation. If you are told to wean, ask for an explanation from the health care provider. Then call a La Leche League Leader or a lactation consultant (IBCLC) for additional information. She can help you explore whether alternatives to weaning may be available in your situation. Health care providers usually are happy to accommodate realistic options to weaning.

When exploring options for keeping your breastfeeding team intact during a hospitalization, your physician or family members may be concerned that meeting multiples' needs by keeping them with you as much as possible may be too taxing. There are several points you may want to make in order to arrange for your babies to be with you.

- Explain as many times as necessary that it is impossible to treat one of a breastfeeding "team" without affecting every member of that team. It may be difficult for some health professionals or family members to understand the benefits of receiving breast milk without interruption. They may not grasp the intimacy of the breastfeeding relationship or that you and your babies work to together to achieve a physical harmony. You must teach them that breastfeeding is more than a way of getting food into babies. It also provides a sick baby with the perfect nourishment for healing.

- Discuss the need you have for your babies, as well as their need for you. Health care providers and family members may be concerned that it will be too difficult for you to care for the babies during a hospitalization. Only you can explain that it is a greater burden to be separated from them, which will cause you to worry about their welfare and feel torn about whose needs are greatest.

The hospitalization of any family member generally is a source of stress no matter when it occurs. That stress may be compounded if such an event takes place when multiples are young and still have an intense need for their mother's presence and her milk. Implementing the strategies mentioned in this chapter may allow a mother to maintain the breastfeeding relationships with her multiples during the family member's hospitalization. If you are faced with a family member's hospitalization and have additional questions about meeting your babies' needs, you also can count on support from a La Leche League Leader or a lactation consultant.

Chapter 17
Full and Partial Breastfeeding

It makes sense that Nature would design human milk to be the perfect food for human babies. Most human infants grow and develop best when fully breastfed for at least six months. And many babies, including some multiples, receive only their mothers' milk for even longer.

Nature also seemed to design the typical human to give birth to only one baby at a time. Technology, not Nature, is mainly responsible for both an increase in the number of multiple births and the improved survival rate for these multiple-birth infants. Although technology hasn't found a way to give a new mother more hours in a day or provide additional arms so she can care for multiple babies more easily, Nature apparently did anticipate a boom in multiple births when it created breastfeeding and human milk.

Human milk and the process of breastfeeding can adapt to the number of babies that need to be fed. Most women are able to produce enough milk for several babies. In addition, human milk produced after a preterm birth is different than milk produced at full term. Breast milk is the only infant food that continually changes as babies grow and develop.

What does a mother do when Nature gives her the ability to breastfeed multiple babies, but she and her babies didn't have ideal conditions for initiating breastfeeding? What does she do when it seems there aren't enough hours in every day to cope with eight to twelve feedings for each baby? What does she do? She does her best. For one mother this may mean she fully breastfeeds each multiple for several weeks or months; another mother may have to offer the babies her milk or an infant formula by another method at times.

The physical demands of a multiple pregnancy and birth, and the round-the-clock care for two or more newborns, creates situations that a mother breastfeeding a single infant never encounters. To make breastfeeding decisions that are best for their multiple babies and for themselves, mothers will want to compare the benefits of full and partial breastfeeding and then examine their particular family situation. It may also help to be aware of some of the pitfalls that can lead to unnecessary supplementation when breastfeeding multiples. When partial breastfeeding becomes the goal, a realistic plan may make the difference between long-term breastfeeding and untimely weaning.

Breastfeeding Definitions

New mothers may be unfamiliar with some of the terms health professionals and La Leche League Leaders use to refer to breastfeeding. Several of these terms refer to breastfeeding "quantity," and other terms refer to aspects of any alternative feedings a baby receives.

Multiples nourished only by breastfeeding are said to be **fully, exclusively,** or **completely** breastfed. Fully breastfed babies receive no other liquids or solids. When a baby is **almost fully** breastfed, the baby may receive vitamins and minerals or an **occasional** feeding of other infant food.

A baby is **partially breastfed** when the baby is given **regular** feedings through an alternative method, such as by syringe, feeding tube, infant feeding bottle, etc. These feedings usually consist of some food other than the mother's milk, including infant formulas or other type of infant food.

When expressed breast milk, infant formula, or any other infant food is regularly offered to a baby after a breastfeeding, it is considered a **complement** to breastfeeding. In some areas to complement a feeding is to "top off" a feed.

A **supplement** replaces all, or most, of a breastfeeding. Instead of breastfeeding first, a baby receives only expressed breast milk or infant formula at a particular feeding.

A baby who is almost fully breastfed may receive an occasional complementary or supplementary feeding. Daily complements or supplements usually are associated with partial breastfeeding.

The term **breast-milk-feeding** may be used when a baby is fed expressed breast milk by an alternative feeding method, usually bottle feeding. Some mothers fully **breast-milk-feed** one or more multiples for days, weeks, and even several months. Other mothers breastfeed directly for some feedings, but one or more babies are breast-milk-fed at other feedings.

Benefits of Full and Partial Breastfeeding

Full or almost full breastfeeding is Nature's ideal, and Nature had very good reasons for designing human milk and the process of breastfeeding to nourish human babies as it did. Human milk creates a balance within the fully breastfed baby's body systems, so the human infant can easily absorb essential nutrients, eliminate any wastage, and minimize exposure to potentially allergenic substances. Introducing a foreign substance, such as infant formula, interferes with that balance. Still, multiples benefit when they receive any amount of the nutrients unique to human milk.

Because of the antibody properties found only in human milk, the incidence rates for many common bacterial or viral illnesses are lowest among fully, or almost fully, breastfed babies. Partially breastfed babies still are less likely to contract many common infant illnesses than babies receiving only infant formula. Almost any amount of breastfeeding/breast milk is associated with better health for babies.

The degree of difference in illness rates depends on the percentage of a partially breastfed baby's diet that comes from mother's milk and the percentage that comes from other sources. The more breastfeeding or human milk a baby receives, the healthier that baby is likely to be. The less babies breastfeed or receive human milk, the more the illness rate approximates that of babies on diets consisting only of artificial infant milk or foods.

In addition to being the optimal way to deliver human milk, the process of breastfeeding ensures close contact with mother. A computer-age mother may not worry as much as her stone-age counterpart about keeping a baby physically safe from saber-toothed tigers and other environmental hazards, but each baby's need for the emotional and physical comfort provided by close contact with mother has not changed for tens of thousands of years.

Multiples must share mother from before birth. Once babies arrive, infant care can too easily become a series of tasks rather than an opportunity for building a relationship with each baby. No matter how much round-the-clock attention multiples require, each still is an individual with the same need for physical contact as any single baby. Any amount of breastfeeding provides an important means of close contact with mother.

Dealing with Temptation

Your multiples have arrived and all are breastfeeding well. The babies' diaper counts are good and each is gaining weight. That still leaves you with eight to twelve daily feedings times two, three, or more. Even if two always breastfeed simultaneously, you are feeding babies for many hours of every day.

There are days, and nights, when most mothers feel willing to try anything if it might calm two or more crying babies. Yes, supplementing is mighty tempting when multiples are howling, they have demanded extra feedings all day, and you are wondering if you have enough milk. Maybe it's the prospect of an entire night's sleep a few times a week that makes supplementing sound so appealing.

Family, friends, and health professionals often pressure mothers of multiples to complement or supplement breastfeeding even when all babies are doing well. Some think it isn't possible to produce enough milk for multiples. Many worry that breastfeeding multiples is too hard on a mother.

No matter what form temptation takes, you aren't alone if you find yourself thinking at times that there has got to be an easier or better way than fully breastfeeding multiples. Many mothers ask themselves at least once a day, and usually before that fifteenth feeding, "Why am I doing this?"

To get past these temptations, answer the question. Why are you doing this? You can remind yourself and others that you are doing this because you want all of your babies to get all of the physical and emotional benefits of breastfeeding.

Repeating "self-talk" statements may help. Some mothers post these one-liners in conspicuous spots.

"This is a short period of time in my life, but it is a crucial time in my babies' lives."

Feedings should meet babies' need to be held in mother's arms as much as they meet babies' need for nourishment. Breastfeeding ensures they receive both. The period of eight to twelve daily feedings per baby lasts a relatively short time. In a few months all will be ready to add other foods to their diets, and they will begin to drop breastfeedings. Before you know it, each will be weaned and off on adventures away from home.

"I know I'm making enough milk because each baby has enough wet and soiled diapers, and each is gaining a normal amount of weight."

Frequent breastfeeding increases milk production. Typically, each baby should breastfeed eight to twelve times a day, but different babies have different breastfeeding needs. It may seem confusing, but it's no cause for concern if each baby has a different breastfeeding pattern.

Babies, like most adults, sometimes want to eat for reasons other than hunger. And like adults, some of the daily feedings each baby requests may be more of a snack than a big meal.

"Look what I did!"

Post this self-talk statement with the babies' latest weights written next to it. Don't forget to pat yourself on the back every time you read it. There may not be a better feeling in the world than watching multiple babies grow—and all on mother's milk.

"It takes time to prepare bottles and clean feeding equipment. I am giving that time to my babies," or *"In the time that it would take to warm a supplement, I could breastfeed and my babies would be satisfied."*

To a mother who is fully breastfeeding two or more babies, supplementing may sound like a way to make life easier. Other feeding methods are often presented as if they can take the time and effort out of multiple feedings. No method can do this. It takes extra time—and extra effort—to feed two or more babies no matter how they are fed.

Supplementing actually can further complicate a mother of multiples' hectic life. If you rarely have help at feeding times, alternative feedings offer no advantage and actually may add work. In surveys, mothers of bottle-fed multiples complained most about the amount of time required for preparation and clean-up of feeding equipment. Mothers who breastfeed multiples after artificially feeding a previous child often say they like the fact that breastfeeding is always "ready to go"—no making a baby wait and no cleaning up.

Some mothers are encouraged to offer their young babies some infant cereal at bedtime. Several studies have shown that this practice does not affect babies' sleep patterns. If given before several months of age, babies cannot digest solid food well, so most of the nutrients are wasted. Also, it may expose babies to an allergen unnecessarily.

Confidence is what a mother needs if she is to avoid unnecessary supplementation. When tempted to offer supplements, keep answering the question of why you chose to fully breastfeed. Remember how you feel when the babies are weighed and you know that all those pounds are from your milk alone.

Recruit family, friends, and health professionals for their support, and ask them to delete any discouraging words. Let them know how much it means to you and your babies to breastfeed. Remind them that multiples require more time and effort no matter how they are fed. If what you need from them is an open ear when you want to vent or their positive comments when you are doubting your ability to breastfeed, tell them.

Partial Breastfeeding

Multiples may be partially breastfed for many reasons. Many mothers planned to fully breastfeed, but partial breastfeeding may have been thrust upon them when babies were born prematurely or one or more was sick at birth. If one or more babies experiences an ongoing breastfeeding difficulty, the mother of multiples may not have the time to work through the problem as a mother with a single baby can. Sometimes a mother's recovery from a multiple pregnancy or birth condition, or the effects of treatment, may affect her ability to fully breastfeed. Other mothers find their family situations simply do not allow the time it would take to breastfeed each baby eight to twelve times a day.

Some mothers decide during the multiple pregnancy to partially breastfeed once their babies arrive. Knowing themselves and knowing their family situations, they know they will need help with some feedings. Mothers sometimes choose partial breastfeeding after several weeks of full breastfeeding so they can begin to have regular relief for some feedings. These mothers may find that having someone offer a baby a supplementary feeding helps them cope when two or more babies "cluster" feedings at the same time of day. Some mothers choose partial breastfeeding so they can get a few hours of uninterrupted sleep. They delegate someone else to handle one of the night feedings on a regular basis. Other mothers initiate partial breastfeeding when they return to an employed position.

Full Breastfeeding as a Goal

The more babies in a multiple set, the more likely it is for difficulties to arise that can affect a goal of full breastfeeding. Don't let that discourage you if you want to fully breastfeed your babies. It may be necessary to supplement with your milk or an infant formula initially, but many mothers have moved gradually to full breastfeeding as babies' ability at the breast or a mother's physical condition improved. (See Chapter 13, "Making Up for a Poor Start," and Chapter 14, "Breastfeeding Difficulties in Young Babies.") This may take weeks, and occasionally months, for any given multiple, especially when babies were extremely preterm.

There are times when fully breastfeeding multiples is never going to become possible. For the mother who wanted to fully breastfeed her babies, this realization can bring feelings of terrible disappointment. Often a mother will grieve for what she and her babies may miss as she "lets go" of this goal. Sometimes it helps to shift the focus to the many benefits of partial breastfeeding and to partially breastfeed in a way that allows babies to breastfeed for as long as they would like.

Partial Breastfeeding as a Goal

Partial breastfeeding is a valid goal. Each mother knows her family situation best, and full breastfeeding may not be a realistic consideration for some mothers caring for multiples. In many cases, the choice is between partial breastfeeding or full bottle-feeding. Obviously, any amount of breastfeeding is the better choice for the babies. Partially breastfed multiples often continue to breastfeed into toddlerhood, and they can experience baby-led weaning the same as multiples that were fully breastfed during their first months.

Successful Partial Breastfeeding

The less "partial" the partial breastfeeding is, the more successful it is going to be in terms of long-term breastfeeding. When possible, establish breastfeeding and adequate milk production by fully breastfeeding, pumping, or a combination for the first week or two after birth. Once milk production and breastfeeding are well established and milk production is plentiful, partial breastfeeding can be initiated. When you plan to breastfeed the babies for several months or longer, bottles should be introduced on as limited a basis as possible.

- Complementary feedings are more compatible than supplementary feedings with long-term, partial breastfeeding.
- Mothers choosing to offer a bottle usually do so in the evening, when babies tend to "cluster" feedings, or during the night. After breastfeeding first, dad might offer each baby an evening feeding, or a baby might be supplemented if he wants to eat again within an hour or two of the last breastfeeding. Another option is for dad to bottle-feed one (or more) during the evening or night while mother breastfeeds the other(s). Perhaps dad bottle-feeds all babies for one night feeding and mother breastfeeds all at the next one.
- Some mothers partially breastfeed, but their babies still receive only mother's milk. These mothers pump their milk once or twice every morning, and dad or someone else offers the expressed milk to the babies later in the day.

Alternating Feeding Methods with Twins

Health professionals or concerned family members sometimes suggest that a mother of twins alternate breastfeedings and bottle-feedings. The mother is told to either breastfeed all babies for one feeding and bottle-feed all at the next, or she is told to breastfeed one and bottle-feed the other at every feeding—rotating which baby is breastfed and which is bottle-fed. With few exceptions, following this feeding plan leads to early weaning from the breast.

Alternating feeding methods can interfere with long-term breastfeeding of twins for a number of reasons. Mothers with twins tend to have less regular household help than mothers with higher-order multiples. Unless someone else takes over the preparation and clean-up of supplementary feedings for her, alternating feeding methods means a lot more work. This mother is investing twice the time as she fully breastfeeds one baby, and then prepares, feeds, and cleans equipment for a fully bottle-fed baby.

In addition, when almost half of the babies' calories are coming from infant formula, milk production drops. Because infant formula takes longer than breast milk to digest, babies don't "ask" to breastfeed often enough. This means even less milk is removed from the breasts, which leads to a further decrease in milk production.

Once milk production decreases, the babies may not seem contented with the breastfeedings they are getting. Most mothers find it is difficult to cope with two "full-time" feeding methods and dwindling milk production. Before long something has to go. Rebuilding milk production can seem a daunting task. So before the mother knows it, her babies are weaned from the breast and both are artificially fed.

If you do breastfeed twins halftime, yet you want your babies to breastfeed for several months, the following suggestions may help.

- To maintain adequate milk production and avoid unanticipated weaning, you still want to breastfeed (or pump) often enough to equal at least eight, and up to twelve, feedings a day. For example, breastfeed (or pump for) **each** twin at **least** four to six times in 24 hours for a daily total of 100 to 120 minutes of breastfeeding/pumping.
- Limit the amount of infant formula in daily bottle-feedings, so babies will "ask" to breastfeed often enough. Although each baby might be willing to take three to four ounces (90 to 120 ml) from a bottle, each may be satisfied after drinking one to three ounces (45 to 90 ml). If weight gain is an issue, monitor the diaper counts and weigh any baby as needed. Then adjust the amount of infant formula to suit the individual baby's circumstances.

This mother of triplets had help from her mother as she coordinated breastfeeding and breast-milk-feeding of her three babies.

- If babies' requests for breastfeeding drop or you notice signs of decreased milk production, begin to pump your breasts as often as needed to make up any difference in the number of feedings.
- As babies begin to eat solid foods, you will probably be able to cut back on the number of bottle-feedings. (See Chapter 27, "Breastfeeding, Starting Solids, and Weaning.")

Alternating Feeding Methods with Higher-Order Multiples

Alternating breast and bottle often works better for mothers feeding higher-order multiples, especially when a household helper manages all aspects of bottle-feeding. A mother may breastfeed one (or two) of triplets for all feedings around the clock, rotating which one or two are put to breast. This routine can be flexible so that two babies breastfeed at some feedings, but only one may be breastfed at others.

Mothers of quadruplets sometimes breastfeed two simultaneously while the other two babies are bottle-fed by a helper. At the next feeding, babies are switched so the two bottle-fed at the previous feeding are breastfed for this one.

- To maintain adequate milk production with higher-order multiples, you still want to breastfeed (or pump) often enough to equal at least eight, and more like 10 to 12, feedings a day. Breastfeed (or pump for) each triplet at least three to four times, and each quadruplet at least two to three times in every 24-hour period. This should equal at least 100, and more like 120 to 140, minutes of breastfeeding/pumping every day.

- When possible, limit the amount of formula the babies receive and pump as needed as per the bulleted items in the previous section for mothers of twins.

- Mothers of triplets and quadruplets sometimes alternate breast and bottle-feedings for part of the day or night, but they breastfeed all the babies for several consecutive feedings at other times. The time of day varies depending on the mother, the babies, and the family situation.

  For instance, one mother fed her triplets on a three-hour schedule during the daytime. She developed a rotation plan, so each baby breastfed twice and bottle-fed once over three feedings. During the night all three breastfed on demand. With her husband's help, the mother simply rotated babies in and out of her bed during the night. (This mother had no household help, so for daytime feedings she would breastfeed two babies simultaneously using the double clutch position. The third baby was given a bottle while sitting in the crook formed by her leg when she rested her left foot on her right knee.)

  Another mother of triplets chose to do the opposite. She fully breastfed all three babies during the day, but her husband bottle-fed one (or two) while she breastfed one (or two) for one or two evening feedings and all the night feedings.

- Some mothers find they are able to continue breastfeeding higher-order multiples only by alternating breast and bottle for all feedings. At least one baby and often two are breastfed at all (or most) feedings, and babies alternate so that all babies get this special time with mother a few times a day.

Breast-Milk-Feeding

Babies who regularly receive expressed breast milk definitely receive the nutrition and antibody benefits available only from human milk, although expressed breast milk is not precisely the same "product" as breast milk obtained directly through breastfeeding. Collecting, storing, refrigerating, freezing, or heating can have a slight effect on some of the nutrients or antibody activity in breast milk. Usually the effects are minimal, and feeding babies expressed human milk is associated with better health for babies than using infant formula.

The "process" of feeding breast milk from a bottle also differs from direct breastfeeding. Having help with feedings is one of the reasons a mother may choose occasional breast-milk-feeding. There can be times when everyone's needs might be better met if a helper holds and feeds a crying, hungry multiple. On the other hand, too much help with feedings can interfere with a baby's social development and the mother-baby attachment process. Mother should be the one holding and cuddling each baby for as many feedings as possible, no matter how they are fed. (See "If discontinuing breastfeeding" in the section that follows.)

Full Breast-Milk-Feeding

Occasionally a mother opts to fully bottle-feed all multiples with expressed breast milk. Usually this occurs when a mother has higher-order multiples and one or more experience an ongoing breastfeeding difficulty; however, twins present a similar situation if both continue to have difficulty breastfeeding. It may not be possible to continue working with two, three, or four babies until they improve their breastfeeding skills while also making sure they receive the complementary or supplementary feedings needed for weight gain—plus fitting in breast-pumping sessions every day in order to produce enough breast milk. Even when one baby breastfeeds well, a mother may find it difficult to breastfeed that baby and still provide the care the others need.

No mother gets more than 24 hours in a day no matter how many babies she has, and a mother may feel physically and emotionally exhausted after days or weeks of trying to "do it all"—juggle breastfeeding, alternative feedings, and pumping sessions. So some mothers breast-milk-feed one or more multiples for long periods. They may pump eight to twelve times a day for six or more months to provide their milk for babies' full or partial breast-milk-feedings.

Physical Conditions that Affect Sucking

When a baby is born with a physical condition that affects breastfeeding ability, such as cleft lip/palate or Down syndrome, a mother may choose to fully breast-milk-feed that baby. A breastfeeding decision should not be made on the basis of a diagnosis alone, since many of these babies breastfeed well with little extra effort. If breastfeeding ability has been affected, a mother may continue to work with that baby at the breast when possible but breast-milk-feed to ensure the baby receives adequate nutrients. (See "Breastfeeding only one" in the section that follows.)

Temporary Breast-Milk-Feeding

When any multiple's temporary breastfeeding difficulty lasts longer than a few days, a mother may choose to breast-milk-feed one or more of her multiples for several days. This "breather" may allow an overwhelmed mother to get some rest after she's been juggling breastfeedings, pumping sessions, and supplementary feedings for two or more babies. Since milk production can decrease when any baby isn't breastfeeding correctly, a few days of only breast-milk-feeding may let a mother focus on increasing milk production. The mother still offers each baby her breast when possible, and she resumes more intense efforts when she feels ready, but the pressure of feeling that one has to "do it all" may be reduced.

Breastfeeding Multiples When Mother Is Employed

Breastfeeding provides additional benefits when a mother works outside the home, and many mothers have continued to breastfeed multiples after resuming full- or part-time employed positions. Because babies fed breast milk are less likely to become ill, mothers generally miss fewer workdays caring for sick babies. This can be a particular advantage for employed mothers with multiples, since illness in one baby often leads to illness for the other(s). After being separated during work hours, breastfeeding is an easy yet wonderful way for a mother and each baby to re-establish physical contact. Mothers say they like the fact that breastfeeding is one thing a sitter cannot do for their babies, so their role as mother remains special.

The increased availability of portable, electric breast pumps has made it easier for employed mothers to continue breastfeeding. Employed mothers of multiples usually recommend renting or purchasing a hospital-grade, automatic, self-cycling model to maintain optimal milk production. Most find they pump more milk in less time when they use it with a double collection kit. If you already have a double collection kit, check the brand name. You may save money if the pump you rent is a compatible brand.

Establishing a pumping routine is especially important for a mother maintaining milk production for multiple babies. Many mothers begin to pump once or twice each morning for a week or two before their return-to-work date. Try to pump every two to three hours when away from the babies, especially if they are less than six to eight months and not yet ready for any solid food. To maintain adequate milk production, your routine may include an additional 10 to 15 minute pumping session compared to that of a mother of a single baby. It may take a couple of work weeks to develop a pumping plan that fits with your workday and with milk production. Once pumping becomes part of your daily routine, however, you probably will take it in stride.

Try to breastfeed before leaving the babies with a sitter, and breastfeed as soon as you and the babies are reunited. Some mothers breastfeed their babies before getting ready for work and then breastfeed one or more again immediately before leaving for work. Breastfeed frequently on any day you have off.

Frequent pumping should maintain milk production, but if you notice signs of decreased production, look at your routine. A feeding or pumping session may have been delayed or dropped inadvertently. Increasing the number of breastfeedings or pumping sessions for two or three days usually takes care of any problem.

Some employers may be concerned about employee productivity when a returning new mother needs to pump as frequently as every two to three hours. They may not be aware that providing breast milk usually means less illness for babies, which means fewer sick days for an employee. Also some studies have shown that employees became more productive when an employer supported their efforts to breastfeed. Employers may be more understanding when they learn that you won't have to take as many pumping breaks once babies have begun to enjoy other foods.

See "Employment issues" in Chapter 7, "Getting Ready: Preparing for Multiples," for additional ideas. For "Human Milk Storage Guidelines," see "Appendix."

Breastfeeding Only One

Breastfeeding means more than food to babies and to a mother. Breastfeeding is a gift of self that a mother gives to her babies, providing babies with close physical contact and the most perfect nutrition available, and it does this in a form that only a mother can deliver. For this reason fully breastfeeding one (or more) and fully bottle-feeding the other(s) **should be avoided** except in extreme circumstances, such as when one multiple has a physical condition that makes breastfeeding that baby impossible.

When any multiple is fully breastfed, it means that this multiple receives perfect nutrition and immunity factors against illnesses. Unless breast-milk-fed, the other(s) is exposed to a potential allergen in a food that is less perfectly suited to human infants and one that contains no disease protection. Most importantly, fully bottle-feeding one while breastfeeding the other(s) may contribute to long-lasting differences in a mother's feelings for her babies, even if the bottle-fed baby is receiving only mother's milk in those bottles.

A better option may be to breastfeed each baby as much as possible and to supplement each as necessary. Not every multiple may require supplementation. Mothers have fully breastfed one (or more) and partially breastfed the other(s). With this plan, all babies are breastfed for at least some feedings.

In the rare instance when completely separate feeding methods are necessary, a mother should be aware of the physical and emotional implications of fully bottle-feeding one baby. Look for opportunities, during and between feedings, to increase skin contact with the bottle-fed baby.

"Kangaroo care" is a good way to increase contact no matter what the baby's age or development. (See Chapter 11, "Multiples in the Newborn Intensive Care Unit.")

When one "loses interest." Occasionally, a mother reports that one of her multiples appears to have "lost interest" and has weaned abruptly or is weaning rapidly, yet few babies naturally wean from the breast before their first birthday. Since this is not a common behavior for a fully or almost fully breastfed baby, suspect some underlying issue if this behavior occurs. Often the baby's feeding pattern, the number of breastfeedings, and the related number of supplemental bottles are at the heart of the problem. If any baby stops "asking" to breastfeed or appears to be weaning prematurely, treat the situation as a **nursing strike** to get the baby back to the breast. (See "Nursing strikes" in Chapter 27, "Breastfeeding, Starting Solids, and Weaning.")

Early Weaning

Sometimes a mother of multiples finds it necessary to discontinue breastfeeding altogether. If you are considering weaning your babies from the breast or from breast-milk-feeding, but breastfeeding had been an important goal for you, first contact an LLL Leader or a lactation consultant to discuss whether there might be other options. The early weeks with newborn multiples can be very chaotic. Family or friends may tell you that other feeding methods would make your life easier. During the first couple of months, mothers sometimes make decisions about weaning that they later regret.

Try to continue your efforts to breastfeed if the babies have been home less than four to eight weeks. (See the discussions above about partial breastfeeding and read Chapter 13, "Making Up for a Poor Start.") Babies change a lot during their first months. Their current breastfeeding abilities probably don't reflect what their abilities will be in a few weeks. Also, you probably will feel better about any feeding decision you make if you wait until you have recovered more fully from the pregnancy and birth. There is no easy way. Multiple babies take more time and effort to feed no matter what method is used. Although mothers say it takes time to breastfeed, they also say it is the easiest method once babies have learned to breast-feed well.

If you decide weaning is best in your situation, you should feel very good about the length of time you were able to breastfeed or breast-milk-feed. No matter how brief it might be, studies have shown that any amount of breastfeeding, or breast milk, has a positive impact on babies' health. Any breastfeeding is better than no breastfeeding, or no breast milk, at all. It may not have been easy in your situation, but you have provided your babies with the best possible start.

It is more comfortable for you, and usually easier on babies, if you can avoid abrupt weaning. There's no switch to suddenly turn breast milk production "off." It takes time for your brain and breasts to get the message to stop production completely. Unless your babies are already getting a large amount of infant formula, you have been producing a lot more milk than the "average" new mother. If you abruptly stop, you could develop severe engorgement.

Gradually decrease milk production by slowly decreasing the number of breastfeedings or pumping sessions. You might begin by breastfeeding one less baby at each feeding or pumping for several less minutes at each session for several days. When your body has adapted, you can begin to delete a feeding or pumping session every few days while increasing the amount in their supplementary bottles by one-half to two ounces (15 to 60 ml). Your babies' behaviors and diaper counts are your best guides.

If you do become engorged or you develop a plugged duct or mastitis, maintain the current number of breastfeedings or pumping sessions. Do not decrease breastfeeding or pumping further at this time. (See Chapter 15, "When Mother Has a Breastfeeding Difficulty," for suggestions for coping with a specific problem.) Depending on the severity of the problem, you may want to increase milk removal somewhat by increasing the number of breastfeedings for some of the babies. You could add brief pumping sessions instead, such as pumping to the point that relieves fullness but no more than this. You can resume the weaning process, but perhaps more slowly, once the problem is resolved.

You still can contact an LLL Leader or lactation consultant for help if you do decide to wean. She may have additional ideas that can help make the process more comfortable for you.

Discontinuing breastfeeding does not change your babies' need for your presence and your touch. Holding them as in kangaroo care, taking turns so each spends time in a sling or carrier, rocking one or more in your arms, bathing with one or another—all are ways to increase contact. Of course, one of the best ways to provide physical contact is to continue to be the one who bottle-feeds each baby most of the time.

To develop a sense of trust and feelings of security, babies need a primary, that means one, caretaker. Babies' feedings are as much a social and emotional experience for them as they are a way of getting food—just as meals are for older children and adults. Babies learn to trust and feel most secure when one person generally replaces their hunger pains with a pleasurable feeling of fullness. No matter what method you use to feed your babies, they need you to hold and cuddle them during most of their feedings.

A mother of multiples is in need of the best possible breastfeeding start, yet she is the least likely new mother to get it. Fully breastfeeding is ideal for babies, and many mothers have fully breastfed multiple-birth infants. However, it is not always possible. Babies' or mothers' physical conditions after birth may interfere.

Breastfeeding does not have to be "all or nothing." Partial breastfeeding and breast-milk-feeding can provide babies with the nutritional and immunologic benefits of human milk—the degree depends on the number of breastfeedings (or amount of breast milk) each receives. Whether you ultimately breastfeed for years or only days, your milk still provides your babies with the best possible start.

Chapter 18
Enhancing Individuality

Most parents want to watch each of their multiples grow into a self-confident, unique individual. At the same time, they want their children to enjoy the special relationship that only multiples can share as they mature. This often leaves parents feeling as if they're walking a tightrope over an alligator pit! However, it is possible for multiples to have both. When each is treated as an individual, each is free to savor the special bond only found among multiples.

Breastfeeding is a wonderful way to begin to appreciate each multiple as an individual because it removes the temptations that could compromise close contact. For two persons to get to know one another as individuals, they must spend a lot of time together. The close contact and interaction inherent with frequent breastfeedings helps a mother slowly form individual attachments with each multiple—whether or not she's aware of it at the time. Breastfeeding on cue, or demand, helps a mother appreciate that from birth the babies have individual needs and approaches to life.

Attachment to Each Baby

The formation of an attachment with each baby provides multiples with the foundation to be individuals and part of a set. The attachment process may be influenced by multiples' type (identical or fraternal), and by the effect their births had on early interaction with each.

Attachment seems to be a very different process with multiples. Nature designed humans to form close bonds with one person at a time. A mother often feels an intimate closeness with her single newborn within hours, days, or at least within several weeks. It takes more time to get to know two or more babies with that same degree of closeness. It's not as easy to fall in love with two persons at the same time. In addition, the attachment process with multiples often is complicated by factors beyond parents' control.

- When healthy newborn multiples can be in a mother's care from the beginning, she may find she feels very close to and protective of the "unit" of babies first. Once attached to the unit or set, a mother (and father) will begin to get acquainted with each unique personality within it. This may take months or even well into the babies' second year.

   1. This may be why some mothers say that during their babies' early months they know they have two (or more) babies. They certainly can see each one. Yet it seems they are caring for only one baby that keeps them busy around the clock. (Only other mothers of multiples seem able to understand this phenomenon.)
   2. "Unit bonding" may be one reason some parents feel compelled to dress multiples alike. When dressed in look-alike clothing, the babies almost take on a single image.

- Many situations common to multiple births may interfere with attachment in that they are more likely to lead to the formation of a stronger attachment, or a "preferential attachment," for one baby.

   1. There has been a reduction in the number of "surprise" twins (and occasionally triplets) since ultrasound and other tests were introduced, but sometimes a women gives birth to a second baby whose presence wasn't detected until the first baby had arrived. Many mothers of undiagnosed twins say they initially felt more of an attachment for the first baby born. Because the bond between a mother and child begins to form before birth, it isn't surprising that a mother may think of the firstborn twin as "her baby."

Multiples do not deserve to be treated exactly the same; each is an individual with different needs.

2. It is fairly common for one (or more) close-to-term multiples to require a stay of several hours to several days in a NICU while a mother cares for the other multiple(s) in her room and at home. When separated from one for even a brief period, mothers often report they quickly feel closer to any baby who was in their care and not separated from them. It seems logical that a mother would bond initially with a baby who was able to respond to her constant care and was with her without interruption before she develops a closeness with a multiple that must always share her with the other(s).

3. Persons who are acutely ill tend to withdraw from those around them. Interacting with others may take too much of the energy needed to get better. As an ill person's condition improves, she regains an interest in her surroundings. The same is true for sick newborns. As with the adult, a newborn will respond more as his condition improves. When multiples are sick at birth, they usually don't make progress at the same rate. Therefore, one may be ready to respond and interact before the other(s). It is natural to feel drawn to and form an attachment first with any multiple able to respond.

Obviously, a long-term preference for one can have profound consequences for the entire multiples set. Ideas for coping with preferential attachment follow later in this chapter.

Other Factors

Generally, the more different multiples are, the sooner parents see beyond the set to the individual persons that comprise it.

- Opposite-sex fraternal twins tend to look and act the most different, which may be the reason they usually are regarded as individuals sooner than same-sex twins. Their differences can lead to unnecessary concern when parents compare babies with very different, yet normal, developmental timetables.

- The physical appearance, temperaments, and growth and development of same-sex fraternal multiples may be very similar or very different, depending on the number of genes they have in common. These multiples may be very close or vary widely in their approaches to breastfeeding and to life in general.

- Identical multiples have all their genetic material in common, so they are always the same sex. They not only look more alike, but they often behave more alike and operate from built-in body clocks set for the same or a similar "schedule." When their clocks are in sync, a mother will usually find she is feeding and handling two at once. This lack of one-on-one time may contribute more to unit bonding than their similar appearances, and it can influence how long it takes to form an attachment to each.

- The more multiples in a set, the more complicated the attachment process becomes. Not only are there more individuals to form an attachment with, but the twin types comprising the set affect getting to know the different babies. In the majority of higher-order sets, all multiples are fraternal due to the use of fertility-enhancement methods for conception. However, any given set may include all multiples of the same sex, or one, two, or several babies may be of the opposite sex. Also, identical triplet, quadruplet, and quintuplet sets occasionally do occur. A combination of twin types, such as a set of identical twins and a fraternal triplet is not uncommon.

No matter how similar multiples' temperament traits may seem, especially identical multiples, they will vary in the degree to which each expresses those traits. For instance, all may be calm or all may be high need babies, but one will be calmer or more high need than the other(s). However, the moment you begin to figure out the difference(s) in degree, the babies will add interest to the attachment process by flip-flopping traits, or taking turns, as to which is calmest or most high need. Flip-flopping seems to be more common with identical multiples. Also, it occurs more often during their first year, although they may continue to take turns expressing traits, or the degree of trait expression, for years—even into adulthood for many sets.

Parents can flip-flop too. Whether unit or preferential attachment better describes the initial process, parents may find they spend more time for a while getting to know one multiple and then switch to pay more attention to another. Because the parental attention ping-pongs from one to another (and back again), it differs from a preferential attachment in which the same baby always is the focus of attention.

Unit Thinking

Watch out for "unit thinking"—a desire to always treat multiples equally. It strikes most parents of multiples at an early date. And it can interfere with individual attachment formation.

Multiples do not deserve to be treated exactly the same. Each is a different person. Each has different needs, and their individual needs will vary and flip-flop as they grow. For instance, today's high need baby really needs the extra time and attention. Another multiple may not need the same amount of your time now or she may need more of you later. Responding as the individual multiples demand helps a parent focus on developing a relationship with each baby rather than simply on accomplishing baby care tasks for a unit.

When you find yourself worrying about spending equal time and attention with each, stop and think. Ask yourself, "Would I be concerned about treating these babies exactly the same if they were a year apart, or would I allow myself to respond to their individual needs?"

Helping the Attachment Process Along

There are many actions a parent can take to enhance attachment with each multiple. Although different "types" of attachment are noted, many of the suggestions might apply to any set of multiples.

Unit Bonding

If you feel closer to the unit, or the set of multiples, there are several things that can help you get to know the individuals.

- Consciously look for differences. There are always differences, no matter how alike the babies may seem. Frequently one of identical twins will have a fuller face or a different look about the eyes. Look for some type of distinguishing mark, such as a freckle or a birthmark.
- Generally, mothers of identical multiples can quickly tell them apart. (Fathers often take longer.) However, if you cannot yet tell one from

another when they are ready to leave the hospital, take an extra set of identification bracelets home and continue to bracelet one until you are certain you know each. Paint a fingernail or toenail of one baby. (Mothers of identical triplets or quadruplets may need to use different colors of fingernail polish for each.) Use different-colored diaper pins for each. Iron the first letter of each one's name on t-shirts. (This won't work if multiples are given alliterated names.)

• Go out of your way to call each baby by name. Every day you have numerous opportunities to make eye contact with each during feedings, diaper changes, and cuddlings. Encourage others to do the same. It may be unrealistic to think the lady up the street or the grocery clerk will remember one from the other(s), but it is reasonable to expect relatives, friends, and close neighbors to call each by name.

Discourage references to them as "the twins" (or "the triplets," "the quads," etc.), "twin" or "twinnie"—especially in their presence, because these reinforce a set rather than the individuals.

Never admit to anyone if you ever have trouble telling them apart, especially when one or more of your multiples are within hearing distance. Can you imagine how it would feel if your parents weren't sure who you were?

• Take photographs of each baby alone, as well as photos of the set together. Unless each baby has a very distinct look, label photos after processing. This helps others learn to identify each baby. If you don't label photos, you may be surprised years later when you also have trouble identifying who is who on some of them.

• Don't feel concerned if you find yourself dressing infant multiples alike. This may be one way of having the babies "take on" a single image. However, if you find yourself changing every baby when only one soils an outfit, you may want to look more closely at your actions.

Many parents say they dress multiples alike because they were afraid others might think they like one baby better if one baby was perceived as wearing a cuter outfit than another.

You can revisit the issue of look-alike outfits as multiples become toddlers. By 18 to 24 months, they can help choose their clothing if given some simple options. Three- to six-year-olds often develop definite, and individual, senses of style that should be respected—within reason.

A solution that combines the urge to dress multiples alike with a desire to treat them as individuals is to color-code their clothing. The babies wear the same outfit, but each dresses in a different color. For instance, one of male twins may be assigned to always wear the color blue and the other would wear whatever other color was available. (For same-sex triplets there would need to be at least two assigned colors, same-sex quads would need at least three assigned colors, and so on.)

Color coding same-sex twins can help others identify one from another. When one of a set of boys is always in blue, other people soon learn to call him by name according to the color he wears. The other boy(s) wearing a different color is identified by process of elimination. It may be helpful if a neighbor can call an escaping toddler by name before he runs into the street. However, it is not good when others come to depend on the color of clothing and never take the time to distinguish the children by other means.

Preferential Attachment

The attachments you feel for your multiples influence your interactions with each. This in turn may affect each one's sense of identity. Because of the long-term implications of a preferential attachment to one, it is crucial for a parent to recognize when feelings of attachment are stronger for one (or more) than for the other(s).

If you do prefer one (or more), remember it is a fairly common feeling, especially if you were able to care for one before the other(s). Don't waste energy by feeling guilty about a situation that began beyond your control. Instead, take action. Invest that energy positively to rectify the situation. It often takes a conscious effort to become as attached to the one(s) with whom you feel less close.

- Go out of your way to listen for and respond immediately to the cues and cries of any multiple with whom you feel less close.
- Make eye contact with that baby and talk to him often.
- Make a special effort to increase close contact with this baby by placing him in a baby carrier or sling more often than the other(s), breastfeeding him skin to skin in bed, massaging him, or taking him in the bath with you.
- Of course, you will still want to meet the needs of the multiple(s) you feel closer to, but most mothers don't find this to be a problem. They usually continue to respond quickly to these babies.

Differentiation

Making Comparisons

Parents of multiples are often told they should not compare their babies. This advice may be well meaning, but it is absurd. Most parents compare their baby with other babies. It's a way of trying to figure out if a baby is growing and developing at about the same rate as peers. It's just that most parents don't have a built-in peer comparison.

Comparisons are a way of examining individual behaviors. Comparison may be part of the attachment process with multiples, because it helps parents sort out their babies' different traits and approaches to life. This sorting out sometimes is called differentiation. Differentiation allows parents to look at their babies' similarities and differences, and note changing as well as ongoing behaviors.

There are a couple of pitfalls to avoid when making comparisons.

- Be wary of labeling multiples. Labels can stick. Saying, "Baby A is the outgoing baby, but Baby B is unsociable," or "Baby A is the dominant twin; he can make his passive brother do anything," unfairly categorizes babies who may very well flip-flop personalities next week. Multiples can switch dominance in the same way they seem to alternate, or flip-flop, temperament or personality traits. A child can carry a label long after a behavior has disappeared or taken a new direction.

- There are variations for most behaviors associated with normal infant growth and development. Multiples may accomplish new tasks on very similar or very different timetables, yet all may be within normal. Invest in a reliable reference on normal infant growth and development, and refer to it when you feel concerned about multiples' different developmental timetables. (See "Resources.")

- When babies are preterm, they may not "act their age" for several months to more than a year of age. Ask their pediatric care provider how much you should adjust developmental timetables to accommodate their original due date rather than actual birth date.

Celebrity Status

By giving birth to more than one baby, parents of multiples gain a sort of celebrity status by default. You may as well enjoy it—sometimes praise from an adoring public can help a mother get through a long day. However, don't let instant celebrity tempt you to reinforce the unit of multiples rather than the individuals. It is normal for the ego to inflate a bit with recognition as a celebrity. There's no reason to feel guilty about it, unless you lose perspective and become a victim of the celebrity syndrome.

You might be taking celebrity too seriously if you find you must always mention the existence of the other(s) even when out with only one multiple. You may be taking advantage of your celebrity if after they've celebrated their third birthday you still often find yourself calling them "the twins" ("the triplets," "the quads," etc.) instead of calling each by name or you're still compelled to dress them alike when you all venture out.

Keep in mind that your children and others are watching and listening. Always announcing a child's status as part of a multiple set could cause him to wonder which you value more—his uniqueness or his place as part of a unit. Relatives and friends take their cues from you. When your emphasis is on the individuals, they will learn to look at them that way, too. If you express unit thinking, they will do likewise.

The attachment process with multiples is different than falling in love with a single baby. Breastfeeding is a positive first step, since it provides many opportunities for close contact with each and it works best when it accommodates each baby's differing "demands" to feed.

It often takes longer to get to know and love two, three, or more unique little persons. Allow yourself the extra time it takes. In the meantime, your babies are learning that you consider each to be special in his/her own right. Once they know this, there will be no difficulty with the concept of individuality for your multiples—or for you, either.

Chapter 19
Comforting a Fussy Baby x 1, 2, or More!

There should be a contract that promises parents of multiples that because they are caring for two or more babies, none of the babies will be a fussy or high need baby. There should be a contract like that, but of course, there isn't.

As with singletons, one or more multiples may have fussy times that last for hours. Multiples can have colic. One or more may be a "high need" baby who needs almost constant contact and attention. If babies fuss at different times during the day, a mother may feel as though each day is one big fussy time. (And she's more than half right!) On the other hand, it is extremely difficult to cope when two or more babies continually cry during shared fussy periods.

Any mother who has felt the helplessness and frustration of caring for one high need baby can only imagine contending with another high need baby at the same time. When only one is a high need baby, it still takes much more energy to meet the needs of that multiple plus the needs of the other(s). It is more than doubly or triply frustrating.

This is often the point when a mother feels ready to throw in the towel, put the babies in cribs or automatic swings, walk away, and let the babies cry it out. It can be very difficult to take a broader viewpoint. However, the only thing babies learn when they are left to cry it out is that no one is there for them when they most need someone.

No matter how frustrated and overwhelmed a mother may feel, her babies are feeling even more so. Babies don't **choose** to be high need or fussy. Imagine how terrible it would be to feel uncomfortable and not know why, much less how to communicate the nature of the discomfort.

Physical Causes of Fussiness

Many babies have fussy periods, especially for the first few months. Rarely is this a breastfeeding problem. However, you may want to check your diet for foods that occasionally affect babies through mother's milk. This is especially true if there is a strong history of allergies on either side of the family. Most foods eaten by mother do not create problems for babies. Breast milk is made from products in a mother's bloodstream, and the foods a mother eats are broken down in her intestinal tract before they are available for making milk. For eons women from different cultures and with different diets have nourished babies at the breast without causing digestive problems for those babies.

Infant fussiness may be more related to temperament or physical causes than to exposure to some substance. However, if you suspect one or more babies is sensitive to something in your diet, work with your babies' pediatric care provider to eliminate one food at a time for a couple of weeks to see if it makes a difference in a baby's behavior. In addition to food sensitivities, there are a few other substances a mother may ingest that can contribute to fussiness because they decrease breast milk production. You also may want to consider whether something in the environment may be contributing to fussy or colicky behavior.

1. Cow's milk and other dairy products are among the more likely sensitivities. Artificial baby milks, or formulas, even in small amounts, can cause some babies to become gassy or frequently act fussy. A baby who is extremely sensitive to cow's milk protein may have a similar problem when mother drinks milk or eats dairy products.
2. Other foods associated with food sensitivity, such as soy, wheat, corn, nuts, egg whites, etc., also have been implicated with fussy behavior.
3. Some babies seem to have negative reactions to something in supplemental vitamins, iron, and fluoride drops.

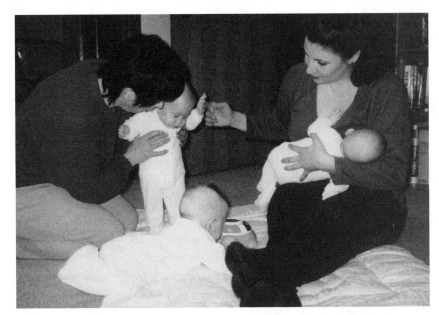

An extra pair of hands can help when three babies need attention.

4. Caffeinated beverages seem to affect some babies, especially when a mother consumes several cups of coffee or tea, or more than two to three soft drinks daily. (Most mugs hold at least two cups.)

5. A few medications mothers take may contribute to discomfort resulting in fussiness. If you have any question about medication side-effects, contact your babies' care provider, an LLL Leader, or a lactation consultant for information.

6. Cigarette smoke irritates babies and nicotine and other chemicals are excreted in milk. Cigarette smoking is also associated with lower milk production, especially for those who smoke more than a half pack daily. Furthermore, babies exposed to secondhand smoke are much more likely to suffer upper respiratory infections, bronchitis, and asthma. If you smoke and truly cannot quit completely, cut down as much as possible, always smoke outside so babies aren't exposed to the smoke, and smoke just after—not before—a breastfeeding.

7. Contraceptive pills and devices that contain estrogen can decrease breast milk production. (Progesterone/progestin-only pills or injections do not appear to affect milk production, especially if they are started after a mother's milk supply is well-established.)

8. Environmental factors may contribute to fussy behavior usually through skin contact or inhalation. Some babies react after inhaling sprays or

powders. Other babies are sensitive to substances added to soaps or detergents. They react to skin contact with a soap or when clothing, bedding, and so on are washed in an offending detergent.

You may have to experiment to discover whether any of these things is causing a baby distress. It is important to remember that each multiple is an individual. One may find a substance irritating when the other(s) does not.

Survival Tips

No matter what the reason for high need behavior, you still have to cope with any fussy babies. The following mother-of-multiples tested ideas may help you and your babies survive the fussy times.

• Hold and cuddle your babies. Skin contact often calms a fussy baby. Try kangaroo care for awhile; take off your shirt and the babies' shirts, and

put one or two of them directly against your chest. You then can place a shirt or a sheet over all of you. Offer the breast. Although cuddling or breastfeeding may not always relieve the babies' discomfort, your actions are at least letting them know you are there for them and you care.

• Dance with a baby. Think waltz. Soft classical or "new age" music usually is the most soothing.

• Place a fussing multiple in a baby carrier or sling. Buy or borrow carriers that may be worn front or back so you'll have more options. It is usually easier to carry a baby in front when meeting only that baby's needs. Although it may help to carry a baby on your back when another multiple needs cuddling or a breastfeeding at the same time, you at least will have a free arm to hold a second multiple when one is in a front carrier. A sling is worn to the side of one hip, which allows you to carry one baby in the sling and hold or feed another on the opposite side. Some mothers have carriers (and bodies) that allow them to carry one in

front and one in back, or both in front, or crisscross slings to carry a baby on each hip.

- When two or more multiples are distressed at once, head for a rocking chair. Keep one on every level of your home, and store a folding lawn rocker in the car. Rhythmic rocking generally calms a fussy mother as well as her fussy babies.
- Go for a walk with the babies. You can wear a fussy baby in a carrier or sling while outside. Dress everyone appropriately and enjoy the fresh air whenever possible. Drive to an enclosed mall and then walk the halls during inclement weather. Keep a book, paperwork, sewing, etc., in the car, because the movement of the car may "rock" the babies to sleep as you drive. If so and when weather allows, you may as well stay in the car and let the babies snooze while you take advantage of the peace and quiet. One mother reported taking her babies for a drive every day in order to help them nap. Since quiet time was hard to come by, she enjoyed her hour or two of sitting in the car. (For ideas about getting out of the house with multiples, see Chapter 22, "Getting Out and About.")
- Perform "colic massage" on any high need multiple during diaper changes. However, massage may help more if performed at times other than during a baby's actual crying bouts. A massage usually takes about five minutes, but feel free to enjoy this one-on-one contact for longer periods if another baby isn't "calling" you. For more information about infant massage, see "Resources."
- Few, if any, childcare experts would suggest picking up and holding two babies at the same time, unless one is secured in a carrier. However, it is unlikely that these experts ever had to listen to the symphonic sound of crying multiples. Carrying two is dangerous because you have no way to break a fall, so you or the babies could easily be injured if you slip or trip. Carrying two while walking up or down stairs is particularly hazardous. **Avoid** such situations as much as possible. However, if there are times when you find you must carry two babies:

    a.) Walk slowly.

    b.) Be constantly alert for objects on the floor or spots in carpet or flooring that could cause you to trip. Sit or put a baby down as soon as possible.

    c.) **Never** let others hold two babies at once. You've probably noticed that your babies practically mold to your body. Because each is often in your arms, you are adapting constantly to minute changes in their weights and each baby's ability to balance her body. Unless another person, for example, your husband, is helping you with the babies daily, it is extremely dangerous to allow anyone else to carry two babies at once.

- Bathe in a tub with one baby at a time. (This is a nice way for a father to get extra skin contact with his babies, too.) The warm water usually relaxes everyone. Do not step in or out of a tub with a baby in your arms because of the potential for slipping. Instead, have someone hand a baby to you after you are sitting. Once seated, mothers have also reached for a baby who was lying on a towel on the floor or in an infant seat next to the tub.

- A few babies become over-stimulated with constant handling and their fussiness continues until they are put down. This baby's crying literally "winds down" once she is put down. If you put a baby down and crying persists with no noticeable winding down within several minutes, it is unlikely that the baby's crying is a result of handling. In fact, the baby may be in need of your arms again.

Equipment That Can Help

High touch still beats high tech every time. However, mothers of multiples aren't given extra arms, so there may be times when you depend on equipment to "console" a baby or two while you care for the other(s).

- You may find you are often breastfeeding one (or two) while coping with another crying, hungry multiple. This is not a relaxing way to breastfeed. It may help to lay the crying baby close to you and touch her as you feed the other(s). Another idea is to place the crying baby in a cradle, buggy, stroller, or rocking infant seat, and use your feet to rock it. Some mothers find the baby in a seat calms if she "wraps" her bare feet around that baby's body. Many mothers of multiples swear by a bouncer seat, since a baby's own movement causes the seat to move up and down. Others find an automatic swing to be a godsend at these times.

- Certain sounds tend to have a calming effect on babies. The same soft classical or "new age" music you waltz to with a baby is also the best choice for soothing background music. Many parents recommend an audio-tape or CD of the sounds a baby heard when in the womb. Rhythmic "white noise," such as the sound of a vacuum cleaner or the static heard when a radio is set between stations calms some babies. There are also white noise recordings on the market.

You may be surprised to find you feel closer to a high need baby sooner than to a less demanding one. This is probably due to the extra contact the high need multiple requires. Mothers often say they feel guilty because they are not paying as much attention to their more patient babies. Actually, you are treating each baby as an individual when you respond to each one's different needs for your time and attention.

You certainly will want to spend any extra time with the calmer baby, but don't feel guilty on those days when there is little extra time. And even the most patient baby will still have time with you during several daily breastfeedings. Also, most patient multiples eventually flip-flop with a fussier baby and demand equal time when it is needed. (See Chapter 18, "Enhancing Individuality.")

Colic generally disappears by the time babies are a few months old. Some high need babies remain high need because of temperament, but they often express their sensitivity in different ways as they grow older. For more information on high need babies and children, see "Resources."

Chapter 20
Getting Enough Sleep

Most mothers of multiples say they can cope with any number of babies as long as they get enough sleep. Sleep also contributes to your recuperation from a multiple pregnancy and birth. Of course, two or more babies wake for night feedings that much more often, so getting enough sleep is no simple quest.

A few babies sleep through the night, a four- to six-hour stretch, within weeks of birth, but most cannot. They need to eat every few hours. Babies aren't born telling time; they don't recognize that activity is associated with daytime while sleep is associated with night. Eventually they will get the idea, but it may be months before one or more can be counted on to sleep for a several hour stretch without waking. Fortunately, most mothers of multiples eventually adjust to babies' sleep cycles and are able to get adequate rest on a "catch as catch can" basis!

Always respond to your babies' cries as quickly as possible no matter what the hour. Your babies are learning to trust the person who answers their calls and learning that they are worthy of your response. Babies who continue to wake at night do not interrupt their parents' sleep on purpose. However, you may want to try some ideas that have worked for others.

Encouraging Sleep

Try waking each baby more often during the day to see if it lengthens the time they sleep at night. Babies wake more easily from light sleep, so watch for signs that a baby is in a lighter sleep state, such as stretching arms and legs, grimacing of the mouth, blinking or movement behind the eyelids, and grunting or making other noises. As with coordinating feedings, some babies are better able to go along with attempts to change their body clocks than others.

If you have been waking your preterm babies every few hours on doctor's orders, ask if you can begin to let each set her night feeding routine as soon as each demonstrates typical wetting and stooling patterns and has continued to gain weight.

Some parents find babies sleep longer when they massage each baby every evening. Infant massage techniques are simple to learn. There are several books that illustrate the movements that babies find relaxing. (See "Resources" for suggestions.)

Unless you find night feedings the perfect time to interact with one baby, and some mothers do, night feedings should be kept as businesslike as possible if you want babies to learn that nighttime is sleep time. Dim the lighting and leave the TV, radio, or CD player off. Cuddle and give a few kisses but keep conversation with babies to a minimum.

Play the same soft classical or "new age" music each evening when you observe a baby getting sleepy. The babies may learn to associate the music with falling asleep. Don't expect this to work immediately; it may be weeks or months before they make this association.

Younger babies may settle more easily if they hear the rhythmic static of "white" noise, such as a vacuum cleaner, a radio set between stations, etc., in the background. Recordings of such noises are available. Also, some babies respond to recordings of "womb sounds"—the soft, rhythmic sounds of a mother's heartbeat and blood rushing through an umbilical cord.

By two to three months babies generally soil diapers less often, and you may be able to double- or triple-diaper babies to avoid the stimulation of nighttime changes. Heavier diaper liners may help extend disposables, although this may not be necessary when more absorbent brands are used.

Co-Bedding

Multiples often sleep for longer periods when at least two share a crib, so you'll probably need only one crib (or none) for the first three to six months. Don't worry that one is disturbing another when you find a baby stretched on top of another. They've been in cramped quarters together long before now, and many sleep for longer stretches when able to touch

Babies can snuggle together in one crib for the first few months.

another. There is no arbitrary time when each baby should be given her own crib. The babies will let you know in no uncertain terms if it is time to separate them.

Co-Sleeping

Whether to bring a baby (or two or three) into the parents' bed may be a matter of debate for parents of a single baby. It's more often a matter of survival when there are multiple babies to care for at night. Human mothers sleep with their babies in almost all cultures, so it isn't anything new. For tens of thousands of years mothers have appreciated that everyone in the family copes better during the day when they've gotten as much sleep as possible the night before.

Babies and young children will not be in your bed forever, so relax. Although parents sometimes worry that they might hurt a baby by rolling on her, such happenings are rare unless a parent is under the influence of some drug or alcohol. When you sleep with a baby in the crook of your arm (or one in the crook of each), it is virtually impossible to roll on her. And co-sleeping is beneficial for babies, as scientists have found that newborns actually regulate their breathing patterns and heart rates better when they sleep with parents. Babies in bed do not affect physical intimacy for new parents of multiples. Most couples are creative enough to figure an alternative "approach" when they wish to be intimate and babies are in their bed. (And most parents of infant multiples usually are thinking of sleep rather than sexual relations when they propose going to bed!)

Parents of multiples have discovered many ingenious ways to get more sleep by bringing babies in bed for all or part of the night. Co-sleeping with two or more babies is a little more complicated than bringing one into bed with you, but with a little imagination, it can be done.

- Remove one side-rail from a crib. Adjust the crib mattress to the level of your mattress and fasten it securely against your bed. One baby can sleep between you and your husband, and another can sleep in the crib. Roll from side-to-side to meet babies' breastfeeding needs during the night. Portable cribs that attach directly to the parents' bed have been developed to give everyone more space when co-sleeping. (See "Resources.")

- Some parents refuse to be limited by standard bed sizes. When even a king-size bed may seem too small with two or more babies sharing it, extend the width of a bed. Simply place two (or more) mattresses side by side, making sure they cannot separate and allow a baby to slip into a crack. It may be safest to place the mattresses (and box springs) directly on the floor.

- If you can deal with only one at a time in bed, it may save steps to set up a crib in your bedroom. You can rotate the babies in and out of it as they wake to eat during the night. Babies may begin nighttime sleep in this crib, in your bed, or in a crib in another room. When Baby A wakes, breastfeed and fall asleep with that baby until Baby B wakes up. Settle Baby A in the nearby crib and fall asleep again while feeding Baby B.

- Instead of bringing babies into their bed, some mothers place a mattress on the floor of the babies' room and go there to feed, and fall asleep, once babies begin waking.

- It becomes easier to prop on pillows in bed and breastfeed two using the side-lying, prone, or a combination position to fall asleep as babies get older, although some are able to achieve this from the start. If you sit up and lean back against a bedrest pillow, you might be able to feed two newborns without getting out of bed.

- Some find they are more comfortable feeding newborns simultaneously when they sit in a more supportive chair, sofa, or recliner. Many mothers call a recliner "bed" and fall asleep in it while breastfeeding for several weeks or months after bringing multiples home. Some mothers place the recliner in their bedroom and others prefer to go to another room.

*The Arm's Reach
Co-Sleeper attaches
securely to parents' bed
to allow easy access to
one or more babies who
wake to nurse at night.*

Mother Sleep Styles

How a mother chooses to cope with night waking and feedings, and getting enough rest, often depends on her sleep style. There seems to be two basic styles: 1) the mother who easily falls back to sleep after waking for feedings, and 2) the mother who has difficulty falling asleep again if she awakens too much or for too long for feedings.

Mother #1 probably will try to coordinate babies' night feedings by waking two to feed at the same time or waking one after the other. She figures this is the best way to get several hours of uninterrupted sleep. Mother #2 will roll toward or slide into bed with her whichever baby wakes first, help him latch on, and then drift back to sleep as soon as possible. If both wake at once, she'll find some way to feed them simultaneously so she can quickly fall asleep again.

Mother #1 may not understand how Mother #2 copes with being interrupted so often at night, and Mother #2 can't figure out how Mother #1 gets any rest by waking for so long several times a night.

Mothers also have different napping styles. Mother A falls asleep at the drop of a hat when the babies (and older children) sleep. Whether she gets a 20 minute or two hour nap, she wakes feeling refreshed and ready to take on the rest of the day. Mother B cannot fall asleep no matter how tired. On the rare occasion she eventually does drift off, she wakes from her nap feeling more tired than when she lay down and is sluggish the rest of the day.

Mother A probably will want to take advantage of opportunities to sleep when all babies sleep, which may range from a daily to a rare occurrence. Mother B may find she gets more rest if she relaxes some other way when babies sleep.

Ultimately, the idea is to meet the babies' needs and get the rest you need—no matter which method(s) best suits your sleep style.

Dad's Involvement

It's amazing how much more sleep you will get if dad gets up to bring babies to you for night feedings when they sleep in another room. He also can change a baby as necessary and soothe a baby waiting to be fed.

If your partner's schedule often interferes with his ability to help at night, you and he may need to discuss ways for everyone to get enough rest. Dad's need for sleep is also important if he is to be alert on the job the next day. He may be unavailable many nights because he travels with his job or because he works on call. Of course, respect for his workload still doesn't give you the rest you need.

Perhaps he can agree to help more on the nights before his day off. You might nap during the day or evening or go to bed several hours early sometimes, and leave dad with expressed breast milk if babies need something to eat while you sleep. When feeling truly exhausted, some mothers express milk for one night feeding so dad can get up and feed one (or more). Mom also might feed one (or more), but she is able to go back to sleep sooner. Or dad might be responsible for feeding all the babies for one feeding so mom can get several hours of uninterrupted sleep one night.

Sleep Deprivation

Sleep deprivation in mothers of multiples can be a real problem. It especially affects mothers during the early weeks postpartum when they are recuperating from pregnancy and birth. And it is physically and mentally draining if weeks or months pass without being able to get a several hour stretch of uninterrupted sleep a few times a week. Some mothers report they begin to feel numb after operating for several days with very little sleep. Many find that small annoyances are magnified and they feel "on edge" or irritable. Occasionally mothers say they became so exhausted that they felt unable to respond to a waking baby; they literally felt paralyzed and could not make their bodies move.

Dad must be ready to help when a mother becomes too exhausted to care for babies. Suggestions for how dad can help are mentioned above. If your husband cannot be relied on to awaken, you may need to ask a relative or friend to stay over when you recognize the signs that you are reaching a critical point of sleep deprivation.

Although exhaustion is understandable when a mother is recuperating from multiple pregnancy and birth, the babies still need someone who can respond when they cry. Parents must find a solution that meets the babies' needs as well as mother's need for sleep.

Even prolonged night waking has its silver lining. You will never take uninterrupted sleep for granted the rest of your life.

Chapter 21
What You'll Need

Infant gadgets and equipment often make life easier for a mother of multiples. Fortunately, few items are needed in double or triple quantities, and most can be purchased after you've begun to care for the babies at home and developed a better sense of what would be useful. When an item is needed for each baby or toddler, taking advantage of relatives' and friends' offers to lend clothing and equipment often is a budget saver. Consignment shops and neighborhood or mothers of multiples club sales may be other sources of used clothing and equipment in good condition. (Uses for various types of equipment are discussed in relevant chapters. Information for certain products is included in "Resources.")

Anticipating the kinds and amount of clothing and equipment you will need to have on hand for multiple newborns can be difficult, but newborns don't need much in the way of material goods. Beyond diapers and several changes of clothing for each, there is little you must have on hand when they are discharged home.

Diapers

Each newborn will require about six to ten diaper changes a day. (Older babies usually require at least four to six daily changes.) Cloth diapers, or nappies, usually must be changed more often than highly absorbent brands of disposable diapers. You will probably want to weigh the advantages and disadvantages of diapering options with potential cost. Since your time is at a premium when you have multiple babies, don't cut convenience for low cost or you may find you pay in other ways.

• Laundering cloth diapers may seem the least expensive diapering option. You won't need a week's worth of diapers, but unless you want to spend a lot of time in the laundry room, you will probably want at least 1½ to 2 days of diapers on hand. Pre-folded diapers are more convenient than unfolded ones, but become costly if you have to invest in different sizes as babies grow. Flushable diaper liners can be purchased to make diaper changes and laundry easier. Include the dirty diaper hamper, laundry detergent, hot water, and wear and tear on appliances when figuring the total cost of cloth diapers.

• Disposable diapers are convenient to use, but the cost of eight diapers times two, three, four, or more daily quickly adds up! However, you can easily change diaper sizes as babies grow. If you're interested in using disposables, ask other parents which brands they like and why. Some discount department store brands incorporate the favorite features of name brands yet are often much less expensive. Most brands are not biodegradable, and many have voiced concern about disposable diapers' long-term effect on the environment.

• Diaper services deliver cloth diapers for a fee in many urban areas. Most of the fee covers the delivery charge. Multiplying the number of diapers for two or more babies often adds very little to the total cost. Most services include the "dirty" diaper hamper(s). Hampers are returned when you cancel the service. Many parents have found diaper service to be the most economical yet convenient option for multiples.

Many parents combine diapering options. They use purchased or diaper service cloth diapers at home, but take disposable diapers for outings or travel.

Clothing or Layette

You'll probably find you change each newborn's clothing two or three times a day due to diaper overflow, spit-ups, and so on. You probably can get by with about five t-shirts or one-piece shirt/diaper covers per baby and an equal number of stretch sleepers or gowns for each. Depending on the climate, each newborn may need a sweater and cap/hat or heavier outerwear. You'll also want at least one larger crib blanket and two smaller receiving blankets for each multiple. Some parents color-code blankets so they know which blanket belongs to which baby.

Babies quickly grow through several sizes of clothing, so parents of multiples often look for durable used clothing at garage sales, flea markets, and consignment shops. Some parents of multiples groups sponsor clothing sales. Lucky parents make a connection with another family having slightly older multiples of the same number and sex(es).

Whether new or used, wash all clothing before the babies wear it. Just throw it in with the rest of the family wash.

You probably won't have to worry about buying "party" clothes. Most friends and relatives love to give dressy matching outfits to multiples as gifts.

Breast Pumps

Few women need to purchase a breast pump prior to giving birth. If you must express your milk for one or more babies, many hospitals now provide a double collection kit and the loan of a self-cycling breast pump for use in the hospital, which will appear on your hospital bill. (Be sure to take all collection kit pieces home with you from the hospital.) Milk collection kits may also be purchased, and pumps purchased or rented, through breast pump company depots. La Leche League Leaders and lactation consultants in your area should know of local depots if 1) a hospital doesn't stock these items for use during your hospital stay, 2) you must continue to pump after hospital discharge, or 3) a need for pumping doesn't appear until after discharge.

Eventually, you may want to rent or purchase a self-cycling pump if you decide to express milk two or more times a day for daily supplementary bottles or you return to a place of employment while your multiples are infants and still rely mostly on your milk for food. However, you should have plenty of time to rent or purchase a pump for these uses after babies are born and breastfeeding is well established. If you find you need to express milk only for occasional complementary bottles, a reliable manual (hand), battery-operated, or mini-electric pump probably will do. Many mothers find that even this expense is unnecessary if they learn the proper technique for hand-expression of milk. (Milk expression in different situations is discussed in relevant chapters. See "Resources" for breast pump company contact numbers.)

Car Seats

One car seat for each baby must be purchased and properly installed in your car before the babies can be discharged from the hospital. In many areas infant car seats are required by law. Some car seats adapt for newborn through toddler ages or weights. Other types are specific for a certain stage, but they can be used outside of the car as seats for strollers, infant swings, and so on. Still others are for use only in the car and for a specific age level, which means purchasing separate sets of car seats for newborn and older multiples.

Age-related car seats may seem less expensive initially, but adaptable car seats often save parents money in the long run. Before purchasing car seats, match the measurements of your car with the measurements of the car seats. Also be certain that the car seats you are considering can be anchored safely in your car according to the manufacturer's directions.

Bedding

Sleepy newborns can drift off in any safe spot. The latest design in nursery furniture is not a requirement for sound sleep. As a matter of fact most newborns prefer to snooze in parents' arms and on their chests. It is not always as easy or convenient to let multiple babies sleep with parents, so you may want to have some type of bed or crib available. A bassinet-size drawer, appropriately padded and placed in a safe spot, makes a great temporary, portable baby bed.

Multiples often sleep better when placed with one or two others, so a single crib for two or three babies may meet the babies' needs for several weeks or months. You will have plenty of time to find additional cribs before the babies let you know, loudly and clearly, that they want more space! Doubling or tripling may not work in bassinets or small portable cribs, however.

Whether you buy or borrow a baby bed(s), be certain that each meets all recommended safety guidelines. Babies have strangled after getting their heads caught between side-rail slats that were too wide and from constricting clothing that became caught on some attachment projecting from a crib. Also, a mattress should fit a crib frame snugly so that a baby cannot smother if its head should become trapped between the frame and mattress.

A bed extender, which is similar to a portable crib, can attach to the side of the parents' bed. This can make it easier to keep babies close during the night. One to three multiples should safely fit in it depending on the length and width of a particular brand and the babies' sizes.

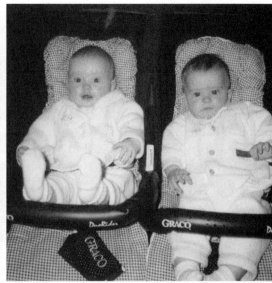

Multiple Stroller

A stroller that safely seats two (or more) babies or children is considered a must by most parents of multiples. They often rely on their special double, triple, or quadruple-seat strollers until multiples are through the toddler or preschool years. It simply is not practical or safe to chase after multiple toddlers and preschoolers running in different directions, so a stroller must be durable enough to last several years. High-quality strollers for multiples can be expensive, but most parents say a well-constructed stroller that adapts as their multiples grow pays for itself many times over. (Many parents ultimately have spent more by having to replace inexpensive, less durable strollers that fall apart from use, or because their original strollers were less adaptable or quickly outgrown by toddler multiples.) A quality stroller also has resale value when your multiples no longer need it.

Many parents delay the purchase of stroller until after the babies' births. They figure the babies will not be going anywhere immediately after discharge, and they want to gain a sense of which stroller, or stroller-baby carrier combination, might best meet their needs before making an investment. Whether you purchase one now or later, ask other parents of same-number multiples which strollers they prefer or which they wish they had bought (and why).

Parents have more stroller options than ever before. Side-by-side models are becoming more compact and some brands offer individually adjusted seat backs. Strollers the width of a single seat come with all seats facing forward, one seat facing another, or adjustable models with one or more seats that may be moved to face backward or forward. There are now stroller frames that allow for the addition of a variable number of seats. Double jogging strollers are also available.

Consider how you might use a stroller before you go shopping. Compare features and cost to find one that best suits your needs. The suburban family that is in and out of the car a lot probably will want a lightweight stroller that folds for easy storage in the trunk or cargo area. On the other hand, the urban family that spends most of its time cruising uneven concrete sidewalks and curbs may be looking for one with a shock-resistant frame and wheels. Both families will want a stroller that easily passes through doorways and shop aisles, which are usually at least a yard (36 inches) to a meter wide. Weight and portability are issues for a family whose flat is on the third floor of an apartment building without an elevator or when public transportation is frequently used. And think about immediate and long-term use. A stroller or carriage that is perfect for newborns may not offer enough room for toddlers to stretch their legs.

"Tandem" strollers were developed for families having closely spaced children—those born more like 10 to 18 months apart than 10 to 18 minutes. This type of stroller may not be the best option with two newborns, but many parents begin using a tandem stroller once one baby can maintain a sitting position. If you have an older toddler or preschooler in addition to newborn twins or triplets, a stroller offering a variable number of seats may be the best option. Linking two umbrella-type strollers with a special stroller connector creates a compact and portable double stroller, yet allows you to have the convenience of a single stroller when you want it. Use connectors with two swivel-wheeled, umbrella-type strollers of the same brand. Measure the combined width of the two strollers and the connector, since you will want the strollers to be narrow enough to pass through most doorways when joined. (See "Resources" for stroller information.)

Rocking and Recliner Chair(s)

No parents should bring multiples home without installing a comfortable rocking chair on every level of the house! A rocker is so indispensable, it should be tax deductible for parents of multiples. Rocking not only soothes babies, the rhythm is also soothing for a frantic mother or older sibling.

A well-designed wooden or upholstered rocker will hold you and your multiples for years. Place the most comfortable rocker where you spend the most time, usually not the nursery. Folding lawn chair rockers are an inexpensive option for other areas of the house and can be thrown in the car to take when traveling or visiting someone.

A comfortable recliner allows a mother to rest comfortably while two babies nurse.

Upholstered recliner chairs have been instrumental in helping mothers learn to feed two babies simultaneously. The semi-reclining position and the upholstery combine to support babies' bodies, so a mother's hands are free to help the babies latch on. Many parents of multiples have gotten extra hours of sleep in a roomy recliner with babies held safely in their arms or lying across their chests. Since many parents find they literally live in a rocker or a recliner for the first six months, you may want to find at least one upholstered rocker-recliner combination.

Baby Carriers

You may want a cloth sling or infant carrier available when you first bring babies home. A carrier allows you to carry and provide close contact with one baby while still having two free hands. A sling may be more practical with multiples because the baby is carried to the side in it, which leaves a breast accessible when another baby wants to feed.

Eventually you might want to get an extra one or two slings or infant carriers, so each parent can "wear" one or two babies. Some parents have carried two multiples at once by crisscrossing slings on their upper bodies; others have worn two infant carriers—one baby on their chests and one against their backs.

Because of the limited market, brands of double carriers have come and gone over the years. If you do find one, the most practical models come apart to form one or two single carriers. Most parents find it difficult to wear a carrier with two full-term babies by three to six months, but parents of preterm multiples may find they can use a double infant carrier longer. However, a double carrier may be impractical to use with some babies even when they are very small.

Other Equipment

There are many infant products on the market that sound wonderful, but you and your babies can usually easily live without them. Consider your budget and the space available in your home for storing nonessential equipment before buying or borrowing.

A **changing table** may be nice to have, but placing a waterproof pad on a carpet, sofa, or bed will work just as well and allows you to change two newborns assembly-line style. Changing babies on the floor eliminates the danger of a baby falling if another baby distracts you during diaper and clothing changes.

Bathing babies in an **infant bathtub** is fine, but laying a newborn on a towel next to a sink for a sponge bath is just as effective for getting a young baby clean. Some infant seats can be used to prop babies for bathing in an adult tub. A parent can bathe with a baby by laying the baby across her/his chest or legs to bathe it. This can be a good way, especially for fathers, to get more skin contact with babies.

There usually is no need to purchase special baby towels or soap, adult towels and soap will do for most babies. Only those with highly sensitive skin actually require special soaps or detergents for their clothing. And breastfed babies have such a nice scent of their own, why spoil it with artificial baby lotions or oils?

A **play yard** or playpen initially may protect one or more newborn multiples from an older sibling. Many parents find it works great as a large toy chest or laundry basket. Older infants usually don't find a play yard or playpen a very interesting place to play.

An **automatic infant swing** can be a great help when feeding one newborn and another is demanding attention, or it can rock one while you meet an older child's needs or prepare supper. However, a **self-rocking infant seat**, or (self) **bouncer seat,** may work as well or better. One swing or bouncer seat on the main floor of the house usually is enough when babies first arrive home. Depending on the individual babies' responses, you may want to buy or borrow additional swings or bouncing/rocking seats.

Caution: In one study of infants and equipment use, researchers found that babies less than two months old were spending an average of six hours—and up to 12 hours—a day in some type of infant seat, such as infant or car seats, swings, etc. Because of their lack of muscular control, the babies' necks bent forward within 20 minutes of being placed in an infant seat. This positioning caused babies to regurgitate more. It also partially blocked the airway, and researchers think this is possibly related to more upper respiratory infections among these babies. It comes as no surprise then that the researchers concluded that babies belong in arms, not in devices.

After three to four months, infant seats may pose a different problem. In some play seats a baby is virtually suspended in the sitting position. When this occurs, it is difficult or impossible for the baby to keep his feet flat on the floor. This may place unnecessary stress on the physical structures in a baby's pelvic area. Watch for this if babies are in walkers, saucer seats, or jumping seats that are suspended from a doorway. If your babies enjoy any of these seats, you may want to limit their use and take a baby out of the seat after 20 to 30 consecutive minutes.

Infant equipment is beneficial, and some may be essential, when parents must meet the needs of multiple babies or toddlers in addition to other family members. However, it is too easy to overuse, or even abuse, equipment that gives a harried parent a break. Ultimately, the babies will suffer.

As a parent of multiples you may have to remind yourself often of the purpose of equipment. No matter what your multiples' current age, equipment is meant to briefly help you—not replace you. A rocking chair or baby carrier will always be better equipment options because they include **you.** Automatic swings, infant seats, play yards, and so on, will never replace your arms. Your babies, no matter how many of them came together, always **need** your touch. The wise use of equipment allows you to stretch yourself a little farther without compromising babies' developmental needs.

Chapter 22
Getting Out and About

It is important for you and your babies to get up and out of the house. However, outings are often more complicated to organize with multiples. Some days you may feel too tired to leave home by the time you get everyone ready for an excursion. When you don't have another adult helper or if all the babies wailed in chorus the last time you were out, you actually may feel scared to leave your house. Yet staying home because of fears, real or imagined, isolates you and the babies.

The entire family benefits from the stimulation of fresh air, new sights and sounds, and meeting other people. Taking a stroll outdoors or in an enclosed shopping mall can help you relax and regain perspective when caring for multiple babies becomes overwhelming. On days when you have begun to doubt it, you will return from an outing believing you have the most adorable babies in the world after so many people have come up to confirm it.

To make outings more fun for everyone, try some of these mother-of-multiples-tested ideas.

Be Prepared

- Find a large **diaper bag** that can comfortably accommodate extra outfits and two diaper changes for each baby, a changing pad, diaper wipes, and several plastic bags for soiled items. Some mothers say a stick-type stain remover is an indispensable diaper bag item. You'll also want to keep several small toys in the bag.

    a. Restock the diaper bag on a daily basis, so you won't have to think about it when you are ready to run out the door.

    b. Consider keeping a separate stocked bag in the car.

    c. Most mothers don't want a bag that can slide down the arm, leaving them to juggle babies and a bag. An expandable backpack with lots of pockets is often an ideal diaper bag. There are also diaper bags designed to fit on strollers.

    d. If you store your wallet, keys, credit cards, and so on in the diaper bag or a purse, your valuables may be at risk when you are preoccupied with babies' needs. Valuables should be kept in a hard-to-reach pocket of the bag. You may want to choose a bag with a long shoulder strap so it can be worn across the chest. A fanny pack for these valuables may be a better solution.

- Your **multiple stroller** may be the most valuable piece of child care equipment parents of multiples ever own. (For buying a stroller, see Chapter 21, "What You'll Need.") A good stroller can be used indoors or out in a variety of ways. However, no stroller is perfect for every outing.

    a. The backs of most multiple stroller seats can be adjusted in several positions. A few strollers have seats with only a flat back position for very young babies, which can cause babies to startle and cry every time the stroller hits a bump in the pavement. Some parents have avoided this by placing infant seats narrow enough to fit in the stroller seats on the flat back and seat. They secured each baby in the infant seats with a seatbelt. Then they wrapped another seatbelt around each infant seat-stroller seat unit. However, **caution** should be used whenever any baby equipment is not used according to a manufacturer's directions.

    b. You'll soon find that two or more babies in a stroller attract a crowd. There definitely are days when a mother can use some attention, but other days a mother may want to keep moving. For uninterrupted outings with twins, place one baby in a baby carrier or sling and let the other ride in the stroller. You could use a single stroller, but with a double stroller you'll have the extra seat for storage. When you "wear" one baby, many people won't notice you have twins until they've passed you.

A mother's helper can make it easier to take multiples out.

Parents of higher-order multiples still have at least two in a stroller, so this strategy won't work as well. However, show-stopping attention may be minimized if you and Daddy each "wear" a baby. One or both of you can push another baby in a single stroller. If attention is unavoidable, at least the babies will enjoy some close contact with you while in the sling or carrier.

Alternate which baby gets close contact in a baby carrier or sling. When one is fussy or high need, you may find you need to "wear" that multiple more often for outings. Also, the pediatric care provider may feel more comfortable about early outings if you wear a multiple that must avoid contact with outsiders as a result of some birth-related health problem.

You may limit the number of times you are stopped by strangers if you attach a sign to the stroller that answers their most common questions. A sign might include: 1) Yes, they're twins (triplets, quads, etc.), 2) They're __ weeks (months, years) old, 3) They're fraternal (identical)-two girls (two boys, girl/boy), 4) No, they're not small (large) for twins (triplets, quads, etc.).

You may be asked questions that are not worthy of a response, such as personal questions about how the multiples were conceived, whether one is your favorite, and so on. For these questions, some parents develop snappy comeback lines; others simply say, "I prefer not to answer personal questions," or "That really is not any of your business."

c. Many families have a toddler or preschooler in addition to infant multiples. It is easier to keep an eye on everyone if a parent wears one multiple in a baby sling or carrier and lets the older child ride in one of the multiple stroller seats.

• When shopping at grocery and discount centers, you may want to take advantage of shopping carts that provide an attached infant seat or a child seat facing the parent. **Warning:** Never leave any baby or child alone in a shopping cart for even a moment.

a. The easiest way to maneuver a shopping cart with twins is to wear one in a baby carrier or sling, and seatbelt the other in an attached infant seat.

b. You may have to place an infant seat in the body of a cart if: 1. there is no attached seat, 2. you cannot wear a baby carrier or sling for some reason, or 3. you have triplets. In these cases, pull a second cart for the items you are going to purchase. If you have triplets or quadruplets, you may have to place an infant seat in the body of the second cart as well. Don't plan on buying many items when babies are in infant seats in the body of the cart. It is **dangerous** to pile items in a cart around babies in infant seats.

c. As the babies grow, you might carry one in a baby backpack while the other is harnessed or seat-belted in the cart seat. (For additional ideas for older baby or toddler multiples, see Chapter 28. "Older Babies and Toddlers: Childproofing and Helpful Equipment.")

• You may need a **mother's helper** when taking infant triplets or quadruplets for a walk or shopping. Although shopping with higher-order multiples may continue to be easier when you take someone along to help, you probably can manage walks alone once the babies reach several months as long as you have a well-designed stroller. A mother's helper still is indispensable if multiples accompany you when you are trying to purchase personal items.

• Arriving on time for appointments can be a challenge for anyone with multiples. If you ever needed an excuse for being late, you really have it now. Besides having the diaper bag ready to go at all times (or keeping a second stocked bag in the car), there are ways to make appointment-keeping more realistic.

a. Ask for appointment times that require minimum periods in a waiting room when scheduling time with the pediatric care provider, a baby photographer, etc. Usually this will be the first appointment in the morning or after a lunch break.

b. Bring someone with you to help with the babies when you take them for pediatric appointments. This is especially important when an office building cannot accommodate a multiple stroller. Even if you can take the stroller, you still will need extra arms to help in the waiting room. Also, you may need to attend to each baby individually during physical exams.

c. When you have an appointment the first thing in the morning, dress the babies in "traveling" clothes the night before. An alternative is to change nothing but their diapers, and not even those if the babies are asleep when you put them in the car, until you reach your destination.

Most people are very understanding and willing to accommodate you once you've explained your reason for wanting a certain appointment and why you might be late. It's a good thing this is so because of **Murphy's Multiples Law.** No matter how prepared you are, the moment you've gotten the last multiple fastened into the car seat or stroller, one of them will manage to spit up or need an immediate diaper change.

Safety Precautions

Develop a **fire evacuation** plan for your home today. Keep a baby carrier, sling (or two), or backpack where the babies sleep, so both you and your husband could carry at least two babies in case of a fire. You may be able to wheel a multiple stroller into the bedroom at night if that bedroom is on the first floor and there are no steps to the outside.

Never drive with the babies unless a baby carrier, sling, or the multiple stroller is in the car. Although the items might not be needed for a particular trip, any of them might prove to be a lifesaver if you have a breakdown or run out of gas.

Getting out and about with multiples takes more planning, but it is worth the effort. You and the babies will enjoy the outside stimulation. Everyone will feel better when you regularly get out and see some of the world.

Chapter 23
For Mothers Only:
Adjusting to Multiples

One dictionary defines the word "intense" as: 1) occurring or existing in a high degree, very strong, 2) strained to the utmost, earnest, 3) having or showing strong emotion, great seriousness, etc., 4) characterized by much action, emotion, etc. With its positive and negative connotations, **intense** is a perfect word to describe life with young multiples. Nurturing multiples can be extremely intense during their first years.

A sentiment often expressed by women during the last months of a multiple pregnancy is the desire to "get back to normal." Expectant mothers tend to idealize babies during pregnant daydreams. Daydream babies seldom fuss, spit up, or have leaky diapers. Pregnant parents acknowledge that caring for multiple babies will keep them constantly busy, but **imagining** "constantly busy" and **living** "constantly busy" are seldom the same.

It can be a shock to discover that the postpartum year is even less "normal" than 30 to 40 weeks of a multiple pregnancy. Who could anticipate the suddenness of all the physical and emotional change that giving birth brings about? Change is always disruptive for routine-loving humans, but change, and the accompanying disruption in household routine, lasts longer when a new addition turns out to be new additions.

The new mother of multiples must begin to cope with two or more unique, yet immature and totally dependent, new human beings in her life, a task that can make the strongest woman feel vulnerable. And she must care for these new, very little persons while recovering from a more demanding pregnancy and birth that may leave her wondering if she's inhabiting a stranger's body. The new mother may be the one most personally involved, but the entire family is affected by change.

A New Role
Oldest but Not Only

If your multiples are first children, you probably will need time to adjust to your new role and the title "Mother." Ambivalent feelings about learning this role with two or more different babies are not unusual; although some first-time mothers think it is easier to have multiples first since they know nothing else! However, meeting baby needs (times two, three, or more) while shifting career gears is a tremendous change.

Of course, your babies do not realize that you have never had one baby before, much less two. They don't care that you may be a bit inept at first—your babies know only that you love them. They come to know this if you answer quickly when they call, when you relieve their hunger in such a pleasant, high-contact way, and by your voice when you talk with them as you look into their eyes. All awkwardness is forgiven.

Recurring Role

If you have an older child, you probably feel relaxed about handling babies and more confident in your mothering. Having multiples is a very different experience, however. In many ways a mother starts all over again—unless this is her second set of multiples.

The thought of nurturing two or more newborns at once may seem almost frightening at times to the experienced mother. You know how much time it takes to meet the needs of one baby, so you have some idea of what the care of multiple infants will entail. Physically managing multiple newborns may require a completely different set of caretaking strategies from the ones you used for a single infant.

Having felt a special attachment with a previous baby, it can be frustrating if a similar intimacy with the individuals within the set of multiples seems to elude you. You truly understand the luxury of having a moment to look into your baby's face. You know the feeling of closeness that develops when you can devote hours a day to one baby.

You may also feel concerned about caring for an older child, knowing that the younger the child, the greater that child's need for mother. Ideas for coping with multiple newborns while helping other children adjust are in Chapter 25, "Older Siblings of Multiples."

Attachment

The process of maternal-infant attachment is very different when a mother must get to know more than one baby. The intimate closeness that develops within hours, days, or at least within several weeks, may take months or even well into the second year with each multiple. It's simply more difficult to fall in love with more than one person at a time. (For more on the attachment process, see Chapter 18, "Enhancing Individuality.")

Fortunately, you are a breastfeeding mother of multiples, which puts you in constant contact with each baby. The increased contact provides opportunities that maximize the attachment process. Perhaps with time at a premium or because it often takes longer to form individual attachments, it may feel as if the emotional benefits of breastfeeding are postponed for you. Something may seem to be missing, which can be very disappointing.

Your need to develop a special relationship with each baby is as important as each baby's need for your special brand of mothering. However, put any disappointment in perspective by remembering that your babies enjoy **all** the advantages that breastfeeding offers from the start. Be patient. Allow breastfeeding and bonding the luxury of time. Accept that breastfeeding may be different with multiples. Let the bond between you and each baby grow in its own time.

Developing a Routine

After the birth of a single infant, a new routine usually begins to emerge after the first four to eight weeks. At the same time most mothers are beginning to feel really in tune with the baby. A mother of a single infant often adapts to slight day-to-day changes in her baby's breastfeeding style and overall development without even being aware of them, because they are so subtle.

It often takes longer—sometimes much longer—for a routine to develop after the births of multiples. Change is constant and usually there isn't anything subtle about it. The developing routine may be dependent on current circumstances. A change in breastfeeding style, the reaching of a developmental milestone, or the onset of a minor illness for even one multiple often has a noticeable effect on the delicate balance in the household. A mother simply cannot adapt as effortlessly as she might have with a single infant. In addition, as a household routine emerges, the busy new mother of multiples may not have time to recognize it for what it is.

Learning to cope with the physical and emotional changes created when multiples are introduced to a household can be a good lesson in flexibility for control-oriented adults. Don't fight to hold onto some old idea of "normal" routine. Let go of expectations. Two babies, three babies, four babies, or more than that can never be like having one baby. Let go, and give a brand new "normal" routine the time it needs to evolve.

The Myth of the SuperMOM

There is a cultural myth that implies that such things as infant-feeding routines, family sleep patterns, and a mother's body should quickly fall into place after giving birth. Help? There must be something wrong with a woman who thinks she needs help. New mothers are supposed to zip up their pre-pregnant jeans, nurture any number of newborns, and energetically resume all prior responsibilities within several weeks of delivery. Right?

Wrong! Few mothers of a single-born infant can meet the unrealistic expectations of this Supermom mythology. Yet mothers of multiples or their family members often impose the same unhealthy myth on themselves and their special situation. At times it may be difficult for you to remember, and your husband, relatives, and friends to understand, that you will continue to need their help. When you or your husband hear that other new mothers seem to have settled into a routine with their babies, you may wonder if you are doing something wrong. You are doing nothing wrong. You simply have two, three, four, or more times as many newborns as the average new mother!

When you find yourself saying, "I **should** be doing...," ask yourself what you are trying to prove and to whom are you trying to prove it? Give yourself a break. You don't have to give in to a stressful mythology that places unrealistic expectations on your shoulders. Let go of all you think you **should** be doing, and do only what really must be done.

- The cultural myth makes it very difficult for most new mothers to ask for help. You must get over it **now** if you are to get the help you need. Your relatives, friends, and acquaintances may never completely understand the intensity of mothering multiples, but you owe it to yourself and your family to learn to ask for their help when you feel pressured or overwhelmed. To others it may appear that you are juggling babies and a hectic household with the greatest of ease. No one can read your mind. You have only yourself to blame if you fail to ask for help when you need it.

  Never deprive someone of an opportunity to do a good deed. Take whatever aid concerned family and friends can offer. Sometime in the future you will have the chance to pay back all the good deeds. Someday others will need your help, and you will have the time and energy to give it. Now it's your turn.

- Feel free to cut extracurricular activities to the bone until multiples are older. The extra tasks add unnecessary extra pressure and take extra energy. The earth will keep turning and the task will be completed if you aren't the one to bake the cookies, collect the donations, or work the auction booth at an organization or school event.

Leaving your babies for meetings or activities means they will have less of you than they already do just by being part of a set. It may seem hard to believe now, but your multiples will be babies for a very brief time. All those activities will still be available when you are under less pressure and your constant presence is a little less important.

Riding the Emotional Merry-Go-Round

A lack of time and routine during multiples' early weeks or months may leave you feeling as if you've jumped on a merry-go-round that can't be slowed, much less stopped. Many mothers of multiples find they experience only emotional highs and lows for quite awhile after the babies' births. They feel as if they've lost any control of the environment. Ambivalent feelings about being the "lucky" one who had multiples are common.

Highs and lows can occur in cycles of days or weeks, and sometimes within minutes. When everything is going smoothly or you've actually gotten several hours of uninterrupted sleep, you feel fantastic. You are proud of the way you are handling the situation and meeting the babies' needs so well. However, there are days when babies take turns crying all day, an older child constantly seeks attention by getting into mischief, the family has been living out of the laundry basket for several days and laundry has piled up again, the last frozen casserole was baked the night before and the cupboards are bare, and you haven't had more than one-and-a-half hours of uninterrupted sleep in a week. On those days you are allowed to feel that you've reached a deep dip on that merry-go-round.

When you are feeling low, feelings of guilt usually aren't far behind. After all, here you are with these beautiful babies. How can anyone so lucky claim the right to complain? All right, so you are lucky. You know it. Still, feeling lucky cannot lessen the intensity of this positive situation. Knowing you are lucky does not give you more time or more sleep.

You're probably heaping on extra servings of guilt if your babies were the result of fertility-enhancement treatment. You are not allowed to feel ambivalent, tired, blue, and so on. Nope, no negative feelings for you. You asked for this. Isn't that right? Never mind that multiple babies mean multiple feedings, changes, cuddling—no matter how they were conceived.

And how are you supposed to feel if you aren't as lucky? Perhaps one or more of your multiples requires extra care for a short-term or a chronic health condition, or maybe one was born with a congenital anomaly. You still have to care for this multiple and the other babies, too. You still have to form a close attachment with each.

The Death of One or More Multiples

The death of a baby probably is the most difficult situation any mother (parent) may ever face. Because of the complications associated more often with multiple pregnancy and birth, the chance that one or more multiple infants may die before or after birth is slightly increased. The death of a baby is not acceptable, no matter how many other babies have lived. Once a mother knows how many babies she is expecting, she begins to attach to those babies. All of those babies.

If one or more dies, mothers (and fathers) grieve profoundly for the one(s) that dies. Yet they also must form deep attachments with each living multiple. It is difficult to grieve and form attachments at the same time, and many mothers seem to postpone one or the other for a period of time. This period may be brief or it may be months or years before they deal with the other emotional task. A mother may also flip-flop between grief and attachment within the same day, week, month, or year.

More mothers appear to focus first on forming strong attachments with any living multiples. Nature probably encourages this, since any living baby's physical and emotional growth depends to a great extent on the attachment that develops between a mother and child. Sometimes mothers are initially overcome with grief for the one(s) that died. In either case, mothers often feel torn and guilty about their feelings.

There are no rules for grief. One feels what one feels. However, if grieving for a multiple that dies is prolonged and interferes with forming an attachment with the other(s), it is probably wise to get professional help. A psychotherapist or grief counselor should be able to provide ideas for coping with grief so that you can also develop the relationships you and your other little one(s) deserve. (See "Grief Support" in Resources.)

Mothers Are Not All the Same

Every mother of multiples is different. Their responses are different, too. Your personality, the number of multiples and their conditions, the babies' temperaments, the number and ages of other children, the amount of help you receive, your family situation, and many other variables all influence your adjustment to multiple newborns.

Don't be surprised, however, if your mood seems to fluctuate between high and low without hitting a plateau for awhile. There is no advice that will eliminate the dramatic ups and downs reported by many new mothers of multiples, but there are ideas that might help you cope.

- Acknowledge and accept your feelings—whatever they are today.

  Multiples are both a blessing and a burden. It is possible to feel glad you gave birth to multiples yet also envy women who have only one to care for. You can feel thankful but overwhelmed, or excited yet isolated and alone all at the same time. You may feel grateful for the help of relatives and friends, yet also resent being unable to manage alone. It's okay to want your children and your house to yourself.

  Positive and negative feelings often coexist. But to paraphrase two old sayings, actions speak louder than feelings. You can't help your feelings; however, you do control your responses to them—and your response is what really matters.

- Remind yourself several times every day that you are doing your best, and no one—not even you—can expect more of you than your best. Say it aloud and listen to yourself, "I am doing my best today to cope with this situation."

  Accept that "best" is a relative term. Your best will differ from day to day. Do the best you are capable of today. If occasionally your best isn't too much, be sure to get help so that babies' and other family members' needs are taken care of.

- Guilt is born along with babies. Mothers feel guilty that they can't give each multiple the same time and attention they could give one baby. They feel guilty that they don't have enough time to spend with an older child. They feel guilty that they are neglecting their husbands, their friends, their jobs. They feel guilty when they have ambivalent feelings.

  Stop wallowing in guilt! It's an unproductive use of needed energy. Make guilt your friend instead of an enemy. It may be trying to tell you that something is out of balance in your life, or you may be falling victim to what you think you should be doing. When you feel guilt, examine it. What is it really about? Is it something you can, or should, do anything about it? If you truly believe the answer is "yes," than ask yourself what you need to do to change the situation. And do it. If you can't do anything about it, accept that you can't do anything. In either case, let go of the guilt once you've dealt with it.

- Enjoy the "highs" when you feel so capable of dealing with everyone and everything. When experiencing a "low," remind yourself that it soon will be followed by a "high."

- Live one day at a time. This may enable you to get more enjoyment out of a "high," and it may help you cope when you feel low. During periods when even one day seems an eternity, try living from meal to meal instead. "I made it through night wakings to breakfast; I can make it to lunch; made it to lunch, so I can make it to supper; made it to supper, I'm sure I can make it through colicky time to bed time."
- Don't look too far ahead. Look behind only to gain some perspective of how far you've come. You may not appreciate how much progress you and the babies have made, especially if you're having a temporary setback today.

Take Care of Yourself

When caring for the needs of multiples and other family members, keep in mind that you have important needs, too. You owe it to yourself, and your family, to regularly recharge your "giving" batteries. The earth will keep turning and your house still will be standing if you do something for you instead of accomplishing some household chore when a few minutes of peace and quiet come your way. A little clutter never caused a house to collapse. Your home will fall apart in a much more crucial way if you fail to take care of you.

- Savor moments alone, but accept that these time treasures may be brief. They add up, however, when used wisely.
- Do something you really enjoy if a few minutes of uninterrupted calm come your way. Forget tonight's supper, the dirty laundry, or the dustballs under the chair. Of course, if you find it relaxing to clean and cook, go to it! Just don't feel guilty if you would rather take those minutes to read, exercise, nap, work on a hobby, etc.
- Find a socially acceptable, physical outlet when you feel tension building. Make bread dough, and when the recipe calls for you to "punch down," really let that dough have it! (This is a very productive tension reliever, since you will also have something for dinner.) Don boxing gloves and attack a punching bag. Hit tennis balls against a backboard or a solid wall. You can jump rope, pedal a bike, jog, or take a walk. (With the proper equipment you can engage in the same activities indoors.) None of these activities has to take much time; all easily fit into any few minutes you can find—or make.

You may be surprised to discover that physical exercise increases rather than depletes your energy stores. However, take it easy at first. Your spirit may be raring to go, but your body may be weaker after a multiple pregnancy and birth. If you were on prolonged bedrest during pregnancy, you may need to consult with a physical therapist to develop an appropriate reconditioning exercise program. (Even short-term bedrest diminishes muscular strength and endurance.)

- Laugh. A lot! Face it. You've landed in a laughable situation. A sense of humor can help you keep babies' needs and breastfeeding marathon days in proper perspective. Laughing is good for you. People who laugh are physically and mentally healthier.

  You say you've just changed the twelfth soiled diaper between babies' alternating nonstop feedings, and the day simply isn't funny anymore? Try videotaping your favorite comedy series, renting a silly movie video, or listening to a comedy CD or audiotape as you feed babies. With the amount of time you spend each day breastfeeding, you should have plenty of time to meet your daily laugh allowance!

- Have you ever been in the middle of describing a ridiculous story about your laughable situation and at a really funny part your laughter suddenly turned to tears? Give in and let go if tears threaten. There's nothing like an occasional good cry for releasing bottled-up tension. Trying to hold it in only gives one a headache, a stuffy nose, burning eyes. Don't think you have to be alone to give in to tears. A cry can be the most effective when others are present. Maybe they finally will get the message that you are feeling a little overwhelmed and a lot sleep-deprived. You will be treated with renewed respect and tenderness for **at least** a couple of hours!

- Your nutritional needs while breastfeeding will be as great, or even greater, than during multiple pregnancy. Producing milk for two or more babies is big business; you burn a lot of calories when making so much milk. Breastfeeding mothers of multiples usually have a tremendous thirst and appetite. Most mothers place this need for extra calories high on the list of personal advantages of breastfeeding multiples.

  Of course, you probably have no time to prepare all that food, much less sit down and enjoy it. When busy with multiple infants, the key to good eating is to select easily prepared finger foods. Eat while breastfeeding a baby or two, and always have a beverage available.

  1. Create a "breastfeeding station" next to the chair or sofa you use most for feedings. Stock a small table with nutritious snacks within arm's reach, so that even on the most hectic days you still can grab a bite or two.

  2. Cut up fresh fruits and vegetables in quantity and store them in individual plastic bags to grab on the run. If you don't have time to

Enjoy those special moments when four tiny eyes are focused on your face with unconditional love.

prepare them, ask someone else to do it. Many supermarkets now have bite-size pieces of fruits and vegetables available in bags or at a salad bar. Take advantage of the convenience, and if these "ready-to-eat" items cost a bit more, remind yourself how much you are saving by breastfeeding.

3. Cheese cubes or slices and shelled nuts are good sources of protein that can be eaten on the run. Both are available in finger-food form at many markets.

4. Eggs are another excellent source of protein, plus a number of vitamins and minerals. Hard boil them to eat as is or to make an egg salad, which can be spread on a slice of whole grain bread. One mother of twins always kept her "egg" skillet ready to go on the stove. (She said she washed that nonstick skillet once or twice a week whether it needed it or not!) She'd quickly scramble or fry an egg, which she then "threw" on a piece of toast. Voila! As her babies breastfed, she'd enjoy a nourishing sandwich.

5. Whip up a pitcher of nutritious milkshakes in the blender every morning. Combine milk, yogurt, ice cream, or ice milk with fruit, wheat germ, etc. Grab a glassful from the refrigerated pitcher throughout the day.

6. Invest in a large sports mug that holds at least 16 to 24 oz (480 to 720 ml.) of liquid. Sports mugs usually come with a fitted lid that has a large straw in the middle. This is perfect for keeping at your "breastfeeding station," since you won't have to constantly refill it, and these mugs are less likely to spill if bumped.

7. If you are drinking a lot of water to keep up with your increased thirst, try squeezing fresh lemon or lime into it. It's more refreshing and both citrus fruits are good sources of vitamin C.

Sometimes breastfeeding mothers are told to drink X amount of liquid a day. Rather than take time to measure what you're putting in, check the color of what is coming out. As long as urine is pale yellow, you probably are getting enough fluid. If urine becomes dark yellow, try drinking a bit more.

8. Talk with your care provider before taking additional vitamin/mineral supplements while breastfeeding. Many mothers say they have more energy when taking higher levels of these supplements. The vitamin and mineral content of breast milk is stable, but high levels of some vitamins and minerals may have toxic effects for you.

- Because postpartum bleeding tends to be heavier and last longer after a multiple birth, postpartum anemia can be a problem. Postpartum hemorrhage, which occurs more often with multiple births, is also associated with anemia. Anemia, or "low blood," can contribute to fatigue, decreased energy level, and lower resistance to some diseases. Diet plays an important role in rebuilding red blood cells and replenishing iron stores.

Exclusive, or almost exclusive, breastfeeding also has an important role in resolving anemia, as it generally delays the return of menstruation. This gives a mother's body time to renew itself without losing additional blood through the monthly flow. Although having two or three times as many babies does not necessarily cause two or three times the delay in a resumption of the menstrual cycle, mothers who have breastfed a previous infant often report a much later return of menses when breastfeeding multiples.

Menstruation does not occur during the months of exclusive breastfeeding because the hormones that regulate copious milk production inhibit the hormones that regulate ovulation and subsequent menstruation. The suppression of ovulation and menstruation by breastfeeding is called "lactational amenorrhea." In many parts of the world, lactational amenorrhea is the chief form of contraception after births. It is extremely effective when a couple understands how it works. Exclusive breastfeeding for several months, frequent feedings, including some at night, and delayed initiation of solid foods all influence the length of lactational amenorrhea for any given woman. Whether complementary or supplementary feedings for multiples affect lactational amenorrhea when the daily total number of breastfeedings still computes to the exclusive breastfeeding of at least one baby is uncertain. For more information about lactational amenorrhea, see "Resources."

Self-Esteem Issues

Body-Image

During a multiple pregnancy, it's not uncommon to hear a woman exclaim, "I can't wait to get my body back!" It can be a shock when she later discovers that the body she gets back seems to belong to someone else. Plus, there usually is little time for personal grooming when caring for multiple infants and other family members. Some days there may not seem to be time for basic personal hygiene.

It can be rather demoralizing to realize that it's 4:30 PM and you are still in a robe. Not to mention the flaps of your nursing bra have been down all day—including the time you opened the front door for a delivery man, one of the babies spit up down the front of that infamous robe at noon, and another waited until 1:30 PM to have an explosive bowel movement when on your lap. Now the flour that spilled down the front of you while you tried to throw supper together is clinging to the dried spit-up. And today you'd planned to have everything organized when your husband walked in the front door, which should occur in about 45 minutes.

It's a good bet that you aren't feeling your most attractive self at this moment. Unlike situations portrayed in movies or on television, you don't have time for a relaxing bubble bath. There is no live-in housekeeper who can watch the babies while you bathe, curl your hair, apply make-up, or give yourself a manicure. Still, when you take a little time for your appearance, you will probably feel better about everything. The following are ideas that other mothers of multiples have used to maintain "neat and clean" even if they don't quite measure up to gorgeous.

- Get a good "wash and wear" haircut a month or two before the babies are due, since multiples have been known to arrive early. Once you've gotten the basic cut, it should take little time to maintain it. With a good cut, the lines fall into place as hair dries rather than depending on time-consuming styling.

- Schedule a shower or a quick wash and wipe bath every day at about the same time. It may be easiest to bathe during a naptime. Any baby still awake can be placed in an infant seat or automatic swing in the bathroom or just outside the door. If you sing in the tub or shower, they probably will enjoy your bath time as much as you do. A bright mobile hung over a crib or play yard may keep them occupied for the time it takes you to shower. As babies get older, putting one or two in a large play yard placed just beyond the bathroom door usually provides a safe environment during the brief time you need to bathe.

- Don't panic—yet—if you find it difficult to drop those last 10 pounds of pregnancy weight gain. Many mothers find it takes months for those last pounds to melt away just as it took months to gain that important weight during pregnancy. It is unrealistic to think it will all magically disappear the moment the babies are born. If you ate a balanced diet during pregnancy and you continue to eat a balanced diet now, you eventually will lose the weight.

If you find your body has been rearranged once all, or most, of the weight is gone, give yourself at least a year to shift back into the shape you remember. Your body needs time to recover from this more physically demanding pregnancy. However, a multiple pregnancy can have lasting effects on abdominal skin and muscles. It's simply impossible to be certain in the first year whether an effect of pregnancy is short term or will have lasting consequences.

If your multiples combined weights were more than 10½ to 11 pounds (4.5 to 5 kg), you may find you suffer from what has become known as "twin skin." It is also referred to as "seersucker skin." The tests for twin skin are: 1) your stretch marks have stretch marks—producing an interesting seersucker pattern, 2) your abdomen looks like it has been accordion pleated, or 3) your abdominal skin can be pulled out several inches and folded/rolled up to be tucked into the waistband of your slacks or skirt!

Like a balloon blown beyond capacity or a rubberband stretched too wide, multiple pregnancy stretches the uterus and the abdominal skin covering it beyond the usual limits, and the over-stretched skin loses some elasticity. This uterine over-distention also causes a separation of the vertical abdominal *rectus muscles,* which is called *diastasis recti.* An extreme *diastasis* gives the abdomen a pendulous, or "potbelly," appearance.

Whether you have a few or many pounds still to lose or you are wondering if your abdomen will be accordion-pleated forever, you will feel better when you look better.

1. Stretch the budget to purchase some new clothing. You will look slimmer in clothing that fits while you **s l o w l y** shrink to your former size.
2. Camouflage twin skin or extra pounds by wearing overblouses, tunic tops, sweaters, and blazers over slacks and skirts. When you tuck a shirt in, lift your hands over your head to loosen material around your waist. Dark clothing makes most women look trimmer than pale colors. Avoid horizontal stripes that make anyone look wider.
3. Abdominal exercises usually improve rectus muscle tone. (Get your care provider's approval before beginning any exercise program.) Start with simple sit-ups. Lie on your back and bend your knees; your feet and your shoulders should be touching the floor. Raise your head, but not your shoulders, as you exhale. Repeat 10 to 20 times. Buttock and leg lifts, and leg rolls also help tone abdominal muscles.

4. Aerobic exercise can help you get back in shape and is a good way to release tension while recharging energy stores. Jogging, jumping rope, and briskly pushing a 10 to 20 pound stroller filled with multiple babies (while possibly wearing one in a baby carrier) are good forms of aerobic exercise.

5. Tummy tuck, or abdominoplasty, surgery sometimes is recommended to repair extreme cases of *diastasis recti* or twin skin. There is also a less extensive variation, but both versions are major abdominal procedures. As with any major procedure, these elective surgeries are not without risks or side-effects. Both require a significant post-surgical recovery period. Generally, a "tummy tuck" is not recommended for anyone contemplating a future pregnancy.

If you are considering such surgery, wait to give your body plenty of time to recover from the multiple pregnancy. Do not expect any surgery to magically transform your abdomen to its prepregnant condition. Although surgery generally leads to some improvement, it is in no way a panacea.

• Depending on your build, you may consider your breastfeeding bustline either a blessing or too much of a good thing during the early months of frequent feedings. Most department stores, maternity clothing shops, and major retail catalog chains carry nursing bras. The best ones have flaps that can be opened easily with one hand. It is hard enough to juggle two babies at once without having to undo tricky clasps. No matter what your size, be sure there is no pressure from elastic or an underwire on breast tissue that might contribute to plugged milk ducts.

Finding nursing bras that fit well and provide proper support can be a challenge for the more amply endowed. There are specialty bra catalogs and breastfeeding equipment companies that sell bras designed for larger-breasted women. (See "Resources.") Some mothers buy a supportive, standard brassiere and cut a circle large enough for the nipple and areola to protrude for easy feeding. If you want to try this, cut the circle large enough so that the baby can latch on deeply, which also allows for skin-to-skin contact during feedings. Stitch around the circle to reinforce the material.

• If you ever have second thoughts about spending some money on yourself for new clothing, supportive nursing bras, a practical yet stylish haircut, etc., remind yourself of all the money you are saving by breastfeeding your multiples. You are worth it! The entire family benefits when you feel good about yourself.

- You are not alone if breastfeeding multiples sometimes makes you think of yourself as some other mammal known for producing litters. Many mothers of multiples experience this "litter" phenomenon during the early months of breastfeeding. Mothers usually consider it to be a negative feeling until they begin to recognize its humorous side. Actually, most human mothers of multiples could learn a lot from fellow mammal mothers who appear to be able to relax and simply accept the intense, but brief, period of their babies' simultaneous demands for frequent feedings.

If you've experienced the litter phenomenon but haven't yet found another mammal to identify with, consider the she-wolf that fed Romulus and Remus, the mythological founders of Rome. In many sculptural renditions, the expression on the wolf's face as she feeds the human twins captures the conflicting wonder and weariness human mothers often feel during the frequent breastfeedings of multiples' first months.

Isolation

Mothers of young multiples easily become physically and emotionally isolated. To "get up and go" with infant and toddler multiples takes more preparation and management than for a single baby. Taking infant multiples out requires carrying around a lot of extra baby paraphernalia, and mothers often worry about what they will do if everyone gets hungry or fussy at once.

Few homes are as childproofed as homes with multiple toddlers. Mothers may stay home because the pleasure of getting out is easily lost when keeping track of two or more "unconfined" toddlers in an unfamiliar environment. In addition, many mothers find the number of invitations to come over to "play" dwindle after someone experiences a visit or two by curious multiples.

Not only do some mothers of multiples feel physically isolated, they often feel emotionally isolated and alone. Have you ever felt no one else understands—not even your husband? Your feelings probably are valid. Unless a relative or friend has had multiples (or the same number of multiples) and been the one responsible for their around-the-clock care, it probably is difficult for anyone to understand.

- Don't allow yourself to become isolated. Make yourself go out. Make yourself take the babies. (See Chapter 22, "Getting Out and About.") It gets easier every time you do it.
- You may feel more comfortable taking multiples out or having others to your home once you've learned to breastfeed one or two babies

Getting together with other mothers of multiples can provide companionship and support.

discreetly. Two-piece outfits are most convenient for discreet feeding. Simply lift a shirt up, or unbutton a blouse from the bottom up, just enough to allow one baby to latch on. Clothing specifically designed for discreet breastfeeding is also available. (See "Resources.") To decrease possible exposure and gain confidence while you and the babies learn to breastfeed with others around, drape a baby blanket, shawl, towel, or diaper (or two) from your shoulder across each baby's body.

Repeat the process on the other side if feeding two at once. Discreet simultaneous breastfeeding may be more difficult to achieve, but many mothers have found a way. The babies' styles and adeptness with breastfeeding influence ability.

Many find the cradle-football (clutch) combination or the double football (clutch) positions lend themselves best to discreet simultaneous feeding with young babies. As babies grow older and latch on without help, you may find the double cradle position allows the three of you to be less conspicuous.

- Grab 30 to 90 minutes and take a walk, relax in a bubble bath, or go to a mall alone when babies are sleeping. (You know you've been in the house too long when a 10 PM trip to the all-night grocery seems like a grand adventure!)

- **Nothing replaces communication with other mothers of multiples.** Find someone who does understand because she has been where you are now. Contact an organization for mothers of multiples and find out if a local chapter holds meetings. (See "Resources.") Ask to be "matched" with a mother who has breastfed the same number of multiples. Attend La Leche League meetings.

If you or your babies are not ready for meetings or there is no group nearby, the telephone and email are wonderful ways to stay in touch. Long distance phone calls with another mother of multiples are relatively inexpensive mental health morale boosters when a mother is feeling alone.

Beating the Blues: Postpartum Mood Disorders

It is important to distinguish the postpartum "blues" and the ongoing merry-go-round ride of the postpartum adjustment period from a true postpartum depression or other postpartum mood disorders, because these disorders can have lasting effects on an entire family. If unrelieved, they take a horrendous toll on a mother and can result in poor mother-infant(s) attachments, disruptive infant (and older child) behaviors, or a marital crisis. Early intervention can save weeks or months of anguish.

Postpartum Blues

During the first week or two postpartum, some of the ups and downs on the adjustment merry-go-round may be a part of the "postpartum/baby blues." Whether a woman gives birth to one newborn or seven, it is not unusual to briefly experience mild depression-like symptoms. Many mothers report feelings of sadness, irritability, and anxiety. They have difficulty concentrating. They may have trouble falling asleep even when their babies sleep. Many suddenly find themselves with tears in their eyes or actually crying, and they often are not sure why. If a new mother is going to get the "blues," the symptoms usually appear within days of giving birth. However, they usually disappear by the end of the second week.

Postpartum Depression (PPD)

Historically, the first recorded observations of postpartum depression (PPD) occurred in mothers of twins. The Greek physician Hippocrates, who is called the "Father of Modern Medicine," documented cases of PPD in mothers of twins when he practiced medicine in 300-400 BC. Besides PPD, other postpartum-onset conditions have been identified in the last century. Sometimes symptoms of one condition overlap with those of another.

Two thousand years later research indicates that mothers of multiples still are at higher risk for PPD. Although depression is related to some change in the brain's biochemistry, other factors associated with PPD are often magnified for mothers of multiples. These include the stress of child care, stressful changes in routine and lifestyle, and a lack of social support. A history of depression, which may have occurred during a pregnancy, a prior postpartum period, or at an unrelated time, also puts a mother at a higher risk.

PPD is different than the postpartum blues because it lasts for weeks or months instead of days. It may seem to begin as a case of the blues, but it doesn't go away after the first week or two. Sometimes a depressive episode occurs later—in the first year or two after a multiple birth.

The signs of depression are similar but worse than those for postpartum blues. When depressed, several of the following symptoms are experienced on **most** days:

1. frequent tearfulness or loss of emotional control;

2. insomnia—difficulty sleeping even when babies sleep, or hypersomnia— sleeping too much and at inappropriate times;

3. extreme fatigue or lack of energy;

4. appetite changes—lack of appetite or overeating;

5. a lack, or loss, of enjoyment in the babies and in pleasurable activities;

6. "foggy" thinking—difficulty concentrating or making decisions;

7. intense or excessive feelings of hopelessness, loneliness, emptiness, worthlessness as a person or a mother, anxiety, insecurity, guilt, or fear of "going crazy";

8. obsessive thoughts of harming oneself, the babies, or other(s).

A mother experiencing PPD may be able to go through the motions of child-care tasks. Babies are fed, bathed, and changed. However, the depressed mother feels detached; she feels unable to love and interact with her babies although she truly wants to. Multiples may be cared for assembly-line style and treated as a unit instead of as individuals.

Postpartum Onset Panic Disorder

Mothers suffering from a postpartum panic disorder experience episodes of extreme and unexpected anxiety, apprehension, or intense fear that occur in conjunction with a panic attack. Symptoms of this condition usually arise within a month of giving birth. It occurs more often among women with a history of an anxiety disorder. This condition may occur alone or it may be a component of PPD.

Usually several symptoms rapidly develop during a panic attack. The heart races or pounds; the chest tightens; and extremities tremble or shake and begin to feel numb or tingly. Sweating may be accompanied by hot flushes or chills. Nausea or stomach upset are common. The person experiencing a panic attack may feel faint, lightheaded, or dizzy. There is a feeling of unreality or a detachment from oneself. The victim may fear losing control or think she is dying.

The frequency and intensity of panic attacks vary. They may occur rarely or several times a day. They may last only seconds or for an hour. Concern about having an attack in public leads some mothers to stay home, which increases their isolation.

Postpartum Obsessive-Compulsive Disorder (OCD)

With postpartum OCD, intrusive and inappropriate thoughts or images plague a new mother. The obsessive thoughts generate feelings of anxiety and distress as the mother tries, but is unable, to "turn off" or ignore them. To minimize anxiety or prevent a dreaded situation, this mother repeatedly or excessively performs certain behaviors or mental acts—behaviors or acts that do not have a realistic relationship to the feared situation.

Women have experienced all kinds of obsessive thoughts. The most frightening obsession, yet one that is fairly common with postpartum OCD, involves horrendous thoughts or images about harming one or all of the babies. Although women rarely carry out such actions, a mother having these kinds of thoughts may become afraid or panicky about being left alone with the babies. She may become overprotective of them, or she may call the pediatric care provider several times a week with superficial questions and concerns.

Getting Help

Women affected by postpartum mood disorders frequently say they knew something was wrong shortly after giving birth. However, many new mothers delay seeking treatment for several months. Many women find it difficult to discuss symptoms of depression, extreme anxiety, or obsessive thinking with others.

Sometimes the mother's feelings and concerns are dismissed when she finally does mention them to a friend or family member. The mother herself may be afraid to face her feelings, or she may be afraid that her children will be taken from her if she discusses them with anyone. Yet some "gut" feeling usually keeps surfacing that tells her she must do something about this problem.

If your mental or emotional state is interfering with living your life, trust your instincts—that gut feeling that won't leave you alone. You need to discuss your concerns with a mental health professional. Don't listen when a friend, relative, or a health professional says you are fine; you know when you are not.

It may take more energy than you think you have at this moment, but you will want to search for a mental health professional who specializes in postpartum disorders. Start by asking your obstetric care provider for a referral. (Ask someone to make the calls for you if you don't think you can do it.) Sometimes it is necessary to interview more than one therapist, but keep calling or looking until you find a comfortable fit.

You may feel less alone and get ideas for coping if you speak with a mother who has recovered from a postpartum mood disorder. Large support organizations often have local chapters that meet regularly, and a member may be available by phone. Members may also be able to refer you to good therapists in your area. (See "Resources.")

Gaining coping skills through psychotherapy may not be enough to treat these disorders. Sometimes medication is necessary to "fix" brain biochemistry. Medications considered compatible with continued breastfeeding are available for most postpartum mood disorders. A La Leche League Leader or a lactation consultant usually has references about such medications. Be sure your babies' pediatric care provider is aware of your condition and knows what medication you are taking, including any plant/herb antidepressant or anti-anxiety preparations.

Get help. Get it today. **Please.** You deserve to feel your best. Your family needs you—and they need you to be your best. The earlier you get help, the sooner you will be on the road to recovery.

A Time of Adjustment

The postpartum period is a time of adjustment as a family's old routine gives way to the new. New parents should be aware that the adjustment period lasts longer after the birth of multiples. Not only are there more babies—each with his own approach to life—having an effect on the household, but a mother must assume her new role as she recovers from a more demanding pregnancy and birth. It is not unusual for a new mother of multiple's feelings to fluctuate between high and low with little in between for awhile. At the same time, she should be aware that postpartum mood disorders are somewhat more common after a multiple birth, and early treatment is the key to a more rapid recovery.

Chapter 24
Adjusting as a Couple

Becoming parents always affects a couple's relationship. Whether the new baby is a couple's first or their tenth, its arrival changes the family. A husband and wife must often postpone meeting their needs as a couple in order to meet those of the baby and any other children. The birth of multiples creates greater change and the adjustment period lasts longer. It takes a great deal of maturity on the part of both marriage partners to put aside their own needs for those of the babies.

Breastfeeding

When expectant parents discuss the advantages of breastfeeding one baby, they often ask whether the new father will feel left out. Few expectant parents of multiples raise this question. They easily comprehend many ways for dad to help out.

Most mothers of multiples say their husband's support and encouragement are more influential during the weeks, months, or years they breastfeed their babies than anyone or anything else. New mothers feel most supported when their husbands recognize that it takes longer to recuperate after a multiple pregnancy and birth, and when husbands express appreciation for the time and attention they give the babies through breastfeeding.

Supportive words mean the most when they are followed by supportive actions, such as a husband assuming more care of any older child and taking over many of the household tasks. Then a new mother can nourish and nurture the babies without thinking of all that must be accomplished around the house. A husband's encouragement often helps his wife maintain perspective on days when babies hold a breastfeeding marathon, an older child "paints" the hallway with colored markers, and the supper hour is fast approaching but the menu is still in question.

Time Together

Both partners still need time together as a couple. It is crucial to keep the lines of communication open, but it may take creativity to achieve this for a while. Of course, "creative thinking" is a stretch for parents who rarely have a moment to spare during the daylight hours and are waking several times at night.

If you and your mate are too tired to be creative, try some of these ideas that other parents of multiples have found helpful.

- When there doesn't seem to be even five minutes in a day to talk with one another between meeting one or another multiple's needs, take a family walk. You and your husband can enjoy relaxed conversation as the changing scenery occupies the babies' and any older child's attention.

- Plan a romantic dinner at home about once a week. Even a sandwich seems special when it is accompanied by candlelight and soft music. Who cares if each of you is holding a baby as you whisper sleep-deprived "sweet nothings" in each other's ear?

- Invite good friends to share the candlelight and soft music occasionally while babies are young and social activities are curtailed. If you tell them the cuisine will be simple or that you're calling for take-out because you can't count on time to cook, it's likely they will offer to bring at least one course. Better yet, simply ask an invited couple to contribute to the meal rather than wait for them to offer. And let friends know that you, your husband, and the babies are free to return the visit almost any time. Some friends may be willing to plan dinner around the babies' bedtime once one is established.

- If you or your husband feel you must have time alone together, keep in mind the babies' need for your presence. Consider going out during the babies' naptime or after their bedtime once either sleep period is fairly predictable. You might think about leaving briefly during a predictable daily "calm" period, especially if babies don't nap at the same time or they don't go to bed early enough.

Going out doesn't have to mean hours away; an hour or two together at a nearby restaurant is often enough time alone to feel refreshed. For example, one couple planned a weekly date at a nearby restaurant for Saturday breakfast—the only calm time of the day—after settling in at home with their second set of twins. A couple with triplets occasionally rented a motel room for an hour. *Where there's a will...*

If you and your husband do plan to go out without the babies, you'll want to be certain that any babysitter is mature enough to manage with more than one baby. Sitters often find it difficult to physically handle two babies, so many couples have one sitter per multiple and then "assign" the care of any older child depending on the sitters' abilities. Consider carrying a cellular phone or digital pager, so you can be contacted quickly if babies really need you before your planned time of return. Also, you may feel more relaxed if you can be called or paged when a sitter has a question or problem at home.

Most mothers arrange outings around babies' feeding times. They leave soon after one breastfeeding and plan to be home in time for the next. Remind sitters not to feed babies if you will be home to feed them. If you may be late, you can leave expressed breast milk in the refrigerator with directions for warming it. Missing a feeding can have more consequences when producing milk for two or more babies. (See Chapter 15, "When Mother Has a Breastfeeding Difficulty.")

- A **father of multiples** needs to feel encouraged and supported in his new role too. There are many ways to offer support.

    a.) Go out of your way to do something special for your husband each day. Ask your spouse what one (realistic) thing he would most like to see accomplished around the house. You may not be able to do it every day, but even the effort usually is appreciated during multiples' early months. Develop an alternate plan if you aren't able to accomplish that one thing yourself. If appropriate, put it at the top of the household helper's list. The important thing is that he knows you care.

    b.) Acknowledge the adjustments your husband must make and the responsibility he may feel after multiples arrive. Not only is his lovely and adoring wife busy caring for babies 24 hours a day, but he may feel a very real financial burden providing for this baby bonanza. "Two for the price of one" definitely does not cover multiple babies!

- Many couples are told to avoid sexual intercourse during the last weeks or months of a multiple pregnancy. Within several weeks of the babies' births, there is usually no physical reason that interferes with making love. However, many women find their interest in the sexual relationship is at an all-time low. Whether this is due to physical recuperation, hormonal influences, fatigue and sleep deprivation, a feeling of being "touched out" after holding babies all day, or some combination of these is not important. Patience and understanding by both partners are important.

Multiples' care tends to leave both parents feeling tired, but the male partner's libido, or physical sex drive, generally is less affected. It may help to know that a couple's physical relationship usually improves as babies get older and require less intense time. In the meantime, it takes communication if each is to understand that the other is sensitive to their differing needs for physical intimacy. Be honest about your sexual needs, and encourage your partner to be the same.

a.) Tell your husband often that you love him and appreciate his understanding even if you don't feel able to express it as often physically.

b.) Creative thinking again is needed to let go of old expectations if you are to meet each other's current physical needs. Babies in bed with you at night? Who cares? In any home a creative couple can find lots of other romantic spots. And who says a couple can be intimate only at night? Both partners can enjoy making love when neither is too tired, which is more likely to occur at some time during the day. Naptime may work. Your babies don't have a reliable naptime? Ask a friend or relative to take them, or just the one(s) that doesn't sleep, for a long stroll. No need to tell that person your plans. Involve older children in an interesting project that will hold their attention. Perhaps they could join the babies for the stroll. (Isn't this the reason someone developed all those children's television programs and "books on tape"?)

c.) You might say to your husband, "I've got 10 minutes free; meet you in our bedroom in two minutes—and be ready!" He knows what you mean, and he will be! Because the male sex drive tends to be more physical, try a physical rather than an emotional approach when you want him to respond more quickly. You might say, "I want you," or "I want your body," instead of "I want to make love." Let him know in a graphic way what you like about his physical attributes. Use your imagination!

d.) There may be times when you can offer your husband a choice between completing a household task or lovemaking. Many husbands would be willing to match a laundry load of socks later for the chance of having some time alone with their wives now.

e.) Whether or not you were built like a Hollywood starlet prior to multiple pregnancy, you may feel self-conscious if your abdominal skin looks like loose seersucker afterward. Discuss your feelings with your husband. He needs to know if you don't feel as physically attractive because of "twin skin." In all likelihood, you'll find it bothers you a lot more than it does him.

f.) Many new fathers of multiples expend energy and relieve tension by taking up or increasing their participation in sports and other healthy activities or outlets.

- It is important to let your husband know if you feel overwhelmed or exhausted at times. He needs to know why you may need some time alone to unwind once the babies and any other child finally are sleeping, since he may think that would be the perfect time to spend together. Just as you want to meet his physical and emotional needs, he will have to accommodate your needs as well.

  a.) Let your husband know that sometimes you really may want to express your affection for him, yet you may not have enough energy for increased physical intimacy. He needs to know if you ever avoid holding, kissing, and telling him how much you love him because you think he considers those actions to be a prelude to intercourse.

  b.) In the past flowers, a romantic card, and dinner out may have seemed the ultimate aphrodisiac. Let your husband know if your ideas about romance have changed. Now you may find it much more arousing when you discover a basket of washed and folded laundry, clean dishes in the cabinets, or the toilets scrubbed without ever having to say a word.

There are no two (or more) ways about it. Multiple babies impose stress on a marriage. However, learning to cope together enhances a good relationship with mutual growth. You will appreciate one another much more for the sacrifices each makes for the good of the children and for one another. It takes maturity for marriage partners to act lovingly in spite of the more intense adjustment of integrating multiples into a family. And believe it or not, the intense investment of time it takes to meet the needs of multiple infants and toddlers lasts a brief time in the marriage of a committed and communicative couple. The increased caring that comes from sharing this intense experience can last the rest of your lives.

Chapter 25
Older Siblings of Multiples

The life of an older child is turned upside down when multiples join the family. The free arm that would have been able to hug an older child when caring for one new baby now holds a second baby. Mother is occupied with babies around the clock, which means she isn't getting much rest—which means her level of patience probably is lower.

Sleep deprivation can lead to a build-up of tension. Everyday child-related occurrences that once were considered only mildly annoying may now loom as major catastrophes. The spilled milk that used to be a minor aggravation may produce tears in a mother coping with the needs of multiple infants and an older child or two. Fitting in a clean-up time may seem too much to add in an already overfull day. The older child who accidentally tipped the milk glass may wonder what happened to the "old" mother who would never "cry over spilt milk."

Multiples are instant celebrities, attracting attention wherever they go. Older sister and brothers are often completely ignored. It can be very difficult to watch an older sibling's face as the minutes tick by and the person gushing over the babies never even thinks to acknowledge an older child.

Many mothers of multiples say the hardest thing for them to deal with is the anguish they feel because of the abrupt changes in the lives of their older children. You probably wish you still had the same amount of time to devote to your older children. But you don't. That can't be changed. When you feel sad for an older child, it can help to remember the firm foundation you've already developed with each. As an infant, each older child never had to share you as multiples always will. Each multiple now needs that same time and attention with you to develop a similar foundation.

Meanwhile, the older children may surprise you with how well they adapt. Mothers of older multiples often report that not only do the older siblings survive, they often develop self-confidence by having to learn to clean up that spilled milk for themselves. Of course, an older child still needs your help while adjusting to life with multiple siblings. And you will have more time for all your children as the months go by. In the meantime, there are ways to provide attention and ease the period of adjustment.

- You do not need any free hands to say to an older child, "I love you." Say it often throughout every day.
- Five minutes of time when an older child **needs** it is often more beneficial than an hour when it is convenient for you. There usually is time for hugs and kisses even when you can't sit and hold a child for a long period.
- No matter who now performs the bedtime ritual with an older child, make time to give each a brief backrub before the child falls asleep. It helps the two of you reconnect, which is important on days when a child managed to spill five glasses of milk, or you've said "wait a minute" (and a minute turned into five or ten or twenty minutes) a hundred times. It's a hands-on "I love you." It says that in spite of any mischief-making or loss of time and attention, you care—a lot.
- Your husband becomes even more indispensable to an older child and to you. As an older child depends more on him for time and attention, don't be surprised to see the bond between dad and that older child grow stronger. You probably will enjoy your time with the babies more when you know dad and an older child are enjoying time together.
- An overnight or weekend vacation with grandparents, relatives, or special friends often allows an older child to enjoy time as the center of attention again. These quick trips also take some responsibility off your shoulders for a day or two. However, the older child's age and stage of development should be considered. One toddler or preschool child might feel "big" going away for the weekend, but another may be able to handle only a few hours away. It may not be a good idea to "push" such

visits when a child's behavior indicates feelings of being "shut out." The idea can always be brought up again later.

- Once the babies develop a dependable naptime, ask your husband, friend, or relative, or hire a babysitter to stay in the house with them while they sleep. This allows you to take an older child somewhere special. An outing may be as exciting as a trip to the zoo or as simple as a walk around the block. Another option is to have a friend take the babies for a walk, so you can read a story or sit in a rocker with an older child without interruption. In either case, take advantage of the opportunity to talk with your older child.

If you have more than one older child, there may be times when you take all of them on an outing while the "poor" babies have to stay home and sleep. You may also want to take turns taking only one older child somewhere. Most mothers have children take turns for some outings and take everyone on others.

Outing time may be limited when the multiples' naps or calm periods are brief. Fortunately, most toddler through school-age children aren't clock-watchers. The older child is only aware of being on a special outing and having your undivided attention—whether for 15 minutes or a couple of hours.

Downplay the fact that family outings may occur less frequently for awhile. It is harder to get up and go with two or more babies. Yet an older child might come to resent the babies if you blame them for any curtailment in social activities. Simply say, "I'm sorry, but we can't go. Maybe we can go some other time." This sounds much different than, "I'm sorry, but we can't go now because of your baby sisters. Maybe we can go when they get bigger."

Behavior Problems

Who wouldn't want to be a baby with all of the attention multiple babies receive? An older child may feel jealous of a new sibling or sad about the loss of his mother's time and attention. When children must cope with the addition of two or more new siblings, it seems understandable that their feelings might be exaggerated. This may lead to "acting out" and regressive behaviors. An older child may release tension through sudden outbursts of anger, thumb-sucking, nail-biting, and so on. Some children go out of their way to find mischief while mother breastfeeds babies. Regressive behaviors, such as wetting or soiling pants long after toilet learning has taken place or waking during the night again are not uncommon.

Although most behaviors associated with the adjustment to new babies occur within the first months of bringing the multiples home, some siblings seem to have a delayed reaction. It may be more difficult for these children when multiples start moving and "invading" their private spaces. And sometimes it takes several months before a child can put feelings into words. What appears to be a sudden acting out or blurting of thoughts and feelings may have been building for months.

- Let older children know you understand it is not always easy getting used to two or more new babies. It is important to acknowledge their negative (and positive) feelings. Sometimes you can open a discussion if you tie a behavior to a related feeling. You might say, "Wow, you looked really angry when you threw the ball so hard it hit the table," or "You're holding your doll really tight, and your face looks kind of sad."

- Take out the family photo albums, baby books, and videos. Point to photographs of an older child as a baby. Describe what you remember about that child's infancy. Let children know how you met their needs and how much time it took. Then remind them that there are two, three, or more babies needing you, and each needs you as much as the older child did as a baby. By preschool age, many children can talk with you about what it must be like to be a baby who doesn't have to share his mother and what it must be like for multiples to have to share her. If you let a child look at the albums or watch a video while you're breastfeeding babies, it may cut down on mischief by an older child who is so inclined! (But keep an eye on photo albums that can be taken apart.)

- Try to stay calm. Change the wet pants. Comfort the night waker. And do it without making negative comments or punishing the regressive behavior. However, it may help to let the child know that you feel tired, which makes you grumpy.

- Emphasize all the things a "big boy" or "big girl" can do that the babies cannot. At times an appropriate consequence of acting like a baby can be the temporary loss of a "big" boy or girl privilege. Of course, the reverse also is true; privileges may be an appropriate consequence of acting one's age.

- If an older child really seems to be acting out, reach for a book that describes general growth and development for children. Many parents worry that their new babies might be responsible for the negative behaviors an older child displays. However, some behaviors simply may be typical for the child's age and stage of development. Often, behaviors that usually would be given little consideration seem problematic because the parents are also trying to figure out the behaviors of two or more babies.

Siblings may need help adjusting to life with multiple babies in the house.

Breastfeeding Activities

Mothers often find it helpful to provide special activities for an older child during breastfeeding times.

- Sometimes a mother gives an older child a gift of multiple dolls so that child can breastfeed and care for his or her babies while mother breastfeeds and cares for the new family members.
- When a child is able to manipulate a tape recorder, mothers can record the child's favorite stories. The child enjoys listening to mother reading those favorites while he or she follows along in the book.
- Many mothers create childproofed play space in the room where they usually breastfeed the babies, so an older child can stay busy while babies eat. They keep toys, books, puzzles, etc., there, but most avoid stocking the area with "messy" activities. Some find it helpful to use a room with a television and video player, so occasionally everyone can watch a favorite program or tape.

Sibling Reactions

Discourage activities that can divide the family into "the (multiple) babies" and "any other child." Within reason, let older siblings hold and cuddle the babies. (Of course, no one can explain why big brothers and sisters always have to cuddle the new family members as soon as the babies finally are fast asleep and mother has a moment's peace.)

Involve an older child in the babies' care. A sibling can fetch diapers, get a snack for you to eat while you breastfeed, or tell a baby that "Mommy is coming soon," when you are busy with another. But when it comes to the amount of help an older child can give, watch out for unrealistic expectations. A child's interest in helping will vary depending on age, stage, and personality. Don't be surprised if acting as "mother's helper" quickly loses a lot of its glamour once the babies are home.

An older child often develops a preference for one multiple. As the babies grow, you probably will see that preference change. If it does not and the preference causes difficulties in the family, you may want to provide opportunities for an older sibling to interact with the "less" preferred multiple(s) alone at times.

Avoid activities that bring attention to your multiples at the expense of an older child.

- Remind visitors that older children are going through a period of adjustment. When arranging a visit, ask them to notice any older child before they ask to see the babies. Post a sign at the door with this request if drop-in guests are a common occurrence.

- Bring attention to an older child when people stop and ask you about your multiples. You might share something special about each one. An older child may enjoy assuming the role of the spokesperson who answers questions about the babies. (See Chapter 22, "Getting Out and About" for other ideas.)

- There may be days when you hope strangers will stop and ask you about the babies. People often express admiration for the parents caring for multiple infants while they ogle the babies. Let's face it, most parents of multiples need a pat on the back at times—but not if it comes at the expense of an older child. When you could use some well-deserved attention, take the babies for a stroll but do it when an older child is not a part of the entourage.

- If multiples become extended family celebrities, you probably will have to remind relatives that an older child is in need of some special attention, too.

- There's no doubt about it, "group" photos of multiples are adorable. However, be sure to include an older brother or sister in some of the group shots and in some separate shots.

Don't be afraid to talk to an older child about your feelings. It's all right to let them know you sometimes feels overwhelmed with two, three or more new babies. Even a young child will understand the emotion, if not always the words. If you find yourself crying, that's all right too. Crying while talking about feeling overwhelmed seems to go hand in hand. Fortunately, no one understands a good cry better than a child. You'll probably find yourself on the receiving end of some much needed hugs and kisses and "I love you" from the older child, which will make you and the older child feel better.

The birth of multiples changes the lives of older children in many ways. Listen to older children and accept their feelings. Look forward to the ways they will grow through the experience of having multiple siblings. In the meantime, liberal doses of physical contact, a frequent "I love you," and the passage of time usually ease the adjustment for older siblings.

Chapter 26
Streamlined Housekeeping

A mother of multiples becomes efficient because she has no other choice! Her time is at a premium. One mother of twins expressed it this way, "It's as if you used to have a whole ship load of time, but now you're in a small lifeboat. You have to throw everything overboard that there isn't room for."

You don't have to be "Supermom" simply because you've given birth to multiples. The arrival of two or more babies is bound to disrupt any family's routine for quite awhile. Forget that you daydreamed during pregnancy of how you would "get back to normal." That pre-multiples "normal" is gone for good, but eventually, you and your family will find a new "normal." Don't expect this new household routine to miraculously appear. Give it a few months, and allow additional months for every additional baby. In the meantime, there are things you can do to help the process along.

Set priorities if you want to meet your babies' needs and those of the rest of the family—including your own! Ask yourself, "What truly has to be done around the house? What can wait?"

The babies cannot be expected to compromise their needs, so caring for them is **top priority.** Other family members are right behind them on the list. Of course, your family will need to eat, and it's nice to wear clean clothes. Beyond this, little actually is essential.

Most mothers of multiples rely on some type of household help and convenience services. **Never forget that your time is money!** When you are hesitant about putting a dent in the family budget to invest in some household convenience, remind yourself that such items or services give you invaluable extra time for your babies, other family members, and yourself. Often the cost of the item or service is more than made up for by the cost-savings of breastfeeding.

Practical Tips

The following suggestions have helped other mothers of multiples keep up with the household and still have time to spend with family members.

Find someone to help with the household. It is unrealistic to think you can meet the needs of two or more babies and those of other family members alone. Chapter 7, "Getting Ready: Preparing for Multiples," includes ideas for finding help. Evaluate honestly any prospective helper's ability to fulfill household needs. You will want someone who frees you to get to know and to frequently breastfeed your babies.

- Be sure your helper understands that the duties may include physical care of any older child, food preparation or cooking, laundry, cleaning, etc., rather than most of the babies' care. Of course, you will want to take advantage of extra hands to help with the babies, too. Be sure the helper knows you are breastfeeding and you are interested only in **positive** comments.

- When full-time help is no longer needed, don't be surprised if you still require part-time help—for years! Having a housecleaning service come once or twice a week still may be a sanity saver when two or more toddlers or preschoolers are finding creative uses for household items. You may also want to have a mother's helper come in to help with older children or babies for a few hours several times a week. Junior and senior high school students are often excellent. Because you would be there to supervise, a younger student may be an option.

Everyone loves to see multiples, but limit visitors during the first weeks or months at home. Be frank when you would rather not have someone over, and let guests know if you feel tired and want them to cut a visit short.

- Let guests know that the role of perfect hostess is low on your list of priorities. Actually, they should wait on you while babies are little—not the reverse. If you want to offer a snack, direct them to the proper spot in the kitchen or tell them what they can put together. And ask them to bring an extra plate and napkin for you. Remind them to pour you something to drink when they are getting something for themselves.

- If drop-ins become a problem, you could hang a sign on the front door asking them to call first. For example, one mother posted, "Mom and babies are napping. Call at 3 PM to see if we're having a good day for company." Record a similar message for the phone answering machine.

- It may be more relaxing to have family gatherings at your home, especially once multiples are mobile, than to monitor two or more moving in opposite directions in someone else's home. After explaining why you want to have the party at your home, ask each family member to contribute a dish. Simplify gatherings by using sturdy paper goods in pretty colors or patterns that will dress up the table without leaving you to face mountains of dishes. Bring the good china back out when your multiples are older.

Offers of Help

When friends and relatives ask how they can help, take them up on their offers! They wouldn't ask if they didn't mean it. And if they didn't mean it, they shouldn't have asked someone with multiples. When people don't follow through with offers to help, it's often because they didn't know what to do. So be sure to share specific "helping" ideas. Also, ask them for a definite "delivery" date.

- Most mothers of multiples say the winner of the "favorite gift" award is the complete meal that arrives after the excitement dies down or the full-time helper has returned home. This gift is appreciated whether multiples are a few weeks or several months old. It's nice to schedule in advance so you know when you won't have to fix a meal that day, but it may be as much a treat when a friend calls at the last minute to ask if you'd like a last-minute surprise. Suggest meals be delivered in disposable containers, so you don't have to think about returning anything.

- It's also fun to have friends bring all the ingredients and prepare a meal in your kitchen. Or plan a dinner party, but ask each friend to bring a prepared dish. Either way you will have the pleasure of their company, and perhaps a few extra arms to help with babies as well, as long as you're not left with the entire clean-up.

- A friend who will do grocery shopping or run other errands can relieve you of what sometimes feels like a great responsibility. If the friend keeps your items separate from her own, the shop clerk usually can subtotal the first order to make reimbursement easier.

- Friends are often willing to run the vacuum, wash and fold a load or two of laundry, clear out a sink full of dishes, or do any other small household jobs. Let them.

Infant Stimulation

Combine infant stimulation with routine baby care and household tasks. Research has shown that most multiples do not get the kind of physical and mental stimulation parents give single-born infants. There's no question that the time of parents of multiples is stretched to the limit, but there is also no question that each multiple still needs this kind of attention.

- Take advantage of the time you spend on baby care tasks to play with each multiple. There are numerous opportunities when changing diapers or clothing, bathing, or feeding each baby. It doesn't matter whether you are handling one baby or accomplishing a task assembly-line style. Make eye contact with one at a time—if only for a few minutes. Reinforce that baby's name. Explain what you are doing as you change, bathe, or feed her. Exercise little arms and legs. Sing to that baby—none of them cares whether you actually can carry a tune. Smile in response to that baby's smile; repeat verbal sounds in response to the sounds that baby makes.

- Place one baby in a carrier or sling before you vacuum, do laundry, prepare a meal, etc. (Take turns with the babies so each often gets to "help.") As you walk through the house, describe the rooms and the objects in them. Explain the job you are doing and what you think about it. Of course, they don't understand what you are saying—yet. However, talking to them now is a large part of how they learn language for later.

- Occasionally, take only one baby to the market or on errands with you. (Again, take turns so each baby gets to go on special outings.) You may be surprised to find how easy and enjoyable it is to get out with only one baby, and each baby is being exposed to whole a new world of sights, sounds, and smells—experiences most single babies often have. Take the time to talk to the baby as you shop, get cash from an automatic teller machine (ATM), or pick up dinner at a fast-food restaurant drive-through window. Describe what you are seeing, hearing, and smelling.

There are many ways to cut corners on routine baby care.

- You can wash laundry less often if you have extra borrowed or bought secondhand baby clothing. When borrowing clothing, ask each lender to put a mark, such as an initial on each item. Wash secondhand items before using. It is less expensive, less time-consuming, and babies are just as happy when you launder their clothing with the rest of the family wash. Cloth diapers should be washed separately, however.

- Few babies get so dirty that they need daily baths. If each baby's face and diaper area are kept clean, most babies can get by with one or two weekly baths. Some mothers bathe a baby (or two) every day, alternating babies so that each is bathed every other day. Of course, a few babies do seem to get grimy enough to need a daily bath. Other babies seem to find a warm bath so relaxing that they drift to sleep soon after the bath and stay asleep longer. In either case, you'll probably want to bathe these babies more often.

Meal preparation can be a challenge when multiple babies request round-the-clock time and attention. The following hints have helped other multiple-birth families continue to eat well.

- Collect recipes that can be prepared in stages. Prepare different parts of a meal at different times of the day. Casseroles are a good example. Meat could be thawing in the refrigerator while vegetables are chopped and refrigerated during a calm period in the morning. Prepare and add a sauce to the meat and vegetables during naptime. You can wait to heat it during the hectic late afternoon or early evening. For other meals you may be able to organize the ingredients early in the day and throw everything together just before supper.

- Look for recipes that eliminate steps. For instance, one recipe might list several ingredients for the casserole sauce mentioned above. Another version asks only for a can of soup and a little water or milk, and voilá— a casserole sauce. The second version saves preparation and pot-scrubbing time. You can go back to the gourmet version when multiples are older.

- Teach your household helper to prepare ingredients, such as chopped vegetables, hard-boiled eggs, or meat patties that can be stored in the refrigerator or freezer for later use.

- In many areas, items such as chopped fruits and vegetables, salad greens, meat patties, and so on are available at a market salad bar or in prepackaged bags or boxes. Buying already prepared fresh or frozen foods can save hours of work in the kitchen.

- Use of household appliances, such as a food processor, blender, crockpot, and microwave is another way to save valuable time. Cooking and baking the old-fashioned way is not always the best way—especially when you have multiple babies wanting all of your time and attention.

- Drive over the route your husband takes to and from his place of employment, and write down which markets and fast-food restaurants he passes. Have him call early every afternoon to see how things are going at home. If it has been a hectic day, give him the shops' names and ask him to stop for groceries or pick up something ready-to-eat for supper.
- Plan at least one night out of the kitchen each week. Keep numbers posted near the phone and order a meal for carryout or delivery. You may feel more relaxed all day when you know you don't have to think about meal preparation later.

You may have to let go of old standards of neatness—at least for a while. However, there are ways to control some of the clutter.

- Keep a laundry basket or two in well-used rooms. A room can be made to look tidier quickly when you collect clutter in one and throw soiled clothing or other laundry in another. Then you can put items away or take them to the laundry area for sorting at your convenience.
- After taking a shower, clean the bathroom when everything already is steamy by simply wiping fixtures, a shower door, tiled walls, etc., with your damp towel.
- Place dirty dishes in the sink to soak in hot, soapy water. The kitchen will look cleaner when countertops are empty, and you can wash dishes when time allows. (If the water gets too cool for effective dishwashing, drain the sink and refill it with more hot, soapy water. Repeat as necessary on any given day!)
- To cut down on dirty dishes, use paper plates, bowls, and cups, and throw the mess away.
- To minimize ironing, read clothing labels for laundry instructions before you make any purchases. Choose easy-care, wrinkle-resistant items for the times when you don't have time to fold clothing straight from the clothesline or dryer.

Look for delivery, drive-through, or Internet services. A grocery or laundry/dry-cleaning shop may add a delivery charge, but you won't pay for fuel to get to the shops. You don't have to dress two or three babies and older children and then strap them into car seats—or figure out how to get all of them into the store, manage everyone once inside, and get babies and purchases back into the car again.

Be a catalogue shopper for the next few years. You can clothe your family, buy groceries, or have holiday gifts ordered and delivered to out-of-town relatives from the comfort of your home. All it takes is a telephone or a computer, and a credit card!

Cut household chores to the bare minimum and get the help you need. You can't do everything, so you will have to decide what household tasks are most important—after taking care of the babies, other family members, and yourself. Housework will be with you always, but your multiples won't be babies for long. (Really!)

Chapter 27
Breastfeeding,
Starting Solids, and Weaning

The breastfeeding routine changes a great deal during the second half of multiples' first year. Babies are introduced to solid foods. By their first birthday, these foods often provide the bulk of babies' diets. Babies begin to join the family at the table for meals. Gradually, they drop a breastfeeding here and there, or they begin to shorten the time spent at the breast for many feedings. As babies reach toddlerhood, they may seem to ask to breastfeed more as a comfort measure than for a meal.

Eventually, one and then another multiple stops breastfeeding altogether. The process often occurs so gradually that many mothers cannot point to a specific day or moment when they knew a baby had weaned completely—that time when a baby no longer needed breastfeeding as a part of their relationship. The weaning process actually begins when babies indicate readiness for solid foods.

Starting Solids

Mothers of multiples sometimes start offering solid food earlier than other mothers. During a particularly overwhelming period, a mother may feel that anything is worth a try. It is often due to pressure from family or friends. Occasionally, a pediatric care provider suggests starting solids before babies are at least four months. However, introducing solid food before babies are four to six months offers no nutritional benefits, does not prolong babies' sleep, and may interfere with babies' intake of appropriate nutrients. This is the reason that associations for pediatric care providers, including the American Academy of Pediatrics (AAP), the Canadian Paediatric Society (CPS), and the World Health Organization (WHO) recommend waiting until the middle of babies' first year.

Because so many sets are born preterm, multiples are often not ready for solid foods until later than many single-born infants. Babies may experience upset stomachs when their digestive tracts are still too immature to handle solid food. Also, the nutrients in solid food may not be absorbed or used well by babies' bodies if introduced too early. Plus, when babies fill up on solids, they take in less human milk—a food containing easily digested nutrients.

Most babies are at least four months, and many are well over six or seven months, before they indicate readiness for solid foods. The multiples in some sets, usually identical multiples, may be ready to begin experimenting with solids at about the same age. However, each multiple may signal readiness for solids at a very different time during the second half of the first year, especially when multiples are fraternal. Pay attention to each baby's signals. There's no reason to offer solids to all when only one baby is ready.

Signs of Readiness

One mother said she knew that each baby was ready for solids when a baby who was sitting on her lap started grabbing at the food on her plate and tried to put it in his mouth. This definitive behavior often coincides with the appearance of the first teeth. Many babies experience signs of a growth spurt at about six months, but if any asks for more frequent feedings beyond a week, you may want to offer that baby a little solid food. (For a description of a growth spurt, see Chapter 10, "Effective Breastfeeding.")

When a disruption in routine or an infant illness coincides with signs of a growth spurt, chances are continued requests for frequent feedings are in response to the stress of the change or illness. Wait to see what happens when the other problem resolves. Increased drooling at about four to five months is thought to be a sign of readiness for solids by some. Actually, it is more a sign that a baby is "getting ready to get ready" for solid foods.

Some have suggested that when multiples reach some arbitrary combined weight they should be given solid food. However, mothers have reported starting one or more babies on solid food when their combined weights were anywhere from 15 to 45 lb (7 to 20 kg).

How to Begin

When any baby first begins to take solids, consider these early meals as "practice." Solid foods are not something a baby eats in addition to your milk. Instead solids replace some of the nourishment your babies have been getting at the breast, so you will want to start very slowly.

Begin by offering one or two teaspoons of a single food, such as a single-grain cereal, meat, vegetable, or fruit. You can add additional bites and a new food once you know a baby is not sensitive or going to have an allergic-type reaction to the first one. Wait several days to a week to introduce a new food, but keep the "old" food in a baby's diet, too.

Be particularly cautious about introducing foods if you or the babies' father come from an allergic family. Avoid typical allergenic foods, such as cow's milk, eggs (whites), nut butters, and citrus fruits or juices until after the babies are at least a year according to the original due date for birth. Canned and processed foods tend to be high in salt (sodium) or sugar (or other sweeteners) and should be avoided. Babies less than a year should never be given honey as it may contain botulism spores, which can make babies extremely ill.

- When first offering solid food, **always breastfeed each baby before offering the solid food,** so babies continue to get enough nourishment and so there is no drop in milk production. Too much solid food too soon not only is a shock to babies' digestive systems, it can also be a shock to your system. If babies suddenly want to breastfeed less often because they are stuffed with solids, you could develop a plugged duct or mastitis.

- Although a baby may act interested, some babies need a few **practice sessions** to get the hang of using their mouths differently to take food from a spoon. However, a baby who consistently pushes food back out of her mouth as fast as you spoon it in may not be quite ready for solid food. You may want to stop giving solids to this baby and try again in a few weeks.

- Many mothers rarely, if ever, offer **commercial baby foods.** Instead they may mash a ripe banana or a baked sweet potato to offer as an early food. If commercial foods offer the convenience you need for some or all of your babies' solid meals, read labels carefully. Choose brands that offer a food without "fluff," such as added sugar, salt (sodium), preservatives, etc.

Mothers who have used commercial baby foods for convenience suggest skipping the pureed "first foods" and moving directly to single-ingredient "second foods." These foods are more economical and offer babies a little more texture, which five- to seven-month-olds often prefer. Because the jars are slightly larger, mothers say one is often the perfect size to split between two babies, which means there is less waste.

- Because of the protein and iron it contains, meat is usually recommended as an early solid food for breastfed babies of six months or older. Additional iron may be recommended for multiples at some time during their first year.

  Babies' bodies store iron during the last weeks of pregnancy, which is then available during babies' first several months. Multiples often miss out—to varying degrees—on this important prenatal development. When their iron stores are limited because of multiples' preterm birth, all of the babies are usually affected. Most full-term twins or triplets are no more likely to need supplementary iron than a single full-term baby, unless uterine conditions favored one of the multiples. Occasionally identical multiples are affected by twin-to-twin transfusion syndrome (TTTS) during pregnancy and the "donor" twin may be anemic. (See Chapter 4, "What to Do If..." for more information on TTTS.)

  Most pediatric offices are equipped to test an individual baby's blood if a parent is concerned that a baby might be anemic. A normal, but borderline low, or an actual low test result indicates a need for supplemental iron for an individual multiple, which may be needed until that baby can get enough iron from solid food sources.

- Mothers sometimes pump a small amount of milk or thaw some frozen breast milk to dilute or soften foods for younger babies. By the time each baby begins to use her thumb and index finger to form the "pincer" grasp, she probably will enjoy being given finger foods with a little more texture, such as unsweetened oat dry breakfast cereal (little "o"s), cooked peas, whole-grain bread cubes, slivers of stewed meat, etc. Don't be surprised if each multiple has her own favorite finger foods.

- If multiples have been **partially breastfed,** you may be able to wean them from infant formula as solid foods are added to their diets. The nutrients in human milk and solids will provide all the calories they need to grow and develop.

- Ask a La Leche League Leader for an information sheet containing additional ideas for introducing solid foods. THE WOMANLY ART OF BREASTFEEDING contains an entire chapter on this topic. (See "Resources" for information.)

Organizing Mealtime

You may want to plan early feeding of solids for a time of day when dad can take over. This is something he can do to relieve you of a feeding or two, so you have time for something else. Handling babies' solid food meals provides dad with a great opportunity to get to know each multiple better while learning to deal with all of the babies at once.

Once two or more babies have gotten used to taking food from a spoon, place them in infant-seats or high chairs side by side, or in their stroller. Use one bowl and one spoon and then alternate bites and babies to **feed them assembly-line style.** If one seems to be getting a cold or other illness, you may want to use separate bowls and spoons for a short time. However, all will usually have been exposed to an illness by the time one develops symptoms.

Bring multiples to the table at family mealtimes as their feeding skills improve. Any baby who sits well in a high chair, or a booster seat with tray, and uses the thumb and index finger in a pincer grasp to pick up particles of food is ready to be part of your family meals. (This occurs at about nine months for full-term babies.) At first it may be easier to place their high chairs side by side at the table and offer them some solids before the rest of the family sits down. Then you can enjoy your meal while the satisfied babies experiment with a finger food.

You could also divide multiples at the table, letting dad supervise one (or two) while you watch the other(s). Older babies often discover that throwing bits of food at one another is great fun, especially if other family members laugh at their antics. Parents and siblings may not think it is quite so funny if it becomes a regular occurrence. Separating babies at opposite ends of the table with a parent or older sibling to intervene before food gets thrown usually halts this behavior fairly quickly. If this doesn't do the trick, remove the food from in front of the babies. You may have to remove the babies from the table, too. Doing this consistently for several meals generally brings an end to solid **food fights.** Occasionally, it is necessary to feed one baby at a time or return to spoon-feeding for a brief period.

Picky Eaters

Toddlers are notoriously picky eaters. One of the advantages of having multiples is that one often encourages another, so that all toddlers eat at least a little of a wide variety of foods. Still multiples are not exempt from picky eating, and some simply are too busy to take the time to sit in a high chair or booster seat to eat a meal. "Picky" eating usually isn't a problem if the foods the babies do eat are nutritious and when each continues to grow and develop at an appropriate rate.

Because of their genetic differences, fraternal multiples may have very different appetites and grow at very different rates yet all may be growing appropriately. It is very important to look at the individual, rather than at the group, growth patterns. Identical multiples may also have different appetites or they may flip-flop picky and hearty eating periods. Their eating patterns and growth rates also should be examined individually. Interestingly, identical multiples often continue to grow at almost identical rates even when they seem to have different appetites and eat different amounts.

Since anything and everything seems to find its way into the mouths of older babies and toddlers, some mothers have taken advantage of this behavior. They have gotten their multiples to eat a variety of solid foods by placing finger foods on a clean plastic cloth on the floor. Don't try this if any pets roam in the same area, and continue to encourage the babies to eat solids at the table with the rest of the family.

Breastfeeding Older Babies and Toddler Multiples

In some Western cultures women have been given the idea that breast-feeding benefits only young babies, so there is no reason to breastfeed beyond a year. Not true. There are many good reasons to continue to breastfeed as babies develop into toddlers. Although the number and length of feedings may decrease, your multiples continue to receive important nutrients and disease-fighting antibodies from your milk for as long as they breastfeed. This is the reason breastfeeding continues well beyond a year in most cultures.

You will discover new or different benefits to breastfeeding as your babies become more mobile. Breastfeeding is better than a band-aid to calm an active toddler who has fallen down or bumped into something, which is a regular occurrence with multiple toddlers. When an older baby or toddler becomes ill, breastfeeding is often the only way a mother can get some food into that multiple.

Once mothers move past any cultural barriers, most say breastfeeding a single older baby or toddler is a personally rewarding and special period in their breastfeeding relationship. Breastfeeding multiple older babies and toddlers is different, yet it is equally rewarding and special. The relationship(s) between or among multiples develops rapidly as they enter toddlerhood, and this creates a dynamic, or multiples "entity," that continues to affect the individual mother-child breastfeeding relationships in many ways.

Finding ways to balance the "give and take" between two persons is an aspect of every human relationship. Breastfeeding offers toddler multiples a unique opportunity to explore this aspect of their growing relationship(s) in

*Your multiples continue to receive benefits from
your milk for as long as they breastfeed.*

positive ways. There is nothing to compare with observing toddler multiples as they drift off side-by-side at the breast, each stroking a cheek, an ear, or an arm of the other. Being part of this circle of comfort fills a mother with a sense of wonder.

Just as there are new or different benefits when breastfeeding older babies and toddlers, there also are new and different difficulties that sometimes arise after babies' first several months. Most of them are rooted in multiples' developing relationship(s). These difficulties, plus ideas for dealing with each, are described below. Fortunately, consistent handling resolves most difficulties, and a sense of humor usually sees a mother through the rest.

Changing Breastfeeding Patterns

About midway through the first year, babies become very efficient and effective breastfeeders. This is a good skill since they also tend to be easily distracted by all the exciting stimuli around them at this age. Older babies become so good at breastfeeding that they may finish a feeding within a few minutes. Mothers sometimes worry that briefer feedings mean they are losing their milk. If that becomes a concern, watch for a decrease in babies' diaper counts.

Increased variation in the babies' breastfeeding patterns is common as multiples reach their first birthday, especially among some fraternal multiples. One may request to breastfeed only once or twice a day, and another may continue to breastfeed several times as often. You may also find one frequently requests to breastfeed only because another multiple has asked.

You may notice that babies seem to breastfeed more for comfort than for food as they reach their first birthday and beyond. They may continue to ask to breastfeed at sleep-related times—just before going to sleep at nap or bedtimes and when they wake—and as a cure for illness or injury.

Biting

Breastfeeding-related biting seems to be more common with multiples than for single infants during the second half of the first year. It rarely is necessary to discontinue breastfeeding if one or more bites when breastfeeding. In most instances, biting is easily overcome by becoming sensitive to changes in older babies' feeding cues and by dealing with the act of biting swiftly and consistently.

Babies do not bite during actual breastfeeding. The two actions cannot occur simultaneously. A typical scenario is that the now more efficient breastfeeder has finished her meal. Mother hasn't yet realized that this baby has figured out how to get a good meal in such a short amount of time, so she tries to keep that baby at the breast when the baby is no longer interested. That is when most babies will bite—at the end of the feeding.

A baby also may bite if feedings are delayed. Mothers often increase outside activities during the second half of babies' first year. A mother may become busier with other activities as babies have gotten a little older without even realizing that this has been happening, or she may have been trying to get all the babies on a certain schedule. In either case, some babies balk and begin biting if this occurs without "consulting" them or if it has caused milk production to dwindle.

To put a quick end to a baby's biting, first review that baby's breastfeeding routine and fix any problems. Watch for signs that this baby may be finishing feedings more quickly so you can end the feeding before the bite. Beyond that, consistent handling is crucial. Don't ignore biting one time and get upset the next. This is confusing for a baby; he won't be able to figure out what you want.

Stop the feeding immediately whenever a baby bites. Without scaring the other one who may be nursing, you can firmly but quietly say, "No," or "Ouch!" (Neither expression requires much thought!) Remove the baby from the breast and put him down. If several minutes later he indicates he would still like to feed, offer the breast again. Any time he bites, repeat the procedure whether it is five minutes, five hours, or five days between bites.

You may find it necessary to breastfeed multiples separately while solving this uncomfortable predicament. Your firm, "No!" may also startle the "innocent bystander" baby. It can be difficult to put one down, and supervise letting him begin again a few minutes later, if you are feeding two simultaneously. However, individual feedings may be difficult to accomplish since biting often coincides with the debut of "jealous" breastfeeding behavior.

Learn to watch for the behavioral cues that let you know when each baby is finished and the cues that one is getting ready to bite. Biting usually is prevented once a mother becomes aware of the early signs preceding the behavior. Of course, some multiples begin to bite each other about the time they figure out you won't let them bite you.

Nursing Strikes

When a baby abruptly refuses to breastfeed, it is called a nursing strike. A nursing strike is more likely to occur during the second half of the first year, although an occasional four- to six-month-old baby will stage a strike. Nursing strikes seem to be more common among multiples than single-born breastfeeding babies, but generally only one multiple in a set—often a more patient multiple—ever goes on strike.

An observant mother usually can help her affected baby resolve a nursing strike within a few days. If a strike occurs, first try to determine its cause. The multiple that has been willing to wait for feedings, or the one who has been more agreeable when rushed through a feeding so that another multiple can be put to the breast, may finally put his foot down by "striking." Frequently, an illness that affected a baby's ability to comfortably breastfeed preceded a nursing strike. Sometimes a teething baby goes on strike. A baby may strike if mother has been doing too much lately and milk production is lower as a result.

Combining breastfeeding with extra skin contact often helps to get a striking baby back to the breast. Feed this baby in a quiet room away from distractions when possible. Breastfeed while nude above the waist with baby wearing only a diaper. Take this baby into a tub of warm water with you. The bath is relaxing, and the breast is available. Put this baby to the breast while he is in a light sleep state—before he realizes he's been "tricked" into breastfeeding. If this multiple prefers a certain breast, assign that breast to him for now. Try to stay relaxed and calm. At least with multiples there is another baby or two to help out with frequent breastfeeding so that you remain comfortable and milk production isn't affected.

For Multiples Only

Although biting or nursing strikes may occur among breastfed multiples, dealing with either issue is no different for one of multiples than for a single baby. There are breastfeeding behaviors that are unique to older baby or toddler multiples. To cope with these behaviors, mothers sometimes employ solutions that seem to contradict a "baby-led" weaning, yet they still can remain "babies-sensitive."

Jealous Breastfeeding

According to child development experts, jealous behavior, or "an awareness of and desire for" another's possessions, is not supposed to occur until some time during a child's toddler years. The experts must not be parents of multiples. Almost any mother of multiples can describe becoming the object of her babies' jealousy as early as four to six months. Interact with one multiple and the other(s) quickly lets mother know she doesn't approve of such individual attention, unless she is the one receiving the attention. Of course, then the other(s) protests. Breastfeeding often gets caught in the middle of multiples' jealous behaviors during the second half of their first year.

This scenario is typical. One baby "asks" to breastfeed because she is hungry or needs comforting. Although the other(s) seems perfectly content playing with a toy or an older sibling, the other multiple(s) soon demands to breastfeed, too. Before a mother knows it, she is never "allowed" to breastfeed only one.

Some mothers are not bothered when jealousy appears to be the motivation for many breastfeedings, but other mothers find this behavior very frustrating. Most mothers have looked forward to a time when they could enjoy the luxury of interacting with only one multiple during breastfeedings. That time seems upon them as the number of babies' solid food meals increases and the number of breastfeedings starts to drop.

When most of older babies' or toddlers' simultaneous breastfeedings are a result of the competition for mother's attention, a mother may begin to resent the double breastfeedings that helped her survive the early months. Few mothers enjoy being the center of this kind of attention if it means they rarely, or never, are "allowed" to breastfeed one without another multiple demanding the same attention at the same time.

There is no easy answer to help mothers cope with multiples' jealous behavior. Multiples tend to become more conscious of one another and the attention each receives throughout the toddler and preschool years. Mothers have found a few ideas to be helpful.

- Some mothers purposefully choose to change their attitudes when they find feelings of resentment sneaking up on them. Although the other multiple(s) may not seem to "need" to breastfeed when one requests it, these mothers redefine their notion of "need" and breastfeeding for comfort. Competing for mother's attention may leave a baby or toddler feeling jealous or insecure, and his requests to breastfeed with another multiple may be a source of comfort and a way for him to cope with his feelings.

- Many mothers encourage slightly different wake-up or go-to-sleep times before or after naps and bedtime, so they may enjoy breastfeeding one at a time. Some mothers say they truly cherish older babies' or toddlers' night feedings, because it allows for individual "cuddle" time with each multiple.

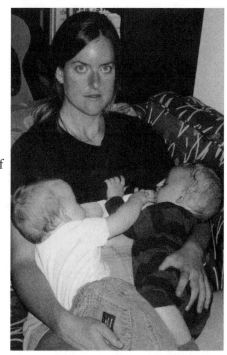

Growing babies take up more space on a mother's lap.

- If one multiple needs to breastfeed after hurting himself, which is extremely common since this time corresponds with increased toddler mobility and the punching, pulling, and poking that characterizes many multiples' interactions, many mothers breastfeed that baby/toddler while standing. (Standing does not always work well, since a mother usually finds the other[s] soon is stuck to her legs like human Velcro®.) Another option is to take the injured party and retreat to an area separated by a doorway gate.

Food Fights

Mothers of multiples are likely to find themselves the center of **food fights, or breastfeeding brawls**, as multiples grow in size. Such food fights may erupt when a mother's lap decreases in proportion to babies' increasing sizes. Jealousy may trigger some brawls. Also, an initial enthusiastic interaction between multiples often escalates to a slugfest.

Growing babies take up more space on a mother's lap, and their movements may be more restless during feedings as they become more mobile. Competing for lap space as well as for mother often leads to a shove here and a kick there. Gentle physical requests to move over soon give way to more vigorous reminders.

Mother may not be the only one who sometimes resents another multiple demanding to breastfeed. The older baby or toddler who hoped to have mother to herself may also not take kindly to another's intrusion. She may then feel compelled to let the other baby know of her displeasure—physically.

The closer multiples move toward their first birthday, the more aware each becomes of the other(s). The babies spend more time interacting, and relationships between, or among, the members of the multiples' set really begin to bloom. Since older babies have limited verbal ability, interactions during this early phase of their relationship tend to be very physical. Each generally continues to interact physically with the peer(s) while sharing mother's lap for a breastfeeding—mother being the forgotten figure as their enthusiasm of learning about each other grows.

Breastfeeding brawling is fairly easy to halt. If you find your lap becoming a battleground, don't be alarmed. Many multiples behave this way as they approach toddlerhood. On the other hand, you don't have to accept this behavior. You have rights in the breastfeeding relationship too, and you deserve to be treated with respect during feedings.

- Some mothers found food fights ended when they distracted each baby with another activity during feedings. For example, one mother tied a small toy to each end of a scarf. She draped the scarf around her neck so that a toy was within reach of each breastfeeding baby. She substituted new toys when any baby seemed to be getting bored with the current distraction.

- Individual feedings are the solution for some. Mothers tell the babies or toddlers that they must take turns. It may be necessary to repeat the message several times to a multiple that is waiting in line for her turn. If jealous breastfeeding is an issue, however, individual feedings may be an unrealistic expectation.

- When physical interaction rates higher than any distraction or jealous breastfeeding interferes with individual feedings, treat food fighting as you would biting. Stop the breastfeeding when you become uncomfortable with babies' physical interactions. You could say, "No, you may not punch or kick during breastfeeding," or "No, I will not be a part of a fight." (You can broaden the explanation depending on the babies' age and ability to understand.) Remove each baby or toddler from a breast and then put both down. Do not "take sides" by allowing one to continue to breastfeed.

If one and then the other indicate they would like to feed again after five to ten minutes, you could offer the breast again. If both want to breastfeed and another food fight erupts, repeat the procedure—whether it is five minutes, five hours, or five days between brawls. Consistency is crucial.

Feeding Frenzies

Sometimes multiples "progress" from the type of jealous breastfeeding where every multiple demands to breastfeed as soon as one indicates the need to what some mothers dub "feeding frenzy" behavior. Instead of waiting for one to signal a need to breastfeed, toddlers descend on mother en masse to request to breastfeed. It's as if each toddler has learned to anticipate that one might ask to breastfeed, so all begin to skip the first step and automatically proceed to the next step of vying for mother's attention.

No matter how busy each toddler acts or how happy each seems, as soon as mother sits down anywhere in the vicinity, she is (or feels) "attacked" by every multiple demanding to breastfeed. Frenzied behavior usually involves toddlers who push and punch one another and their mother in order to be first in position to breastfeed.

This behavior differs from "food fight" behavior, because toddlers already act frenzied when they ask to breastfeed. Food fights are more likely to erupt after multiples have begun feeding. Also, feeding frenzies rarely develop before multiples are of toddler age, whereas food fights are more common during the second half of the babies' first year. If you end up in the middle of feeding frenzies, you might try the following ideas.

- Mothers of toddlers report they stand—a lot—during their multiples' second and third years when their toddlers have a tendency toward feeding frenzies, as sitting down appears to invite a swarm!
- A mother has a right to be respected as a member of the breastfeeding "team." As with biting or food fights, consistently refusing to participate when toddlers display frenzied behavior often limits this behavior or puts an end to it. If multiples begin shoving or slapping as they approach you to breastfeed, simply stand up and announce, "No one may breastfeed* when both (or all) of you hit and kick." Then walk away and wait several minutes before sitting near any multiple. Repeat the action as necessary. (*Insert whatever word you use for "breastfeeding.")
- When feeding frenzies continue frequently in spite of other actions, mothers may limit breastfeeding to a specific area of the house or to certain feedings that seem the most meaningful to the toddlers.

Weaning

Weaning is a slow process rather than an abrupt event. It actually begins the first time a baby is offered something other than mother's milk. When multiples are partially breastfed, the process may begin within days, weeks, or months of the babies' birth. Fully breastfed multiples don't begin the weaning process until they are introduced to solid foods during the second half of their first year. The age(s) at which complete weaning occurs may be the same whether multiples were partially or fully breastfed during early infancy.

When babies are the ones to set the pace, the process of weaning generally occurs gradually over many months or years. There is no natural "rule" specifying that complete weaning must occur by a designated age. Some societies seem to have developed such rules, but complete weaning at or before one year of age is unusual in most cultures. Children do not wean completely until at least two to four years of age in most cultures.

There are a lot of good reasons to let each child set the weaning pace. Gradual weaning is easier for mother and for babies. Only each baby knows when she no longer needs the breastfeeding relationship—when other foods and other forms of maternal attention are preferable. Babies' bodies are given the opportunity to slowly mature and assume the tasks of digesting "foreign" foods and developing an immune system more capable of fighting diseases.

Many mothers also prefer to have breastfeeding gradually taper off, as this allows a mother time to adjust to changes in each mother-multiple relationship. Also, a mother's body adapts easily to a slow decline in milk production, whereas an abrupt weaning often results in engorgement with the potential for plugged ducts and mastitis.

Multiple older babies or toddlers affect the entire breastfeeding process, including weaning. The increasing interactions and growing relationships between or among multiples, their differing individual needs for breast-feeding, and jealous breastfeeding are a few of the factors that influence the way a mother of multiples views and responds to the weaning process.

Baby-Led Weaning

The need to breastfeed varies for older babies and toddlers just as it does for newborns and young babies. Most babies tend to ask to breastfeed less often as they grow older and more of their diet consists of solid foods. The wise mother doesn't offer breastfeeding as a distraction or a way to quiet the older baby or young toddler, but she doesn't refuse the child when he indicates the need to breastfeed.

Baby-led weaning is realistic with many sets of multiples. It seems to work best with fraternal multiples that have very different temperaments and very different breastfeeding needs. When multiples' approaches to life are dissimilar, jealous breastfeeding tends to be less of a factor and individual breastfeeding is more the norm. As with many other behaviors, opposite-sex multiples also seem to vary more in their approaches to the weaning process.

When multiples wean according to a baby-led approach, they occasionally stop within days of each other. However, the time when each completely weans usually varies by weeks to years. The difference(s) in ages is a reflection of their differing needs for breastfeeding and the respect a mother has for her multiples as individuals.

Mother-Encouraged, Babies-Led Weaning

Many mothers of multiples find their toddlers' jealous breastfeedings and the development of feeding frenzies affect their desire for, or their ability to go along with, baby-led weaning. Although a mother of multiples may do her best to let each baby set the pace for weaning, a mother may sometimes find it necessary to refuse one toddler who seems to need to breastfeed because of the behavior of the other(s). Also, she may impose more restrictions, or "rules," on breastfeeding in order to limit the effects of her multiples' jealous behaviors, which in turn often limits their requests for breastfeeding.

A La Leche League Leader who is a mother of twins gave a name to a weaning process that acknowledged each multiple's individual needs yet recognized that multiples also form an entity affecting toddler breastfeeding. She called it "mother-encouraged, babies-led" weaning. The term sums up this modified process neatly.

Mothers who agree with the concept of baby-led weaning, especially those who have enjoyed this process with an older child, may find a modified version difficult to accept. They often express feelings of ambivalence. It may have become obvious to a mother that a plan of "don't offer but don't refuse" must be modified due to her set's "entity" behaviors. At the same time she, like many mothers, may feel guilty because she cannot figure a way to meet each toddler's individual needs and those of the entity created by the multiples set. She also may think there is something wrong if she feels resentful of entity behaviors that interfere with the enjoyment of breastfeeding each.

If baby-led weaning is possible for each multiple, it is obviously the best option for everyone. Weaning "guidelines" that are ideal for most single-born toddlers may not always work for sets of multiples. When baby-led weaning is not realistic, accept the differences that may be inherent for breastfed multiples and accept the feelings that probably are normal under the circumstances. Then move forward accordingly. Do your best and let the rest go.

For some, "mother-encouraged" means they begin to set flexible limits on certain aspects of breastfeeding as their toddlers begin to understand spoken language. This usually occurs by about 15 to 18 months for full-term babies. Toddlers who have developed this "receptive" language ability can follow simple directions and their behaviors show an understanding of the words "wait until we get home."

- One of the first limits imposed by mothers of toddler multiples usually addresses breastfeeding in public or breastfeeding at another person's home when strangers are present. Breastfeeding older babies or toddler multiples simultaneously easily turns into a "spectacle" that may become uncomfortable for a mother as well as for those nearby. Multiples' restless behavior and their interactions are attention-getting under any circumstances. No words adequately describe the same situation when jealous breastfeeding, a feeding frenzy, or a food fight occurs in conjunction with simultaneous feeding. Therefore, some mothers limit breastfeeding to home or to situations where everyone is familiar and comfortable with toddler multiples' breastfeeding behaviors.

- Some mothers find they reduce the number of jealousy-related feedings when breastfeeding is designated to a specific room in the house—one that is quiet, dark, and one that requires leaving the scene of most family "activity"—a very boring room. A toddler who truly wants or needs to breastfeed will be willing to walk to the less stimulating environment. A multiple that asks to breastfeed only because another wants to is less likely to make the move to the assigned room.

- Imposing a rule that limits breastfeeding to a certain position, such as lying down, may encourage toddlers to limit requests. Except for sleep-related feedings, many toddlers quickly lose interest if they must lie down to breastfeed.

- An idea that has worked for many mothers is to tell multiples they may breastfeed but only to the count of a certain number, such as "20." When a mother has time, she may count aloud very slowly. She may count more quickly when certain behaviors or interactions escalate.

If the situation warrants a "mother-encouraged, babies-led" weaning approach, offer toddlers a distraction when one signals a desire to breastfeed but limits have been set. You might read a favorite story to them or ask each if she would like a cup of juice or water instead. Usually an activity with another multiple proves to be the best diversion.

Toddlers are more likely to completely wean within days or weeks of one another when using a "mother-encouraged, babies-led" approach. Whether the short time span is related to this approach or the behaviors that warranted using it, it's difficult to say. Either possibility seems logical.

Partial weaning. Sometimes a mother is more ready than her babies or toddlers to wean completely. It may be due to her multiples' behaviors, preconceptions about the age when weaning should occur, a feeling a mother has that she will never get her body back, and so on. A mother may think her only option is to completely wean each baby or toddler, but many mothers have found an alternative. By partially breastfeeding, these mothers were able to meet a personal need to decrease the number of feedings while meeting the needs of their babies or toddlers to some extent. Although partial breastfeeding usually is more restrictive than a "mother-encouraged, babies-led" approach, it still is more gradual and easier physically and emotionally for multiples or their mother than abrupt weaning.

Several suggestions listed above for "mother-encouraged, babies-led" weaning still may apply to toddlers when partial breastfeeding is the goal. Often counting to 20 to restrict the length of feedings or limiting breastfeeding to a particular room or to a certain feeding position is enough to make breastfeeding enjoyable again for all concerned—including mother. When multiples do not yet understand spoken language, or the suggestions for "mother-encouraged, babies-led" weaning do not meet a mother's needs, some mothers temporarily or permanently limit their multiples' breastfeedings to the one or two daily feedings that appear to be most important to them. For most multiples this would be a sleep-related feeding, either immediately preceding sleep or following waking.

Abrupt Weaning

Abrupt weaning, or suddenly stopping all breastfeedings, is a difficult way to end the breastfeeding relationship due to the physical and emotional implications for babies and mothers. Occurrences when it may be unavoidable, such as a maternal health condition requiring immediate treatment with one of the few medications that are incompatible with breastfeeding at any time, are rare. When possible, it is better to try other weaning options first.

Mother-Initiated Weaning

A mother may wean older babies or toddlers abruptly due to a health condition, but more often it is initiated after a "mother-encouraged, babies-led" approach or partial weaning have not had the desired results. If you have reviewed the options and still decide to wean your multiples abruptly, go out of your way to offer other forms of comfort and attention. Watch each closely for any adverse physical or emotional effects. You may want to reevaluate the decision if any multiple has real difficulty with the loss of breastfeeding.

When a mother suddenly stops breastfeeding her older babies or toddlers, she may be surprised to discover she still is producing a significant amount of milk. Although physical problems for mothers are usually less severe when abruptly weaning older babies or toddlers, they can occur. Intervene immediately if you develop breast engorgement or a plugged duct. One option is to let multiples breastfeed again and take steps toward complete weaning, but take steps more slowly. Other options include applying cold compresses or ice packs to engorged breasts to reduce swelling. You also can pump your breasts as needed—but you may want to do this only to the point that relieves breast fullness. Use massage to "move" a plug downward, starting above the plug and then firmly massaging over it. Sometimes it helps to pump that breast after or during breast massage. You may use hot or cold compresses over any plugged duct, depending on which feels more comfortable. (For abrupt weaning of young babies, see "Early weaning," in Chapter 17, "Full and Partial Breastfeeding.")

Abrupt Baby-Initiated Weaning

It is unusual for a single-born older baby or toddler to abruptly stop when still breastfeeding several times a day. Although multiples typically follow their single-born counterparts and wean gradually, a "natural" abrupt weaning seems to be somewhat more common at about 10 to 15 months of age for one or more in a set of multiples. This type of weaning takes mothers by surprise, since the babies usually had been breastfeeding happily at least two or three times a day prior to abruptly stopping. Also, it often occurs before a mother imposes limits, such as ones for "mother-encouraged, babies-led" weaning.

A nursing strike is the most likely reason for a baby younger than 15 months to suddenly stop breastfeeding. (See information about nursing strikes in a previous section.) When multiples abruptly wean, they tend to behave somewhat differently if breastfeeding is offered than a baby on a nursing strike. Still the possibility of abrupt baby-initiated weaning should be considered only if none of the factors commonly associated with a nursing strike is present or when interventions for a nursing strike have had no effect after several days.

The reason that abrupt baby-initiated weaning may be more common among multiples is unknown. It may be that the subtle limitations imposed by the situation of breastfeeding more than one, limitations that may be associated with an increased number of nursing strikes among multiples, also lead to earlier and abrupt weaning more often. Perhaps the growing interest multiples have in each other as they reach their first birthday diminishes the need to breastfeed for some babies.

In spite of its abruptness this is a form of baby-led weaning, since the baby chose to stop breastfeeding. Therefore, the weaned baby is unlikely to experience negative physical or emotional effects. A mother may develop engorgement or a plugged duct, but this is less likely if another multiple continues to breastfeed. Mothers often express feeling an emotional "shock," since the decision to wean was taken out of their hands. Many mothers also feel a profound sadness, because they were not yet ready for any of the breastfeeding relationships with their multiples to end. Also, some are concerned that they somehow caused the abrupt weaning, or they worry that they may feel closer to any multiple(s) that continues to breastfeed.

To paraphrase an old saying, you can lead a baby or toddler to the breast but you can't make him drink—even if you'd still like him to. Imagine how secure a baby must feel and the amount of confidence it must have taken for him to suddenly stop breastfeeding. Allow yourself to feel sad, but also celebrate what you've given this baby or toddler through breastfeeding and your milk. You still have every right to enjoy breastfeeding any other multiple, but find other ways to enjoy skin contact and one-on-one time with the baby who weaned. Back rubs and cuddle time shouldn't be limited to the period when a baby breastfeeds.

Breastfeeding multiples continues to differ from breastfeeding a single child as multiples grow and develop into busy toddlers. Many of the joys, benefits, and problems of breastfeeding older babies or toddlers are similar whether you have one or several toddlers; yet many joys, benefits, and problems are also unique to this special situation. As with younger babies, issues related to parenting multiple toddlers sometimes become confused with breastfeeding them. A mother who breastfed multiples into toddlerhood, a La Leche League Leader, or a lactation consultant may be able to give you new ideas and a fresh perspective about breast-feeding even as your babies grow and develop into fast-moving and independent children.

Chapter 28
Older Babies and Toddlers:
Childproofing and Helpful Equipment

Older babies need room to practice new motor skills. They also become curious about the environment and want to explore everything within reach. By the time they are toddlers, multiples can figure out ways to explore everything—including places or items that parents think are far out of their reach. It is crucial for the development of their minds and bodies that multiples be given room to roam and to discover the exciting qualities of everyday objects. At the same time, safety is a priority when multiples are in the vicinity.

Safety and Childproofing for Older Babies

Basic Safety

Injury prevention involves anticipating the unanticipated. For parents of mobile multiples, childproofing is the first intervention to protect babies and toddlers from physical injury. No matter how thoroughly parents childproof, injuries sometimes do occur. Are you prepared? Have you:

- Taken infant-toddler cardiopulmonary resuscitation (CPR) and first aid classes?
- Posted a personal phone pad on or near all phones for writing the number where you can be reached if away from home?
- Posted the number for your children's pediatric care provider?
- Posted emergency (911 or police, fire, emergency medical transport, etc.) and poison center numbers on or near all phones?
- Bought syrup of ipecac in case you or a sitter is instructed to give it to any multiple by someone at a poison center or your children's pediatric care provider? (**Never** give syrup of ipecac unless instructed to do so by an appropriate health care provider. Some toxic substances cause even more physical damage when vomiting is induced.)
- Created a first aid kit and shared its whereabouts with any helper or sitter?
- Placed smoke alarms in bedrooms and other appropriate locations in your home and periodically checked the working condition of each?
- Developed a household fire emergency plan?
- Interviewed any helper or sitter for their level of knowledge of safety and first aid?
- Reviewed with any helper or sitter the childproofing and safety interventions you've established in your home?

Childproofing

Parents have a responsibility to make their home as physically safe as possible for babies, toddlers, and older children. This is called "childproofing." Childproofing the home begins before babies actually move themselves from place to place. Since injury prevention is the major theme of childproofing, it begins even before babies arrive home from the hospital.

Often more intense precautions must be taken in homes of multiple explorers. Adapting a home for this higher level of environmental safety is sometimes called "twinproofing" or "multiples-proofing." Some parents consult with professional childproofing experts for help, as they are trained

Older babies are compelled to examine everything with their eyes, their hands, and their mouths.

to see potential dangers that parents could miss. For information about professional childproofing services, check the yellow pages of a nearby city, ask someone in the parent education department of the nearest children's hospital, or search the internet for "childproofing experts or services."

Pre-mobile childproofing. The word "never" applies to few situations in life, but most existing applications probably pertain to caring for children— whether newborns or toddlers. For example, it is **never** safe to leave a baby of any age on a surface off the floor. This would include changing tables, beds, sofas, etc. Babies' movements can cause a shift in their positions so that a fall can occur long before they are able to roll or crawl. And the baby who couldn't roll yesterday may suddenly develop the ability today. Leaving a toddler alone on a high surface is the same as daring her to jump, or climb higher, or fall.

It is **never** safe to leave any baby or toddler in a tub with any amount of water for even a moment. Do not depend on sponge rests, seat rings, etc., to keep any baby safe in water. Babies' and toddlers' heads weigh proportionately more than the rest of their bodies, so babies and toddlers are top heavy. Should any baby find herself on her tummy in even a minimal amount of water, that baby is in danger of drowning because she may have difficulty keeping her head up in that slippery tub. Also, don't trust that faucets really are out of babies' or toddlers' reach. A determined baby will find a way to get to them one unexpected day. As an extra precaution to avoid accidental burns, check the temperature on the hot water heater to be sure it is set no higher than 120°F (approximately 45°C).

Mobile childproofing. Older babies are compelled to explore with their eyes, their hands, and their mouths. This compulsion is a vital step in learning about the wider world. Once multiples can crawl, their home becomes the original new frontier. To each baby it is virgin territory just waiting to be explored and conquered. Until parents of multiples are issued extra eyes for the backs of their heads, they must anticipate the movements of little explorers who are likely to wander off in different directions.

To make your home ultra-safe, get down on the floor yourself and view it from the babies' level **before** any takes off rolling or crawling across the floor. Replace standard electrical outlet coverings with covers that don't allow older babies or toddlers to stick fingers or other objects into them. (Safety caps that fit over the individual electrical outlets or sockets are not enough; multiples eventually figure a way to remove them and then they become a potential choking hazard.) Since electrical wires may be bitten or pulled and babies may be shocked or injured when hit by a falling object, eliminate the wires that are dangling from lamps and other electrical items. Childproof window blind cord roll-ups allow parents to use the blinds normally, but prevent babies from getting tangled in any that lay on or close to the floor or hang over a crib.

Specially designed plastic control panel guards may protect expensive stereo and television equipment, remote controls, etc., from older babies, but they are unlikely to stop curious toddlers. Moving these items plus any breakable or heavy knick-knacks to higher ground now may save you from saying the word "no" a lot, and you're much less likely to someday find an item in pieces.

Babies love almost anything made of paper—books, magazines, newspapers, catalogs—all are in jeopardy. Paper makes a great noise when wadded in the hand and most babies seem to think it tastes good. Unfortunately, the ink used for some printing may be toxic and a small wad of paper can lodge where it shouldn't and cause choking.

If anyone can find the proverbial "needle in a haystack," it is marauding multiples! Look on the floor, and under any sofa, on carpets and through any bordering fringe, chairs, and tables for coins, crumbs, and other mouth-size odds and ends, and remove them.

Adult smoking is not an appropriate behavior in any home with children. Children exposed to secondhand smoke have much higher rates of respiratory illnesses, and children of smokers are more likely to smoke later in childhood. Therefore, cigarettes, cigars, pipes and tobacco, matches, lighters, ashtrays with butts, and other smoking-related items should not be in a home that has older babies or toddlers. There should be no possibility that older babies and toddlers may be burned, eat a tobacco-containing object, or start a fire because of such paraphernalia.

Toxic substances. Go to the kitchen and start looking in cabinets and the pantry. Unless you use an item every day, move anything toxic out of the kitchen. **Lock** these items in the highest cabinet or in a container on the shelf in the laundry area or garage. Dishwasher soap or powder, medications, vitamin and mineral supplements, and alcoholic beverages can be toxic, so place them inside a high, locked kitchen cabinet. Items with the potential for injury or illness—plastic garbage bags, dishwashing soaps, heavy cans or pans, breakable bowls, and so on—should be moved to higher, locked cabinets or containers on shelves. Then move items that aren't necessarily harmful, but if spilled could create a mess you'd rather not have to clean! Next, open kitchen drawers and inspect each as closely as you did the cabinets.

To prevent children from opening cabinet doors and drawers, attach specially designed guards or locks after you have moved dangerous or risky materials. **Never** depend on such guards, however, to keep like-minded multiples from getting into cabinet doors or drawers—sooner or later they will combine their brains and brawn to figure out how to manipulate such locks. Also, you may want to skip a few drawers when attaching safety guards. Many mothers fill lower drawers with unbreakable items, such as small pots, pans, plastic storage containers, and plastic lids to keep babies busy when mommy is working in the kitchen.

Measure the space between banister spindles. Older babies or toddlers could wriggle through and fall or get their heads trapped if there is too much room. It's best to use a gate to limit access to stairways or outdoor decks so babies or toddlers do not have the opportunity to become trapped in banisters.

Helpful Equipment

Infant equipment assumes a new role as babies become mobile and begin to explore. Different items can help or hinder your efforts to keep multiple babies safe. Certain items can also help or hinder babies' development.

Infant seats for younger babies. Babies often outgrow infant seats and automatic swings between four and six months (based on full-term birth). At this age babies begin to arch their backs in a way that can propel them out of such seats or cause a lightweight seat to tip over. Therefore, each must be carefully supervised when in such seats.

As babies gain the ability to sit more erect, it may be necessary to readjust car seat placement and car seat safety belts or harnesses. The same may hold true for the positioning of some stroller seats and the placement of stroller safety belts. No matter how content a particular multiple may seem when in the stroller, **never** use a stroller without first securing all babies with safety belts.

Play yard. A standard play yard is a fairly dull place to play, especially once babies begin to crawl or learn to pull themselves to a standing position. The standard play yard is soon outgrown when it is shared by two or more budding explorers. Expandable play yards are available. Look for play yard pieces that link together and form play yards of varying sizes. These play areas provide more functional space—enough space to practice new physical skills as well as a safe space to play indoors and out. (Avoid models with crisscrossing slats, however, as children's heads and fingers have been caught in the them.)

Doorway gates. To create larger indoor play areas, use gates to block doorways or stairways and extra-wide gates for hallways or room entryways to keep babies in—or out—of rooms and other household areas. A gated area provides more of the space babies need to practice new physical skills and a wider expanse to roam. Properly used, gates meet the babies' needs for exploration and parents' need to safely contain their multiples' curiosity.

You will save money long term if you purchase gates with toddlers' increased mobility in mind. The less-expensive 24-inch (60 cm) pressure-mounted gates may be ideal for older babies or single toddlers, but multiple toddlers will think of ways to crash through or climb over them. Look for gates that are several inches above standard height. For gate stability consider the wall-mounted rather than the pressure-mounted type. For reasons of safety, choose gates with vertical slats. Little body parts can become trapped or pinched when slats crisscross. Gates with a mesh panel are usually safe for older babies, but the mesh can provide toddlers with a toehold for climbing up and over.

When blocking stairways, some mothers leave a few (two to four) stairs open for climbing practice. By carpeting any exposed stairs and the foot of the staircase, there is little risk of injury when babies take the inevitable tumbles.

Walkers and other play seats for older babies. It may be tempting to put one or more multiples in individual walkers, especially when it seems to keep any baby busy for awhile. Yet walker use is associated with one of the highest rates of emergency room visits among older babies. The average baby moves three feet (almost one meter) per second in a walker. It doesn't matter if yesterday a baby couldn't move, or only moved backward in the walker; today that same baby suddenly may figure out how to move forward and toward the stairs. Also, walkers' wheels easily catch on uneven spots or breaks in a floor, grass, or pavement, which cause many "tip over" accidents every year.

Many pediatric care providers think walkers should be banned for safety issues alone, but the overuse of walkers is also associated with problems or delays in proper growth and development. Walkers may become a substitute for more appropriate opportunities for infant mobility. When babies are in walkers, they aren't learning to move by themselves. Walkers ultimately may interfere with babies learning to walk properly. Babies in walkers move forward by shuffling their feet, which may interfere with babies learning to use their lower extremities for "alternate stepping," or placing one foot forward and then the other as with a normal walking gait.

Play seats in which a baby is virtually suspended in a sitting position may affect development adversely. As noted in Chapter 21, "What You'll Need" when it is difficult or impossible for a baby to keep his feet flat on the floor, it may create undue stress on the structures in a baby's pelvic area. For this reason babies should not be left in walkers, saucer seats, or jumping seats suspended from a doorway for more than 20 to 30 consecutive minutes.

High chairs. You won't have to purchase high chairs, booster seats with trays, or seats that attach onto the adult table, until babies are able to maintain an erect sitting position. Because most high chairs are exactly that—high off the floor—they should be used only during mealtimes. **Always** secure each baby by fastening the seat or shoulder belts that should be built in to the high chair. **Never** turn away from, or leave babies unattended in high chairs or other types of seats. A large number of babies and toddlers are seen in emergency rooms for falls from high chairs every year.

If you use high chairs at home and plan to take the babies to grandma's or a restaurant for mealtime, you may want to invest in cloth restraints that are designed to hold baby in a secure sitting position in adult dining chairs. Some slings and harnesses are also designed to secure older babies and toddlers in straight-back chairs, grocery cart seats, etc.

Purchasing multiple high chairs can be a big expense. Some parents find they save money and have a more versatile item by purchasing multiple booster seats with trays or seats that attach to the adult table. Parents find many are easier to clean than high chairs and either type saves space in the dining area. And since most brands take up little space in the car, the seats can go to grandma's or a family restaurant. Toddlers often prefer these seats, because they enjoy sitting at the table with the rest of the family. If booster or table-attaching seats sound like a good option, look for a brand that has safety straps to restrain a child in the seat. Booster seats should have safety straps that attach it securely to a chair, and trays should be easy to use. Some parents recommend brands that adjust in height to accommodate a growing child.

Out and about. One of the pleasures of older babies is their ability to sit upright in stroller, car, or grocery cart seats. They are able to enjoy the world from a new, more visual perspective. Their newfound preoccupation with all they can see from a sitting position usually makes it much easier to take them out.

As babies move into toddlerhood and develop new physical skills, they may be less content viewing the world from a sitting position.

- Older babies and toddler multiples may be able to climb (or fall) out of some stroller or grocery cart seats. **Harnesses** that zip up the back and have straps that attach to the stroller or cart frame will safely "hold" multiples in their seats.

- You may be able to carry one curious older baby or toddler in a baby sling on your hip longer than in a backpack. Some mothers find multiples eventually become too heavy, or it simply becomes too difficult to manage multiple toddlers with one "riding" on a hip while shopping. However, some mothers are able to crisscross slings and hold two multiples—one on each hip—for their first several years.

- Some chain stores now have carts with **double child seats.** If you find one, grab it! (Be sure to let the manager know why you've just become a regular customer.) The shape of these seats and the attached safety belts may deter some climbers, but don't depend on these features alone. The seat shape may interfere with harness use, but it is possible to purchase extra safety belts.

- If you use two standard carts, form a train—push one and pull the other, so at least two multiples can ride in the individual seats. Avoid putting two or more children in one cart. **Warning:** Never let any child stand in the body/basket of a shopping cart. Most cart accidents occur when a standing child wants to touch some item on the shelves and then leans too far forward. Multiples standing in one cart present an additional danger. If two or more rush to the same spot, the cart could become unbalanced and easily tip over. **Never leave any child alone in a shopping cart for even a moment.**

When forming a two-cart train, don't forget to make "choo-choo" noises to keep multiples entertained. Also, many mothers find the train is easier to manage when they put heavier items in the cart they are pulling.

Childproofing and Equipment for Toddler Multiples

There is nothing quite like rediscovering a familiar world through the eyes of a toddler, unless it is rediscovering the world from multiple new viewpoints. For many parents it seems only minutes before multiples progress from crawling to walking to running and climbing. Older babies' increasing mobility offers only a peek at both the excitement and the challenge two or more toddler explorers provide.

Individual safety becomes the major issue as active multiples become even more mobile toddlers. In the blink of a father's eye or the turn of a mother's head, toddler multiples will run in opposite directions to investigate different fascinating objects. Count on all of them to still consider the popping of those different objects into their mouths, or a toilet, as a crucial aspect of their investigations.

Together two can do what one toddler could not, such as drag a chair over and climb onto a shelf or cabinet to reach a knife or that jar of vitamin tablets. Three or more multiples contribute even more interest to the pool of toddler ideas and escapades. Perhaps this explains the response of one mother of toddler twins when asked the question "What do you do for a living?" "I save lives—all day, every day," she said with a straight face.

Basic Safety

Keep your first aid skills fresh, those emergency numbers posted, and the syrup of ipecac in a high but convenient cabinet. An emergency fire plan may need to be updated. Toddlers are heavier and taller, and a home evacuation plan must continually be adjusted for their current sizes. Even if you no longer use a sling or backpack carrier for outings, it may be a practical means of carrying an extra child if you should have to leave your home in a hurry.

Toddler multiples are notorious for figuring how to get out of car safety belts, although the improvements in newer model car seat belts make them more difficult to undo. If any multiple aspires to a career as an escape artist, it is crucial that each learn no one will be going anywhere unless everyone's safety belts are in place. This requires consistent handling by parents. Any time a child releases the safety belt, pull off the road and stop the car immediately. Refasten the belt and resume the drive. Repeat your actions each time one releases the belt system no matter how many times it occurs. Multiples rarely continue this behavior for long when parents are consistent. It may be aggravating, especially if it takes a few car rides, but taking care of this behavior now will make for safer and saner car trips long term. And your toddlers are watching you, so be sure to buckle your own seatbelt every time you get into a car.

Childproofing for Toddler Multiples

Home. Whether your multiples' activity levels are best described as sightseers, wanderers, trailblazers, or a combination of two or more, it can only make family life easier to childproof as if all are trailblazers. Trailblazers constantly explore. The higher or more out of reach an object is, the more they seem compelled to attain it. Trailblazers seem to relish the challenge of finding ways around or over every childproofing barrier their parents erect to keep them safe. (See Chapter 29, "Parenting Toddler Multiples," for toddler activity level descriptions.)

Multiple trailblazers and trailblazer-wanderer combos frequently work together to execute actions that a single trailblazer has neither the strength nor range to even attempt. Two wanderers or wanderer-sightseer combinations may also gain confidence together and engage in risky trailblazing behaviors. However, they probably will do so less often. In spite of close parental supervision, the following escapades are common and frequent occurrences for trailblazing multiple toddlers, are regular occurrences for wanderers, and may be occasional ones for sightseers.

- Multiples can help one another drag a chair alongside a shelf, the stove, or the dining table and then stand on it to reach objects formerly out of reach. A well-placed chair also makes it easy for them to climb onto countertops and other furniture.

- With one on either end of a bureau or chest of drawers, each can grasp a drawer pull or knob to open it. Both then use the drawers as a stepladder—usually after they've emptied them of their contents. Once on top of the furniture, they will be likely to use it for jumping practice. A greater danger occurs when climbing toddlers cause a heavy chest of drawers to become unbalanced so that it topples forward, which can crush the small children using it for a ladder.

- Multiples quickly learn to stack pillows from beds, a sofa, and outdoor furniture against doorway or hallway gates, stairway banisters, or deck rails in order to climb over.

- Two will find a way to open almost any kind of door—to different rooms, the refrigerator, the oven, the dryer, a basement stairwell, and one leading outside.

- Knobs of any kind draw toddlers like magnets. To multiples, knobs are irresistible. There are knobs to adjust stovetop burners, turn the oven on, and control the stereo, television, or other electronic equipment. Water— cold or hot—goes on and off with the turn of a knob in the bathroom and kitchen. And of course, once doorknobs are mastered, toddlers go where someone probably didn't want them to go. In fact, many knobs can be used to gain a toehold when multiples are moving vertically.

- A toilet is the only thing multiples seem to find more compelling than a knob. Water play is always fun, but multiples also like to top one another by finding interesting items to flush. This is not only a plumbing problem; every year toddlers drown because their heads become trapped after they fall forward into a toilet bowl.

As older babies become increasingly mobile you face the challenge of two or more toddler multiple explorers.

- If an item can fit in a toddler's hand, chances are another multiple will encourage him to eat it or drink it. It doesn't matter how inedible or unsafe that item is. Unfortunately, toddlers don't think of choking or poisoning as possible consequences when they pop interesting objects into their mouths.

- Most multiples will at some point use a wall or one another's body as their canvas. (Some clever parents attempted to curtail their multiples' artistic efforts by rolling paper over, and taping it to, the walls at toddlers' arm level. The multiples quickly learned to draw above and below the paper.) In addition to such standard mediums as pens, pencils, colored markers, crayons, etc., many sets have helped one another remove diapers and then used the contents as finger-paints.

- Most parents can count on one multiple to run ahead and another to dawdle behind during any walk out of doors. This is likely to result in a parent wondering whether she should first stop the multiple that appears to be chewing the mysterious berries he's just pulled off a neighbor's shrub, grab the one balancing on the stone retaining wall, or tackle the one who is running toward the street.

- Almost all parents with trailblazing multiples have stories of the time a neighbor found their toddlers wandering up the street after they'd escaped the safety of their home by doing such things as pushing a screen out of a window (and not always one on the first floor), figuring out a deadbolt lock, scaling a six foot fence, or whatever. Usually parents' heads sported several new gray hairs immediately after the episode.

- Older toddlers or preschoolers may become intrigued with fire. Many parents have a frightening tale of the day their multiples stumbled on to a pack of matches or suddenly decided to prepare lunch on the stove. Likewise, older toddlers and preschoolers may become more and more interested in any firearms that parents keep in the home.
- Besides climbing and investigating areas where they don't belong, toddler multiples can become frustrated with one another's behaviors which often leads to pushing or punching. Multiples may be injured in a fall from some perch on a countertop or from hitting a body part, usually one's head, on the floor or a corner of a wall after being pushed or punched.

Indoor solutions. Assuming the childproofing interventions for older babies are already in effect, what can parents do to make homes safer short of emptying one's home of all furniture for several years? First get down on your knees to look at your home from your toddler multiples' perspective. Once you've done that, you may decide removing some furniture is a good idea, especially if the items in question have any sharp edges, pointed ends, or protruding pieces. Books, electrical equipment control panels, electrical wires, window blind cords, lamps, knick-knacks, etc., that were out of reach when babies were on all fours, may now be within the reach of toddlers who able to move vertically as well as horizontally.

Sometimes it is possible to place some items even higher, but many parents choose to store unsafe furniture and items out of sight in a locked attic, cellar, storage closet, or rented storage area. To avoid injuries related to electric-related equipment, lamps, and other objects with wires, keep these items to a minimum and be certain no wires are dangling or out in the open on a floor. It probably isn't possible to eliminate all edges and corners, but cushioned strips are available commercially and can be applied to the sharp edges and corners of tables, a fireplace hearth, and so on. If investing in any new furniture, purchasing pieces with rounded edges may save a lot of trips to the emergency room for stitches.

You may want to empty one room completely of "grown-up" items and designate it as a playroom. Choose a room that is carpeted, easily gated, and one that is either near, or actually is a part of, the center of most family activities. Toddlers like to be near mom or dad, so a playroom in a distant part of a home is unlikely to be used. To give young artists an appropriate outlet for their talents, some parents paint all or part of one wall with "chalkboard" paint. The fact that the chalk used on this wall washes off more easily when multiples decide to decorate one another may be considered an added benefit. **Warning:** No matter how well parents "multiples-proof" a room, two or more toddlers still require adult supervision when in a playroom.

Trailblazers and wanderers usually enjoy practicing large motor skills. To keep these multiples busy, happy, and off the furniture, many parents purchase durable, hard plastic indoor-outdoor gym equipment, such as seesaws and slides with attached steps and platforms. Parents tend to stock their multiples' playroom with toys having the least number of removable, and therefore swallowable or flushable, parts. Toys in the hands of active multiples easily become weapons, so avoid any having sharp or pointed edges. Rubber or spongy toys are less likely to cause an injury when used as weapons by one multiple to hit another. However, not all spongy toy materials are equal. Avoid toys made of any spongy material that is easily bitten and swallowed. (A parental taste test rarely is necessary. A pinch test usually will do!)

Warning: Toddler multiples maintain a "non-discrimination policy" when it comes to eating and choking on or flushing small toys (or parts) belonging to any older sibling. If a toy (part) fits inside a cardboard tube of a toilet paper or paper towel roll, consider it a potential choking or flushing hazard that should be kept in a restricted area, such as the sibling's "off limits" locked bedroom.

Never trust toddlers in a loft area or on a deck. Open banisters on indoor stairways or outdoor decks pose a danger for toddlers, since they are associated with a significant drop to the ground. Banisters on cellar stairways may be little more than open holes. Some toddlers may be able to squeeze through smaller banister spaces, others could get their heads trapped between slats, and many are likely to give climbing over banisters a try. Also, toddlers may use the space between slats as a hole to drop things through to the floor or ground below. In addition to wall-mounted gates that already block access to stairways or decks, consider attaching special shields or netting to open banisters designed for this purpose. **Caution:** Ask before purchasing netting that might allow a toehold that could help rather than hinder climbing.

Toddler multiples consider an open door as an invitation to an older sibling's or parents' bedroom, the cellar, any bathroom, or the outdoors. Slamming a door to slow a multiple, or an angry sibling, hard on another's heels can be great fun—unless someone gets hit in the head or gets fingers pinched in the process. Closed doors are the safest doors, but keeping them closed yet accessible to other family members can be a problem.

Childproof locks that fit into the space at the top of a door may work perfectly for doors that lead to a cellar or the outside, since most mothers also want to know if an older sibling has gone through these doors. These locks may be less practical if parental help is required to open doors when an older child wants to use a room, such as a bathroom or the child's bedroom. One solution is to bolt small slide locks into these doors that are too high for a toddler but within reach for an older child. When in locked position, these locks are difficult for toddlers to maneuver but a preschool sibling can easily open them. For cellars with an open banister on the stairway, consider installing a slide lock plus a childproof lock at the top of a cellar door to provide additional safety. **Caution:** Don't waste money on hook-and-eye locks. Many sets of toddler multiples have figured out how to use a pole, such as a broomstick or mop handle to open hook-and-eye locks set high on doors within an hour of installation. Low placement of these locks is a breeze for them to figure out! **Warning:** Check doors and slide or childproof locks frequently to be certain other family members are remembering to use them.

In addition to locking doors to keep multiples out of bathrooms, toilet-seat lid locks provide extra insurance for keeping small objects or a multiple from falling in. Lid-locks may be opened easily by adults or an older sibling.

To avoid injuries from tipping furniture, install childproof braces/brackets to help protect multiples from furniture pieces they may use as steps. These braces/brackets may be installed on all chests of drawers, bookcases, shelves, and so on.

Parents often use a higher gate to remind multiples where they are to confine their energy when it is time for them to sleep. Some parents have found it more helpful to cut the multiples' bedroom door in half to create a Dutch door. Many parents strip their multiples' bedroom of chests of drawers, curtains, window blinds, artwork, and so on to create a safe and less-stimulating sleep room once any toddler is able to climb out of a crib. (See "Night waking," in Chapter 29, "Parenting Toddler Multiples.") One or more may still sleep in a crib, but often the one who can climb out quickly teaches the other(s) how to do it, too.

Once two are climbing out of cribs, multiples could share a mattress, which often is safest when placed directly on the floor and away from a wall with a window. Be certain screens are intact and locked in place on any bedroom windows. **Warning:** Don't install bars or anything else that could block access or escape through a bedroom window; this is a dangerous fire hazard and in some areas it may be illegal.

Kitchen appliances and equipment may pose particular dangers for multiple toddlers. Kitchen doorways are often open, so many parents use a higher gate to completely block multiples' access to this room. When multiples are in the kitchen with a parent, some parents have used bungee cords or installed padlocks to keep multiples from opening refrigerator, oven, and dishwasher doors. (Yes, the parents carefully drilled holes in these appliances to install the locks.) Many parents store all knives, scissors, food processor blades, pointed tools, matches, etc., in a locked chest, such as standard tool chest. **Caution:** Be sure to hide an extra key to open any padlock or chest—one is bound to get lost.

Childproof stove shields can help prevent toddlers from reaching stove controls or touching burners or hot pots and pans. Some parents are able to remove control knobs. They use only one knob for all the burners or they replace the knobs only when a burner is to be used. Teach other cooks in the family to use only back burners when possible and to always turn pot handles away from the front; pots are less likely to be tipped when facing the middle or the back of the stove.

To minimize multiples' use of chairs as stepstools to tables, appliances, and countertops, some parents eliminate most or all lightweight chairs in their homes for a couple of years. They store their dining or kitchen chairs in an attic, cellar, or rented space. In place of the typical chairs, they use folding chairs during meals, which are folded and placed on top of a dining table or in a locked closet between meals.

A space heater or a wood-burning stove may be an economical way to warm a drafty room while stretching heating costs, but either can be extremely dangerous if touched by curious toddlers or preschoolers. Also, there is a danger that one could push another into a space heater or stove accidentally. Parents must weigh the risks versus the benefits of using such appliances. If using a space heater, check it daily for safe, out-of-reach placement. Be certain there are no flammable objects touching it. If a fuel is used, be sure it is safely stored in an inaccessible, remote area of the home. A wood-burning stove may be difficult or impossible to install in an out-of-reach spot, so treat it as the fire and burn injury hazard it is.

Having firearms in a home with older toddlers and preschool multiples can be extremely dangerous. If you own any type of firearm, whether hand held or rifle, keep it in a locked cabinet or closet. It should not be kept loaded. Ammunition may be stored in the locked cabinet or closet, but it should in a separate container. **Warning:** Never clean or load any firearm in the presence of one or more young multiples.

Outdoor solutions. Toddlers love to go outdoors, and parents usually like it when multiples can expend their energy playing on gym equipment, scooting around on wheeled carts, or splashing in a small pool. **Warning:** No safety device can replace constant parental supervision when multiples play outdoors.

To supervise two or more active toddlers, it helps to fence any open yard directly connected to the house. If installing it new, consider purchasing fencing material with older toddlers and preschool multiples in mind. If motivated to explore the world beyond their yard, multiples usually succeed in getting a toehold in the fencing material which allows them to scale most standard-height fences. To minimize this problem, many parents buy fencing that is one to two feet higher than the norm. Some parents don't install a gate, so access in and out of the yard is possible only via the house entry (or by climbing over the fence). Of course, a parent should be outside whenever multiples play outdoors—no matter how high the fence!

Preventing falls through banisters or over railings on outdoor decks was discussed with "Indoor solutions." Falls could also occur on steps or through stairway banisters leading from the deck to the yard. A gate mounted at the top and bottom of a stairway may be necessary to keep toddlers where a parent currently can watch them. Netting or protective shields on stairway banisters may also prevent injuries, although netting is more likely to provide a toehold for climbers.

Pools, ponds, and fountains of any kind and any depth are particularly dangerous outdoor hazards. Although it is extremely important to install tight pool covers and pool alarms on any nearby body of water, do not depend on these safety devices to keep multiples out. Children have managed to get past them and drown or be injured by a fall into a pool, pond, or fountain. When possible, a pool should be surrounded by a separate fence. It should not be accessible from the main play zone. Ponds or lakes should be drained or fenced separately. Any fountain within the play zone should be drained. (Besides making the yard safer, parents will have less dirty water messes to clean up.) If you have a pool, pond, or fountain, be sure you know resuscitation skills used for drownings.

Many older toddler and preschool multiples have been known to escape through a door left partially opened by an older sibling or to pry or push a loose screen and climb outside. Escape may be of particular concern when a home is on a busy street, but it is good for more than a few parental gray hairs no matter where a family is located! To avoid premature gray, many parents install alarms on all doors leading to the outside—even to areas enclosed by a fence. The alarm emits an audible signal anytime someone goes through a door. Get in the habit of regularly monitoring window safety by choosing certain days of the week to check that screens are locked in place and haven't been exposed to recent wear-and-tear by multiples. (See "Indoor solutions" above for other considerations regarding window safety.) Ask neighbors to call immediately if they see any or all multiples out of their fenced play zone. If multiples have wandered from the yard, neighbors should be advised to ensure the toddlers' safety and then call.

Providing a stimulating yet safe environment for mobile older babies and toddler multiples can be a challenge for parents. Each multiple has the same need as any single older baby or toddler to explore the environment, but multiples often combine brains and brawn to explore in ways that wouldn't be possible for a single child. Many of the challenges to babies' or toddlers' safety are due to the multiples' interactions. Thoroughly multiples-proofing the home and yard does help; older babies and toddlers can explore and parents can relax—but just a little. There still are no child-proofing interventions that will ever replace constant parental supervision.

Chapter 29
Parenting Toddler Multiples

So much to discover in every direction they look! So many lightbulbs blinking on at once! Parents can almost watch the switches being flipped "on" inside their toddlers' heads. With newly developed mobility and growing sensitivity to each other's cues, there isn't any direction that appears uninteresting—whether they set off to explore together or separately. There isn't anything they wouldn't seek together—no matter where or how high it is located. There isn't anything they can't reach when they are of like mind, which they frequently are. It must have been parents of multiples who coined the phrases "two heads are better than one," "all for one and one for all," and "divide and conquer."

Guiding multiples through toddlerhood can be a challenge, but it is never dull. Multiples' social situation is unmatched by any other setting or circumstance, since each is constantly interacting with an exact age-mate(s), a peer(s) of precisely the same developmental level. This leads to unique situations for parents, some of which are great fun and others that are extremely frustrating.

Multiples' Interactions

Most parents anxiously wait for the time when their multiples will begin to play together. Multiples often notice one another and they sometimes interact during their first year, but it is during the toddler years when the bonds between multiples seem to cement. Because of the closeness they share, multiples are often the best of friends but also the worst of enemies. Most multiples appear to share a special bond, but temperament also plays a key role in the degree of closeness experienced by the individuals within any set.

A bond is more likely to develop between pairs of multiples. Twin multiples are a custom-made pair. Among higher-order multiples, pairings may take different forms. Parents of odd-numbered multiples often say there really is something to the adage "two's company, but three's a crowd." Two may get along so well that once bonded they are inseparable throughout childhood. Others may interact more with another particular multiple for awhile, but days, weeks, or even months later the pairings shift so that each multiple now spends more time in the company of a different multiple. In time the pairings shift again. What this can mean for odd-numbered sets, such as triplets and quintuplets, is there can be an "odd one out"—briefly when pairings shift often or long term if two develop a special bond.

Multiples have been constantly in each other's company since sharing a womb, and during toddlerhood many sets develop mutually understood verbal and nonverbal cues. These cues allow multiples to communicate long before they can express themselves through language.* A toddler multiple plays with a fellow multiple; they do not merely play alongside one another as two single-born toddlers tend to do. Parents of multiples usually report social behaviors between, or among, their toddlers that child development books generally list as typical for preschool children.

Multiples often treat other children as they treat one another, and they expect these children to understand the interactive cues they've developed for the set.

Multiples often demonstrate a deep caring for one another.

- Each will **comfort** the other(s) when one is upset. It is so sweet to watch multiples hug and pat one another, establish eye contact to send a look of reassurance to another, or listen to one whisper soothing sounds in another's ear. If one is injured, the other(s) may cry harder than the one who is hurt.

(*The development of these cues is not the same as the development of *idioglossia*, or a special language, by multiples. It is more similar to the repetition of certain phrases and unspoken signals used by two adults sharing a close relationship.)

Multipes share a special bond that lasts for all their lives.

- Multiples **share** with one another. When mother hands a treat to one, that multiple often points to the other(s) and waits until mother has handed over a treat for each. (However, that multiple probably will be smart enough to inspect each treat and take the largest piece when applicable!)
- Multiples often **defend** one another if an older sibling or an outsider bothers any of them—usually by physically or mentally ganging up on the offender. If any multiple is in trouble with mother or dad, the other(s) may become angry or upset if a punishment is involved—even when the one being punished is in trouble for biting or hitting the one now complaining about the consequences.

    Multiples may express **hostility** toward one another, too. Imagine how frustrating it would be to have shared everything with the same person(s) since in the womb. Who wouldn't feel hostile at times?
- If one multiple is enjoying a toy, a snack, or some individual time with mother or dad, it is likely to lead to a **jealous** display by the other(s). Or there could be a hundred red balls in a room yet every multiple in the set will want the same ball.
- Multiples may **compete** to take possession of a toy, be the first to reach the countertop, or gain mother's attention. (About the time parents are able to treat each multiple as an individual, their multiples reach a developmental stage when they demand equal time and attention.)

- Many multiples **fight**. Since most toddlers don't yet have the vocabulary for verbal sparring, disputes are often settled physically. Unfortunately, toddlers haven't grasped the concept of a "fair" fight. Most don't appreciate their own strength. A gentle but purposeful nudge or poke by one and another is pushed into a piece of furniture or a wall and lands on the floor with one more scrape, bump, or bruise.
- **Biting** is extremely common among multiples. Most sets have at least one biter. Often it occurs apart from brawling behavior. The combination of toddler frustration and minimal coping skills can lead to this aggressive behavior.

Multiples' individual temperaments, and related activity levels, influence whether they interact more by reassuring or wrestling one another.

Toddlers' Temperaments

Temperament refers to an individual's behavioral and emotional approach to situations. An individual's temperament is genetic, so it is something a baby is born with. When a young baby is described in terms of the "calm" baby, the "average" baby, or the "high need" baby, adults are actually referring to behaviors that reflect a baby's inborn temperament. As babies become mobile and begin to explore the environment, temperament is also reflected in a child's level of activity and approach to exploration.

Toddler Activity Levels

Toddlers come in a variety of normal activity, or exploration, levels. Since behavioral styles and activity levels have a genetic basis, it isn't surprising that identical multiples usually share a similar level of activity. The activity levels of fraternal multiples may range from very similar to completely opposite ends of the spectrum, and opposite-sex, or boy-girl, multiples tend to be the most different.

A toddler's level of activity usually fits in one of several basic categories. However, the lines between the categories are blurred, because level of activity progresses along a continuum. The majority of a multiple's characteristics may place him in a specific category, yet another category may better describe particular aspects of that toddler's activity level. One way to describe toddler activity level categories is to use an analogy for different types of tourists.

- **Toddler sightseers** are usually content to go along with the tour guide's agenda. They seem able to learn about their environment by simply observing the persons, places, and things they encounter all around them.

Although sightseers sometimes engage in more active exploration, they are usually content to stick to the designated route. In fact, they will reverse course if a recommended activity requires too much exertion or some element of it frightens them. Sightseers actually take hold of mother's or dad's hand when told to do so and stop doing something when a parent says "no." Many sightseers are focused more on developing their fine motor/muscle skills than on the large motor development used for advanced physical exploration. These children are first to build tall towers of blocks, spoon food into their mouths without losing one pea, and figure out how pieces fit together to solve a puzzle.

- **Wanderers** generally enjoy the guided tour, but they also experience a bit of wanderlust. They feel drawn toward the horizon and the discovery of what lurks just beyond. One day they may happily work on a block tower and will stick to that task no matter what distraction arises. The next day they may be busy with a new block tower, but in a flash they are off and running to investigate some new sight or sound. Although they may balk at holding mother's hand or being attached by a wrist cuff when out and about, most will settle down and save exploration for items within easy reach. Nonetheless, a parent must expect the unexpected walk-about from these mini-adventurers.

- **Trailblazers** cannot merely observe something of interest in the environment. Touching and tasting are crucial aspects of learning for them, and they let nothing come between them and any item they consider worthy of investigation. When no obvious path exists to reach the object in question, they forge ahead and create their own roads. They will break away when holding a parent's hand, find a way out of a wrist cuff, or climb out of a stroller if something catches their eye—and something always does.

Few trailblazers are satisfied only in attaining out-of-reach objects. Compelled to master large motor muscle coordination, they seem to enjoy the challenge of testing the limits of their newly achieved mobility. Trailblazers quickly abandon quiet projects for more active pursuits. Most seem as comfortable moving vertically as horizontally. Excellent climbers, these toddlers see almost everything in their home as a mountain. Impulsive exploration lands them literally in one scrape after another. To identify the trailblazers, look for toddlers with bumps and bruises on their foreheads and scrapes on their knees.

Whether a multiple is more an observer or a participant, all definitely are aware of and enjoy one another's exploits. **Multiple sightseers** sometimes encourage each other to roam a little farther on, or off, the designated path. The combined courage of **two or more wanderers** easily propels each to discover what is waiting around the next bend. With the slightest support from **fellow trailblazers,** all are ready to run faster and climb higher!

A multiple's level of activity may be affected by another's activity level. Usually a less active toddler takes direction from one who is more active. Often each member of the combined duo or trio then behaves at an increased level of activity, and the combined energy of the duo or trio almost seems to form a "multiples" entity with its own separate activity level.

Typically, a trailblazer inspires a wanderer to pick up the pace and follow his lead—frequently right into mischief or danger. Sometimes a wanderer encourages a sightseer to explore farther afield. Such influence does not appear to work in reverse. A more active multiple rarely decreases activity to join in the calmer play of a less active one. Apparently, a mover's got to move.

Are They Hyperactive?

When caring for more than one trailblazer or a trailblazer-wanderer combination, parents sometimes worry that their toddlers are hyperactive. Also, a trailblazing multiple may seem hyperactive when compared to another in the set that is a sightseer. Although parents should discuss this concern with the toddlers' pediatric care provider, multiples' combined activity level does not necessarily mean one is truly hyperactive. When parents have an opportunity to spend several hours with only one multiple, they may be surprised to find that a single trailblazer is not as difficult to watch as two. Also, many trailblazers settle down when alone and act like more easily supervised wanderers. When multiples' activity levels are extremely different and parents are tempted to compare, it may help to have a book that discusses the ranges in normal toddler development within easy reach. Frequent review is often reassuring.

Dominant vs. Passive

Parents often express concern when the dynamics of the multiples' relationship(s) seems uneven. They may worry when one toddler is a show-off, directs the set's activities, gets his way every time, starts, or at least ends, most of the fights, etc. On the other hand parents feel equally concerned about another multiple that goes along with anything another initiates, easily gives up when the other(s) demands it, rarely or never defends himself, etc.

Some parents observe a different form of dominance between multiples. In this instance none is passive, and parents report a physical or mental struggle, or competition, for dominance. Their struggles often play out in jealous behavior and the strong desire for the same toy, treat, or parent's attention. It seems to occur more often among identical multiples and same-sex, similar-temperament fraternal multiples.

Depending on the direction each multiple's dominance or passivity takes, parents may feel confused as to whether they should intervene. Avoid the temptation to intervene. In many sets, multiples take turns or "flip-flop" taking the dominant or passive role every few weeks or months. Whether one or another's dominance or passivity lasts briefly or for years, multiples are testing these characteristics within the confines of their developing relationship. Allow them the freedom to build that relationship on their own terms. Their relationship belongs to them—not to their parents. For better, and perhaps for worse at times, multiples need lots of time to learn when to give and when to take in that relationship. It is not always easy, but **avoid rescuing or saving them from each other.** They can handle their relationship even as toddlers. Really. They can.

The increased **verbal ability** of one multiple is often a factor when one seems dominant. The more verbal multiple becomes the set's spokesperson and sometimes continues to assume this role long after the other(s) is speaking well. Generally, girls lead boys in verbal ability, and many parents have described how the girl takes charge of boy-girl sets' activities.

Finally, it helps to **think positive.** The words "dominant" and "passive" both have a positive and a negative connotation in American culture. When parents are concerned about a multiple's dominance or passivity, they often focus on the negative aspects of those words. A dominant toddler may act bossy, but that bossiness may reflect self-confidence, assertiveness, and the beginnings of leadership. That passive multiple may be more flexible, more easygoing, or more self-assured. Look at the positive sides of both traits.

High Need Flip-Flopping

Many toddlers go in and out of periods when one (or more) will stick to mother like super-glue as each vacillates between the quest for independence and the familiar security of the mother's arms. For each multiple this is part of the normal process of learning one is a separate individual. What may be a surprise is the way in which this behavior can flip-flop between or among multiples. Often a multiple that had been a "needier" baby becomes a more independent toddler, and one that had seemed more easygoing or woke less during the first year begins to cling and wake more at night as a toddler.

Dealing with this flip-flop can be difficult because many mothers find that a clinging toddler has a much different "feel" than a clingy, high need baby, and they often had expected high need behaviors to decrease once multiples were playing and interacting more. When a mother has less patience for the toddler who had waited more than a year to take his turn as the higher need one, she may feel guilty about her response and sad for that multiple. Ideas for coping are included in several of the following sections. Related information about toddler breastfeeding is discussed in Chapter 27, "Breastfeeding, Starting Solids, and Weaning."

Discipline

Babies usually begin to learn that their family "society" has rules when they become mobile and their adventures take them into unsafe territory or they discover another family member's private property. Since dangerous activities can have life-threatening natural consequences and because each family member is entitled to personal possessions, parents must impose certain limits or boundaries on their older babies' or toddlers' explorations. Setting physical limits is the beginning of discipline, and parents must now assume a more active role in guiding their children toward safe and responsible behavior. Self-discipline is the eventual goal, but many years will pass before each multiple achieves it. Expect multiples to test the limits and push all boundaries for at least a couple of decades!

As their children's guide on the road to self-discipline, parents explain the behaviors they expect, reinforce and reward appropriate behaviors, halt inappropriate behaviors while diverting a child to appropriate ones, and identify the consequences of inappropriate behaviors. Consequences may be a natural result of an action or behavior, but sometimes they may be in the form of a "punishment" imposed by parents (and later by society). Whether the term "punishment," "consequences," or "corrective measures" is used, it is only one small aspect of discipline.

After months of parenting two or more, it should come as no surprise that **discipline is affected by the dynamic of multiple, same-age children.** Just as some multiples-related issues may be confused with actual breastfeeding problems in the early months, now many so-called discipline problems in toddlers actually are related more to the multiples' interactions and their combined energy-activity level.

Parental guidance will be more effective, and parents will feel less frustrated, when the rules or limits they set and the ways they choose to reinforce them reflect their multiples' current stage of development and individual temperaments. In addition, it helps to learn about the capabilities and the limitations of the normal toddler's thought processes, which is referred to as cognitive ability. It's too easy to label behavior as "purposeful" or "willful" when actually multiples simply got caught up in the "thrill" of the moment and acted, or reacted, impulsively.

In spite of any challenges, toddler multiples still want and need limits on their behaviors. Defining and continually reinforcing the limits that have been set is a serious parental responsibility. Reinforcing rules often requires parental action. It isn't enough to remain seated on the sidelines and merely remind toddlers about a rule or the consequences of breaking it; parents must be ready to get up and physically intervene when toddlers push the limits. This is not an easy task day in and day out, especially when parents are responsible for guiding multiple children to adulthood. Those multiples sometimes may work individually in different areas of the house, work together to perform incredible physical feats at other times, and frequently disagree physically on which method might work best or which multiple should go first in the performance of those feats.

Models of Behavior

Parents are their children's first, and remain their most important, models of appropriate behavior. From birth, infants constantly observe their parents. They listen to what parents say and how they say it long before they understand the actual words. An older sibling also provides an example for a younger one. The behavior of an older child provides the younger one with the opportunity to see what happens when someone with a little more experience follows or breaks a rule.

Multiples have a built-in buddy, and unless they have very different temperaments, toddler multiples tend to model their behaviors on each other. And who can blame them? Another toddler's ideas are usually more interesting—and definitely a lot more fun—than those that mommy, daddy, or a big brother or sister may come up with. They lovingly guide one another toward all kinds of mischief. Reinforcement from one's fellow multiple(s) often seems to have more meaning, and result in repeated behavior, than any positive or negative reinforcement from parents. In spite of the creative benefits for the multiples, modeling another toddler has major drawbacks!

Because multiples' interactions affect many, if not most, of any problematic toddler behaviors, interventions that are generally effective when reinforcing behaviors for a single toddler often do not work with multiples. Receiving positive reinforcement from the other multiple(s) for behaviors that parents consider negative is one aspect of this interactive effect, and it may be demonstrated in a variety of ways.

- Because toddlers enjoy receiving praise or approval, single-born toddlers will often adjust behaviors that don't please parent to ones that do. Toddler multiples appreciate praise from parents, but they often forget and will forgo parental approval when mutual approval impulsively draws them into an activity.

- Active multiples join together to dream of adventures that parents would likely discourage. Unlike most single toddlers, multiples' combined abilities mean they actually can—and frequently do—implement ideas that are far beyond a toddler acting alone.

- Multiples cheer each other on. Whether they try something together or only one actually follows through, the support of another toddler spurs many to try something that would inspire caution in a single toddler.

- Multiples may be playing happily or enjoying a treat one just shared with the other(s). As they mutually enjoy the activity or treat their behaviors escalate and they get sillier and sillier. Before a mother can say "uh oh," one of two things has probably occurred. In the first, the multiples' laughing banter has led to a poke. Another takes umbrage and follows the poke with a punch. Soon it becomes an all-out boxing match and each is crying. Or the escalating giggles translate into a corresponding escalation of physical activity. Soon something is thrown or knocked over as multiples careen through the room.

- Due to limited verbal ability, many toddlers express pleasure and displeasure physically. A single toddler may pound the floor or throw an object into the air if angry. A multiple is more likely to pound on or throw an object at another multiple when feeling the same way. (Happy pounding still hurts the other!)

- When parents impose consequences for inappropriate adventures, whether all participated or one cheered another on, multiples often begin to socialize when given a "time-out" or "calm-down time" or one who is not involved will come over to keep the isolated multiple company.

- When interaction results in one multiple biting, hitting, or kicking another, the "victim" multiple may become more upset with the parent reprimanding the "perpetrator" than he was with the multiple that hurt him.

  A demand for equality by many toddler and preschool multiples can result in interactive behaviors that try their parents' patience. Multiples often demonstrate jealous behavior or an apparent struggle or competition for "dominance" in these situations. The following are some common situations arising from the demand for equality.

- One seems to be happily occupied with some activity but every time another multiple asks to be held or breastfed, the busy one is over in a flash demanding to be held and breastfed, too. A few minutes later the situation reverses. The one who first asked to breastfeed is now playing, and the one who was playing now asks for some of mother's attention.

Toddler multiples have great fun together!

Still the one who seems to be enjoying a toy or activity leaves it immediately to demand equal attention from mother.

- A parent may have gone to a lot of trouble to locate two (or more) of the same toy in different colors so that each multiple will be able to easily identify his toy, only to find that all the multiples fight over the same toy of a particular color.
- No matter what the circumstances every multiple wants the same toy at the same time every time, and nine times out of ten a battle erupts to determine which multiple has first "playing" rights. If a parent diverts the attention of one or more to a different toy, multiples will soon fight over the diversion. Remove the toy in contention and multiples will compete for a different toy.

There Are No Easy Answers

Imposing corrective measures for toddlers' misbehaviors can be challenging for parents of multiples, and often laughable as well.

- By 18 months many multiples have figured out how to respond when a parent asks, "Who did it?" Each simply points to the other in an eloquent, nonverbal "He did it."
- Knowing that retreat is often a better form of valor, those same 15- to 18-month-olds will run in different directions when they hear a parent coming. They've already figured out that one parent cannot catch two (or more) if they split up.

- If told to sit in a specific chair to minimize socializing during a "time out," few multiples will actually remain in that chair unless a parent restrains each by using a seat belt or harness. Often too much time is lost between the behavior and the consequences for the last multiple to be restrained on a chair. The point of demonstrating the consequences for a behavior often seems lost.

- To eliminate socialization during a "time out," a parent may try to separate and then supervise multiples in different rooms; however, this is not always feasible. Unless each is isolated in a room with a gated door or a shut door, which often isn't appropriate for toddlers, the first multiple will have left the room to rejoin the other member(s) of the set before a parent can settle a second one in a different room. Again, too much time may be lost between the behavior and the consequences for the last multiple placed in a separate room, and the toddlers miss the point of being isolated.

- When interaction results in one multiple biting, hitting, or kicking another, parents often don't know whether to first comfort the "victim" or correct the "perpetrator." The victim deserves to be comforted, but the perpetrator probably won't make the connection between the action and the corrective measure a minute or two after an incident occurs. (And the victim is likely to forget the incident and soothe or comfort the perpetrator when corrective measures are taken, so the parent now appears as the "bad guy" and the point of correction is lost—again.)

If any of these scenarios sound familiar, what are parents to do? Although parents may be tempted to throw up their hands and walk away, each multiple still needs and deserves limits. Parents of multiples must be more vigilant and they have to expend more effort to keep up with two or more same-age toddlers, especially if a trailblazer or two is part of the set. A child's temperament influences how that child responds to the limitations or boundaries parents impose. It also affects how a child responds to the consequences for different behaviors.

Strategies That Work

Fortunately, there are interventions that parents have found to be helpful.

- **Super-childproofing,** or multiples-proofing, may be the greatest disciplinary action parents of multiples can take. (See Chapter 28, "Older Babies and Toddlers: Childproofing and Helpful Equipment," for specific childproofing ideas.) By making the home and yard a safe place for toddlers and other family members, many incidents that would require parental intervention can be avoided. This also means the word "no" will be heard less often.

Hearing "no" too often might lead some children to eventually lose their wonderful sense of adventure, or worse, lose the confidence to try new things. During childhood, active multiples hear the word "no" many more times than single-born children. Each multiple hears the "no" meant for him alone, the "no" meant for every other multiple alone, the "no" directed at multiples' joint ventures, and the "no" for the activities that only multiples can dream up and implement. Keeping the word "no" to a minimum is especially desirable in a household with toddler multiples.

- Sometimes parents limit outings, especially outings to others' homes, if trailblazing or wandering multiples are too difficult to supervise away from their super-multiples-proofed environment. To curious multiples, going to someone else's home may seem like a visit to an exotic foreign land. Their need to investigate by climbing, touching, and tasting may be overwhelming. Keeping track of multiples is crucial to avoid dangerous or seemingly mischievous situations, but parents may then find they don't have much of a chance to talk with the friends or relatives they came to visit. Often it's easier to ask friends and relatives to visit your house for the time being.

- Offering each multiple simple choices often reduces misbehavior that may be due to toddlers' feelings of frustration and helplessness. Choices allow each to have a voice and gain some control in various situations. Limit the number of options offered (two is usually enough) and don't offer an option if you aren't comfortable with it. Some of the forms choices may take include:

  1. The "either/or" choice—"Would you rather have carrots or peas with supper?" Count on at least one multiple to change her mind once she sees that another multiple made a different choice. Sometimes it takes no effort to accommodate a change of mind and a parent may want to avoid the hassle of insisting each multiple stick with the choice already made, but this may set a precedent for future choices when it may not be as easy to adjust.

  2. The "conflict of interest" choice—"Do you want to walk to your room in three minutes when it's time to get ready for bed, or do you want me to carry you to your room then?" (Going to bed is not a choice, but each may control some aspects of it.)

  3. The "best behavior" choice—"Are you ready to choose a different toy now, or do you need me to take you to your room so you can be alone to calm down?"

  4. The "no decision is a decision" choice—"Three minutes are up and it's time for bed. Did you decide whether you want to walk or have me carry you?" (No response from toddler.) "I guess you're telling me you

want me to carry you." Be prepared to pick the child up and follow through immediately.

- Multiples may sometimes act "wound-up" or become frustrated and start fighting because one or more is overtired or over-hungry. Respecting each multiple's body clock for food and sleep helps avoid some of these situations.

- When toddlers are interacting or are involved in an activity, they may have difficulty abruptly switching gears. Giving a several minute warning often helps them to readjust and move on to the next item on the parent's agenda. Announce what they will be expected to do next (making certain they are listening to you), tell them when they are expected to make the transition, and set a timer for the number of minutes (not more than five to ten minutes for toddlers). When the timer rings, tell them it is now time for the next activity so they must stop whatever they've been doing. Be ready to help them end the current activity and move on if they ignore the timer.

- Try interrupting an inappropriate behavior by wrapping a toddler in a gentle but firm bear hug. If the child is upset, continue the hug until the child calms down. During the hug, a parent can whisper "sweet nothings" to explain why the behavior was not the best choice and other options that might have been better.

  Jealous behavior can be a drawback to the bear hug. Often the other(s) want to join in the corrective measure. Depending on the parent's and toddlers' sizes, a bear hug may lose its effectiveness as a corrective measure when another one or two are added. However, including the other(s) can be a lot of fun and it often demonstrates a positive way to resolve a conflict.

- A variation of the bear hug for older toddlers is to have the multiple being corrected place her hand in a parent's pocket. The hand has to stay in the pocket until the parent releases it. Until then the child must go wherever the parent goes.

- A parent and each multiple will feel much better about any day that includes kisses, cuddling, and an "I love you, (toddler's name)" for each.

- Except for the multiple that only bites another when alone with the other multiple(s), most parents quickly learn the cues that indicate one is about to bite. Some parents find it helps to stop pre-bite jaw action by cupping the toddler's lower jaw in a parent's hand. They do this by placing the thumb of one hand at the temple by one of the toddler's ears and the index finger at the temple by the other ear; the child's jaw rests in the "sling" made by the palm of the parent's hand. It isn't necessary to apply pressure with the thumb and index finger. The action itself stops the behavior.

Another technique is to place a pliable, plastic container lid in the toddler's mouth just when he is about to bite another. The parent then explains that if a child feels a bite coming on he may use a plastic lid instead of the other's body part.

- Fights over the same toy can lead to placing that toy on the "time out" shelf until a plan for sharing has been worked out. Three strikes— or three squabbles-over the same toy places that toy in "time out" for overnight or longer.

- Although younger toddlers may squabble over the same toy even when two identical toys are available, older toddlers and preschooler multiples often want to play with individual, yet identical, toys. After a couple of episodes when every multiple wants the same toy and in the same color and with the same markings, it may be time to respect their collective wishes and buy each the exact toy for the next occasion. Work with each to find a way to place an identifying mark on identical toys, so everyone knows which toy belongs to which child. (Eventually they will request different toys.)

- No matter what kind of day everyone had, no matter how many times you said and your toddlers heard the word "no" today, positive feelings can be restored by saying to each "I love you, (toddler's name)" and massaging each toddler's back and head at bedtime.

Strategies That Don't Work

- **Corporal punishment,** such as slapping or spanking, sends mixed messages to multiples. Children cannot comprehend the reasoning that makes it all right for a parent to hit them for something the parent doesn't like, yet they are not supposed to hit one another when one doesn't like what the other(s) is doing. It's doubly confusing if any is spanked for hitting another. (The same applies when a parent bites a multiple that just bit another.) How are children with their immature thought processes supposed to interpret parental actions that say, "I'm hitting you for hitting your brother" or "I'm biting you because you bit your sister"? When a multiple's physical "dominance" is an issue, corporal punishment only reinforces that someone bigger, stronger, and more powerful is allowed to physically hurt another.

- Constant parental intervention for **multiples' disagreements or physical fighting** may only aggravate the situation. Avoid intervening unless one toddler is in immediate danger from another. Then intercept the punch or push, describe more appropriate ways for resolving differences, separate both/all if necessary, but again stay out of it as much as possible. Avoid passing judgment about who did what unless you witnessed the entire squabble from build-up to blow-up.

When parents stand back, stay out, and simply observe their multiples, they are often surprised to find that the seemingly more mild-mannered toddler goaded the other until the allegedly aggressive toddler finally had enough and lashed out. Parents are also pleasantly surprised to discover that multiples tend to fight less often when toddlers (or older multiples) receive less parental attention for those fights.

- Multiples deserve to be treated as individuals. Unless a parent witnesses the multiples' misbehavior, consider what multiples may be learning when they are reprimanded collectively but the parent is uncertain whether all actually contributed to the mischief.

- When any multiple repeats an inappropriate behavior but a parent only repeats a verbal warning rather than following up by active intervention, multiples quickly figure out that there is no real consequence for the behavior. They quickly tune out the meaningless parental noise, and repeat the behavior.

- Labeling children, instead of their behaviors, is hurtful. Avoid labels, such as the "good" or "easy" twin and the "bad" or "difficult" quad, which imply that that each multiple purposely chooses a positive or negative course of action. Toddlers (and older children) don't choose their temperaments and activity levels. They don't yet possess the cognitive ability to consciously scheme, consider all the implications, or comprehend the consequences of what adults consider as "good" or "bad" behaviors.

- **Giving up** and allowing physically active toddlers to do whatever they want to do may seem the easiest course at times, but it is a disastrous long-term solution. Later parents will discover how they have shortchanged themselves, the society multiples eventually will live in, and especially their children who someday will interact in that much wider society.

  When trying to keep up with trailblazers or wanderers, renew your energy by taking regular brief breaks. (See "Brief separations" and "Gaining support" in the sections below.) Then continue to give each multiple the guidance he needs. If you gave up today, begin again tomorrow.

- Multiples' escapades may not seem amusing at the time, but they often sound hilarious in retrospect. If you share the details with anyone else within any multiple's hearing range, be prepared to deal with repeat performances! Generally, multiples are more than ready, willing, and able to make you laugh about such incidents—again and again!

Other Toddler Issues

Language Development

It is during the toddler period that language ability blossoms. By the time multiples are 15 to 18 months, parents should be aware of the increasing receptive language ability of each even when multiples were preterm. **Receptive** language is the ability to understand what is said, and it is demonstrated when a parent asks a child a question and the child responds in a way that indicates she understood what was asked. For example, a parent could ask a child if he would like some juice and the child responds by running to the refrigerator, or a parent might ask a child to get his shoes and immediately the child gets the shoes and brings them to the parent. If a child is not indicating the ability to understand language between 15 to 18 months, parents may want to ask the pediatric care provider whether an evaluation by a speech-language expert might be valuable. Early intervention can make a difference in a child's overall development.

The timetable for the development of **expressive** language, the ability to actually speak, is broader. Some toddlers have a vocabulary of 50 or more words and are speaking in clear, several-word sentences at 18 months, and some are almost three years old before they speak in sentences. However, both toddlers are probably within the normal range of development. Generally, girls develop speech a little earlier than boys. Still, all toddlers should be able to speak a number of words clearly by age two, and all should be forming sentences by age three. If any is not speaking at this level by the appropriate ages, ask their care provider about a referral for a speech-language evaluation. Again, early intervention can make a huge difference in later development.

There is some evidence that a delay in expressive language development occurs more often in multiples. Preterm birth and its consequences are implicated in some instances. Studies also have found that multiples tend to receive less individual attention from parents, so multiples are not spoken to as parents speak to a single-born infant or toddler. Since multiples have been in each other's company from before birth, they don't always have to rely on words to communicate. In addition, toddler multiples may reinforce one another's poor speech patterns. Depending on the cause and the degree to which language ability is delayed, speech therapy may be necessary.

Encourage each multiple to speak. Talk to each as you change diapers or give baths. Describe a room as you walk through it with a baby or toddler. Identify items on grocery shelves for them. Praise attempts at new words by repeating the word correctly. Let the child watch your mouth make the word.

Frequently, one multiple is more verbal than the other(s), and that multiple may take over as the set's spokesperson. As long as a less verbal multiple demonstrates receptive language ability by 15 to 18 months and continues to add words and simple phrases to his vocabulary he probably is within normal range for speech development. However, allowing one to be spokesperson may delay the speech of the other(s) since the spokesperson often eliminates another's need to make his wants or needs known. Fortunately, this is easy to halt when parents consistently encourage the verbal ability of each multiple.

Make a conscious effort to speak to each multiple separately and then wait for a response from the one addressed. If the verbal multiple answers for the one spoken to, gently say something to the effect of "It is nice that you want to help your brother, but I'd like him to let me know what he wants." Then repeat the statement for the multiple originally addressed and again wait for a response.

Night Waking

It is not unusual for a toddler to still be waking at night, and multiples are simply two or more individual toddlers. Therefore, it isn't unusual for two, three, or more individual toddler multiples to wake at night. Sometimes multiples have been waking since birth, but the family co-sleeping arrangement that worked with babies is not working with larger or more restless toddlers. Often parents say multiples had been sleeping for several consecutive hours and parents had gotten used to their uninterrupted sleep. Then one or more multiples begins waking during a bout of illness or a period of teething, and they continue to wake when the illness is long gone or the teeth are through.

Sleep is not a luxury for parents caring for active multiples during the day. Coping with one or more multiples that wake at night, especially if any wake off and on through the night, can affect a mother's ability to lovingly deal with all of them during the day. When two or more wake at night and a mother never feels rested, she may not feel able to provide the day-to-day guidance her toddlers need. Many mothers say they feel guilty because they quickly become impatient, yell, and react inappropriately to their multiples' normal toddler behaviors when they are sleep deprived. Accidents can happen when a too-tired parent tries to rest her eyes for a few minutes. Also, sleep-deprived mothers of multiples more often report they experience frequent colds or other physical symptoms.

There are no easy answers. Parents want to meet their toddlers' nighttime needs, yet parents also need adequate rest if they are to be awake, alert, and ready to provide the loving and safe guidance multiple toddlers need during the daylight hours. Different solutions have worked better for different families.

To revise a family co-sleeping arrangement, parents sometimes make more space by adding another mattress or two, which they line up alongside their bed. Once multiples' receptive language is apparent, some parents find they can lay sleeping bags on the floor of their room for a multiple that joins them at night. They tell the toddlers that "big" children may sleep next to, but not in, the parents' bed. Other parents set up a mattress in the multiples' room and mother or dad joins a toddler in their room if any wakes at night.

Some parents find toddler multiples sleep with less interruption when they are able to sleep together. Usually these toddlers will be found touching or hugging each other during their sleep. A mattress on the floor of the toddlers' room may be the easiest way to implement this idea. Bed rails can be attached if a mattress is set on a bed frame. (See "Indoor solutions" in Chapter 28, "Older Babies and Toddlers: Childproofing and Helpful Equipment," for additional information about childproofing multiples' bedroom.)

Other multiples sleep more soundly when apart, so parents will set up a crib or bed in a separate bedroom or in a room with an older sibling. Creating separate space works well when a home has extra bedrooms, but it can be difficult to implement when space is limited. It often means completely multiples-proofing a second bedroom. If this means altering an older sibling's room or storing the older child's "treasures," this option is unlikely to be well received.

Get into the routine of rubbing each multiple's back and head at bedtime. (Some toddlers may want a full-body massage.) Many parents report their multiples sleep longer when massage is a regular part of the toddlers' nighttime routine. Parents often find they relax as they help their toddlers relax. (See "Resources" for books about infant-toddler massage.)

Some parents find they can talk multiples out of night-waking once the toddlers demonstrate receptive language. These parents first prepare the toddlers for the change. For instance, the day they plan to implement the new night routine parents repeat information about the change numerous times, "You are now big boys (girls), and big boys don't need 'milkies' (insert the multiples' name for breastfeeding here) at night. So if you wake up tonight, Mommy or Daddy will bring you a drink of water and rub your back for a couple of minutes while you stay in your bed." When the child wakes, the parent reminds the child of the plan they'd spoke of earlier in the day. "Remember we talked about bringing you a drink of water if you woke up during the night? Here's your drink of water. When you're finished, you can lie down again and I'll rub your back for a few minutes."

Parents are surprised when this method works without a hassle or a single tear. But they need to decide ahead of time what they will do if any toddler continues asking to nurse or crying to come into the parent's bed. Many parents find it helps to initiate any plan such as this when dad has a few days off work, so he can take over the nighttime drink of water duty. Some parents choose to keep taking a new drink of water and the offer of a backrub to an awake multiple every five to ten minutes, but they don't take the toddler into their bed. Sometimes a mother will go in and offer a brief breastfeeding to a toddler, but that toddler remains in her own bed. Other parents take the toddler into their bed if the plan doesn't work immediately, because they aren't comfortable with continuing the plan for this particular toddler or they know the disruption is likely to wake the other toddler(s).

The idea behind the "drink of water-backrub" plan is that a parent meets the toddler's need for a parent's presence; it simply isn't met in the way the child has come to expect. When it works, the multiple begins to sleep longer within three to five nights (or less). It may be necessary to reconsider this option when any toddler continues to wake beyond this time. That multiple probably is saying he isn't ready; perhaps he's in a "clingy" phase and needs more reassurance. Parents can always try this again later. Something that doesn't work now may work well in a month or two.

There probably is no perfect solution when multiple toddlers still wake at night. Parents must weigh each multiple's nighttime parenting needs with their own ability to cope lovingly and consistently with multiple toddlers during the day. Ultimately, the idea is to meet each multiple's overall needs best.

Brief Separations

Toddler multiples, especially those of similar temperaments, tend to develop a close bond with the other multiple(s) as well as with their mother and father. Many are not bothered by brief separations from mother. Unlike a single-born toddler who lets mother know she prefers to stick by her as she shops, visits at a friend's home, or eats lunch out, multiples may be happy if left at home as long as they are left together. They may become upset, however, if they are separated from the other multiple(s). There are exceptions, and it is necessary to consider each multiple as an individual with needs that may be different from the other(s). Sometimes one or more multiple is upset when separated from mother.

Because it takes a lot of parental energy to keep up with energetic toddler multiples, parents may need to reenergize—together and separately—by taking regular brief breaks. Go to lunch or a movie with your husband or with friends. Run away from home—literally but briefly—or engage in some other regular exercise. Meditate in a park or a church. Shopping or running errands alone may provide a brief respite. In addition, a mother may find she can run errands and be back home in half the time it takes to dress multiples for a trip, get them in and out of car seats, grocery carts, or a stroller, push one cart while pulling another when both carts are piled high with items, and she is also dealing with normal toddler interruptions—multiplied.

When multiples don't mind brief separations, it is important that any care provider or sitter clearly understands their individual and interactive activity levels. Daddy can assume more of his multiples' care as they develop into toddlers. When a father is left alone with multiples for several hours on a regular basis, he usually gains a better understanding of the fantastic job you accomplish every day.

When you and your husband plan a few hours out together, many parents still prefer to ask or hire two or more persons to watch multiples while they are away. Parents must be very certain of a single sitter's ability to supervise multiples, especially when there is a trailblazer or two in a set. It can be very difficult even for an experienced care provider or sitter to appreciate multiples' joined capabilities.

Potty Learning

After changing two, three, four, or more times the usual number of diapers, most parents are eager for multiples to learn to use the toilet. Helping a child learn to use the toilet usually is easy and doesn't take long when the child is ready. Most children gain the physical control and mental readiness needed to use a toilet between two to four years of age. Girls generally indicate they are ready to use a toilet earlier than boys.

Multiples may be ready for potty learning at about the same time or at very different times. It is important to respond to the individuals within the multiples set for this developmental issue. Identical multiples are more likely to achieve physical readiness at about the same time, but they may not be interested at the same time. However, a spirit of competition may spur a less interested one once the other(s) begins to use the potty. Fraternal twins, especially boy-girl sets, may vary widely in physical readiness and in interest. When one seems ready but the other(s) is not, go ahead and begin with one. It is often easier to deal with this process one at a time, anyway.

Teaching the basics is easy and takes very little time when a child is ready and willing to use the toilet. If it is taking weeks (or months) for a child to learn to use the toilet, it probably is best to take a break and try again when the child is more ready or interested.

A twins study conducted years ago found there was no benefit in pushing a child who was not yet ready. Parents began "training" one twin to use the toilet between twelve and eighteen months. They waited for signs of readiness before beginning to train the other twin, and readiness varied, but for most it occurred between six and eighteen months later. Researchers found both twins were able to use the toilet consistently at about the same time. This reinforces the notion that when parents put children on a potty chair for weeks or months before those children are ready, parents are training themselves—not the child. Most parents of multiples have better things to do!

When any multiple appears to be getting "toilet ready," mothers have recommended some or all of the following ideas.

- If possible, wait until weather allows multiples to wear fewer clothes. Then there is less laundry in case of accidents. (Expect accidents and you are less likely to feel frustrated.) On the other hand, don't delay when any really wants to learn to use the potty!

- Consider taking any "trainee" out of super-absorbent disposable diapers. Replace them with cloth diapers or training pants. (Training pants are available through some diaper services and there are also disposable brands.)

- Start with one potty-chair for twins, but you may need a second if you have triplets or quads. Multiples rarely need to use the potty at the same time. You can always get another if you find they do time bathroom breaks close together. A potty seat that fits on an adult toilet may work better for older toddler or preschool trainees.

- Once any is going on the potty, dress that multiple in "potty-friendly" clothes. Elasticized waistbands on pants and skirts or dresses that lift easily work best, because toddlers and preschoolers often don't think about using the toilet until the urge to go to the bathroom builds in intensity and requires immediate use.

- Be ready for all to tell you they have to go to the bathroom within moments of buckling the last one into a car seat. Expect to stop—and stop immediately—at every restroom any spots when they are out and about.

A Need for Support

Parents coping with multiple toddlers, especially when any are trailblazers or wanderers, often think they must be doing something wrong when their toddlers are involved in one disaster after another and they create mess upon mess. Parents of single-born children cannot understand what it is like to try to keep up with multiple toddler explorers. It is hard for them to appreciate the interactive effect of multiples and how it affects parental coping day to day. Because many mothers deal with sibling interactions that occasionally result in similar situations or they have single trailblazers that keep them hopping, they may be able to identify with mothers of active multiples but they just can't comprehend the constancy of multiples' behaviors and the wearing effect it can have. Parents of sightseer multiples may not need as much support as parents of more physically active multiples do, and they may also have difficulty relating to the experiences of mothers of trailblazing multiples.

If you think other mothers don't understand what you are dealing with or you wonder if something is wrong with your parenting, find another mother of multiples to be a phone friend. It helps if she shares a similar parenting philosophy, has the same number of multiples, and is dealing with multiples that have temperaments similar to your toddlers. Some prefer to talk with a mother whose multiples are slightly older, which can help put multiples' current antics into perspective. In any case it helps to know that other parents of multiple trailblazers usually feel several messes behind!

A La Leche League Leader or mother may be aware of a potential phone friend. Officers of a "mothers of multiples" organization may be able to help you link with another mother. Also, the Internet has created new opportunities for meeting with other mothers of multiples worldwide.

Multiple toddlers generate unique parenting issues. Parents of multiples may experience both joy and frustration as they care for two or more individuals and the interactive multiples "entity" that forms within many sets. Solutions for guiding one child at a time through toddlerhood don't always work when a family has multiple toddlers. Still each multiple needs and deserves a parent's loving guidance the same as any single toddler.

Limits and boundaries for toddlers often focus on their activity levels and a related need to explore, as these behaviors are most likely to result in injury for a toddler or damage to household property. Whether any multiples are sightseers that easily go along with the limits parents set or a set includes trailblazers that frequently seem oblivious to limits, there are valuable aspects to every activity level and behavioral style—even the ones that are more challenging for parents! Every style also has its weaker points. To recognize and help each child capitalize on his/her strengths while mastering weaknesses may be the essence of discipline.

No wonder a mother (and a father) may feel overwhelmed at times! When this occurs, call an experienced LLL Leader or another mother of multiples for understanding and support. Remind yourself as often as necessary, "I am normal. It's the situation that is not normal!" Before you know it, your multiples will move into the "easier to watch" preschool years when even trailblazers begin to listen first and act second.

Resources

This list is not intended to be inclusive for all organizations, references, products, or product brand names for multiples-related items. Inclusion on this list does not imply author or LLLI endorsement, or guarantee, of any organization, reference, product, or brand name.

International Associations for Parents of Multiples
Australia: Australian Multiple Birth Association (AMBA), c/o The National Secretary, PO Box 105, Coogee, New South Wales 2034, Australia; phone: 049 46 8030
website: http://home.vicnet.net.au/~ambainc/amba3.htm

Canada: Parents of Multiple Births Association of Canada (POMBA), 240 Graff Avenue, Box 22005, Stratford, Ontario, Canada N5A 7V6; phone: 519-272-2203
email: office@pomba.org
website: www.pomba.org/index.html

France: Jumeaux et Plus, l'Association, 28 Place St. Georges, 75009 Paris
phone: 01-44-53-06-03
fax: (telecopies) 01-44-53-06-23
email: info@jumeaux-et-plus.asso.fr
website: www.jumeaux-et-plus.asso.fr

Japan: Japanese Association of Twins' Mothers, c/o 5-5-20 Minami Aoyama, Minatoku, Tokyo, Japan

New Zealand: New Zealand Multiple Birth Association, PO Box 1258, Wellington, New Zealand. Liz Blake (President), 29 Friend Street, Karori, Wellington, phone: 04 476 2207

South Africa: South African Multiple Birth Association (SAMBA), 46 Lockwood Road, Erindale, South Africa 5066; phone/fax: (08) 38 364 0433
website: www.span.com.au/multiplebirth/index.html

United Kingdom: Twins and Multiple Births Association (TAMBA), PO Box 30, Little Sutton, South Wirral, L66 1TH England; phone: 0173 286 8000 (TwinLine), 0870 121 4000 or 0151 348 0020; fax: 0870 121 4001 or 0151 200 5309
email: tamba@information4u.com
website: www.surreyweb.org.uk/tamba/

United States: National Organization of Mothers of Twins Clubs (NOMOTC), PO Box 23188, Albuquerque, NM 87192-1188; phone: 505-275-0955; 800-243-2276
website: http.//www.nomotc.org/

National Online Fathers of Twins Club (English speaking/writing)
website: www.nofotc.org/

Associations for Parents of Higher-Order Multiples

International Society for Families with Triplets and Higher Multiples (German-language countries), c/o Strohweg 55, D-6100 Darmstadt, Germany; phone: 6151 59 58 57

Mothers of SuperTwins (MOST), PO Box 951, Brentwood, NY 11717-0627;
phone: 516/859-1110; fax: 516-859-3580
email: Maureen@MOSTonline.org
website: www.MOSTonline.org/

The Triplet Connection, PO Box 99571, Stockton, CA 95209;
phone: 209-474-0885; fax: 209-474-2233
email: tc@tripletconnection.org
website: www:tripletconnection.org/

Childbirth Preparation for Multiple Birth

Marvelous Multiples, Inc., PO Box 467841, Atlanta, GA 31146;
phone: 770-242-2750; fax: 770-242-2721
email: marvmult@aol.com

Doula: Birth and Postpartum Support

DONA (Doulas of North America, information and referral), 1100 23rd Avenue East, Seattle, WA 98112; phone: 206/324-5440
email: askDONA@aol.com
website: www.dona.com/

High-Risk Pregnancy/Bedrest

Sidelines, PO Box 1808, Laguna Beach, CA 92652;
phone: 949-497-2265; fax 949-581-5266
email: sidelines@sidelines.org
website: www.sidelines.org/

Grief Support: Miscarriage, Stillbirth, or Infant Death of a Multiple(s)

Center for Loss in Multiple Birth, Inc. (CLIMB), PO Box 1064, Palmer, AK 99645;
phone: 907/746-6123
email: climb@pobox.alaska.net
website: www.climb-support.org/

Twinless Twins International Support Group (for multiples who have experienced the death of a co-multiple), c/o 1122o St. Joe Road, Fort Wayne, IN 46835;
phone: 219/627-5414
email: twinless@iserv.net
website: www.fwi.com/twinless/index.html

Twin-to-Twin Transfusion Syndrome

Twin-to-Twin Transfusion Syndrome Foundation, Inc., 411 Longbeach Pkwy, Bay Village, OH 44140; voice mail: 216-899-ttts; fax: 216-899-1184
email: tttsfound@aol.com
website: www.tttsfoundation.org/

Zygosity Testing

Affiliated Genetics, Inc. (cheek swab kit and DNA analysis; worldwide mailing), PO Box 870247, Woods Cross, UT 84087-0247; phone: 801-298-3366; fax: 801-298-3352
email: btanner@burgoyne.com
website:www.affiliatedgenetics.com/

Hindmilk Feedings for Preterm Multiples

Information and Support

Lactation Support Program and Milk Bank, Texas Children's Hospital, 6621 Fannin, Feigin Center, Suite 730, Houston, TX 77069; contact: Nancy Hurst, RN, MSN, IBCLC (Director); phone: 713-770-3612; fax: 713-770-3633
email: nhurst@msmail.his.tch.tmc.edu

Lactation Center and Milk Bank, WakeMed, 3000 New Bern Avenue, Raleigh, NC 27610; contact: Mary Rose Tully, MPH, IBCLC (Coordinator); phone: 919-250-8599; fax: 919-250-8923

Rush Mothers' Milk Club, Rush-Presbyterian-St. Luke's Medical Center, 1653 West Congress Parkway, Chicago, IL 60612; contact: Paula Meier, RN, DNSc, FAAN (NICU Lactation Program Director); voice mail: 312-942-4932; pager: 800-980-7478; fax: 312-942-3355

Human Milk Banks

Human Milk Banking Association of North America (HMBANA), c/o Wake Med 3000 New Bern Avenue, Raleigh, NC 27610; contact: Mary Rose Tully, MPH, IBCLC (Coordinator); phone: 919-250-8599; fax: 919-250-8923 email: milkbank@capecod.net

Canada: Breast Milk Service, British Columbia Children's Hospital, 4480 Oak Avenue, Vancouver, BC V6H 3V4; phone: 604-875-2345, ext. 7607

Mexico: Banco de Leche, Xalapa, Veracruz; phone: 52-55-14-45-10, ext. 204; fax: 52-55-14-45-51

United States: Central Massachusetts Regional Milk Bank, Memorial Massachusetts Medical Center, Worcester, MA 01605; phone: 508-793-6005

Community Human Milk Bank (hospital clients only), Georgetown University Hospital, 3800 Reservoir Road, Washington, DC 20007

Wilmington Mothers' Milk Bank, Medical Center of Delaware, PO Box 1665, Newark, DE 19579; phone: 302-733-2340
Mothers' Milk Bank, WakeMed, 3000 New Bern Avenue, Raleigh, NC 27610; phone: 919-250-8599

Mothers' Milk Bank, Columbia Presbyterian/St. Luke's Medical Center, 1719 East 19th Avenue, Denver, CO 80218; phone: 303-869-1888

Mothers' Milk Bank, Valley Medical Center, PO Box 5730, San Jose, CA 95150; phone: 408-998-4550

Outside North America: see HMBANA (above) or check with breastfeeding/lactation support organizations in specific country

Other Organizations for Parents of Multiples

Center for the Study of Multiple Birth, 333 E. Superior St., Suite 464, Chicago, IL 60611; phone: 312-266-9093
email: lgk395@nwu.edu
website: www.multiplebirth.com/

International Twins Association (ITA), c/o 6898 Channel Road NE, Minneapolis, MN 55432; phone: 612-571-8910 or 612-571-3022

International Society for Twin Studies, Louisville Twin Studies, School of Medicine, University of Louisville, Louisville, KY 40292; fax: 502-852-1093
email: apmath01@ulkyvm.louisville.edu

The Twins Foundation (twin registry), PO Box 6043, Providence, RI 02940, phone: 401-729-1000; fax: 401-751-4642
email: twins@twinsfoundation.com

Twin Services (parent support; information in Spanish), PO Box 10066, Berkeley, CA 94709, phone: 510-524-0863
email: twinservices@juno.com

Twin Studies Center, California State at Fullerton: Dept. of Psych, PO Box 34080, Fullerton, CA 92634-4080, phone: 714-773-2568 or 714-773-2142
email: nsegal@fullerton.edu

Twins on Twins

Twinspace, website about twins for twins and parents: www.twinspace.com/

Related Organizations

Breastfeeding/Lactation

La Leche League International (referral to local LLL Leaders in United States, Canada, and other countries), 1400 N. Meacham Rd., PO Box 4079, Schaumburg, IL 60168-4079; phone: 847-519-7730 or 800-LALECHE; fax: 847-519-0035; in Canada phone: 800-665-4324.
email lllhq@llli.org
website: http://lalecheleague.org/

International Lactation Consultant Association (referral to international chapters or local IBCLCs), 4101 Lake Boone Trail, Suite 201, Raleigh, NC 27607; phone: 919-787-5181; fax: 919-787-4916
email: ilca@erols.com
website: www.ilca.org/

Nursing Mothers of Australia, PO Box 4000, Glen Iris, Victoria 3146 Australia; phone: 61 3 9885 0855; fax: 61 3 9885 0866
email: nursingm@vicnet.net.au
website: http://avoca.net.au/~nmaa/index.html

Childproofing/Infant-Child Safety Equipment
U.S. Consumer Product Safety Commission (CPSC), Washington, DC 20207; phone: 800-638-2772
email: info@cpsc.gov
website: www.cpsc/gov/

Children/Multiples with Special Needs
Special Children (for parents [of multiples] with special needs), S. Devo, PO Box 8193, Bartlett, IL 60103; phone: 708-213-1630
email: spclchldrn@aol.com

Infant Care/Infant CPR Classes
American Red Cross (child care classes; local referral), 11th Floor, 1621 N. Kent St. Arlington, VA 22209; phone 703-248-4222
email: info@usa.redcross.org
website: www.redcross.org/index.shtml

Infertility Support and Information
Resolve, Inc. (local referral), 1310 Broadway, Somerville, MA 02144-1779; phone 617-623-0744 (HelpLine), 617-623-1156 (business office); fax 617-623-0252
email: resolveinc@aol.com
website: www.resolve.org/

Organizations That Offer Support

The American Academy of Husband-Coached Childbirth—The Bradley Method
Box 5224 Department CB, Sherman Oaks CA 91413-5224
phone: 800-423-2397 or 800-4ABIRTH
website: www.bradleybirth.com

Cesareans/Support, Education, and Concern, Inc.—C/SEC
22 Forest Road, Framingham MA 01701
phone: 508-877-8266

Couple to Couple League
Post Office Box 111184, Cincinnati OH 45211
Phone: 513-471-2000
website: www.ccli.org

International Childbirth Education Association—ICEA
Post Office Box 20048, Minneapolis MN 55420
phone: 612-854-8660
fax; 612-854-8772
email: info@icea.org
website: www.icea.org/

International Loving Touch Foundation, Inc.
Post Office Box 16374, Portland OR 97292-0374
phone: 503-253-8482
fax: 503-256-6753
email: children@lovingtouch.com
website: www.lovingtouch.com

Lamaze International (formerly ASPO/Lamaze)
1200 19th Street NW, Suite 300, Washington DC 20036
phone: 800-368-4404 or 202-857-1100
email: lamaze@dc.sba.com
website; www.lamaze-childbirth.com/

Vaginal Birth after Cesarean—VBAC
10 Great Plain Terrace, Needham MA 02192
phone: 617-449-2490

Postpartum Depression or Anxiety Disorders
Depression after Delivery, Inc., PO Box 1282, Morrisville, PA 19067;
phone: 800-944-4773 (information request line) or 215-295-3994 (professional inquiries)
website: www.behavenet.com/dadinc/

Postpartum Support International (postpartum depression or anxiety disorder information),
927 N. Kellogg Avenue, Santa Barbara, CA 93111; phone: 805-967-7636
email: thonikman@compuserv.com
website: www.iup.edu/an/postpartum/postpart.humlx

Equipment

Breast Pumps/Other Products
Ameda Breastfeeding Products/Hollister Incorporated (hospital-grade, self-cycling
breast pump purchase or rental, double collection kit, etc.), Hollister Incorporated,
2000 Hollister Drive, Libertyville, IL 60048; phone: 800-323-4060 (USA) or 800-263-7400
(Canada)
website: www.hollister.com/

Bailey Medical (Nurture III) (adjustable cycling double pump, milk storage bags,
instructional video) 800-413-3216
website: www.baileymed.com

Medela, Inc. (hospital-grade, self-cycling breast pump purchase or rental, double
collection kit, electronic scale rental, alternative feeding devices, nursing bras,
pillow, stool, etc.); PO Box 660, McHenry, IL 60051-0660; phone: 800-435-8316;
fax: 800-995-7867
website: www.medela.com/

White River Concepts (hospital-grade, self cycling breast pumps, alternative feeding devices, pelvic support devices, etc.), 924 C Calle Negocio, San Clemente, CA 92673; phone 800-342-3906 or 949-366-8960
email: custsvc@whiteriver.com;
website: www.whiteriver.com/index.html

Electronic Scales
Medela, Inc. (hospital-grade, self-cycling breast pump purchase or rental, double collection kit, electronic scale rental, alternative feeding devices, nursing bras, pillow, stool, etc.); PO Box 660, McHenry, IL 60051-0660; phone: 800-435-8316; fax: 800-995-7867
website: www.medela.com/

Nursing Fashions/Bras
Bravado Designs, Inc. (maternity/nursing bras up to 46G), 1159 Dundas St. East, Suite 140, Toronto, Ontario, Canada M4M 3N9,
phone: 800-590-7802, 416-466-8652,
fax: 416-466-8666
website: www.bravado.org

Breast is Best (catalog of nursing fashions), Post Office Box 66031, 1355 Kingston Road, Pickering, Ontario, Canada; phone: 877-837-5439; in Toronto, 905-837-5439
email: breastis@interlog.com
website: www.breast-is-best.com

Elizabeth Lee Designs (sewing patterns of nursing fashions), Post Office Box 696L, Bluebell UT 84007, phone: 800-499-3350
email: eldesign@uwin.com
website: www.snj.com/eldesigns

Family Resources (clothing, bras, slings, pillows), phone: 888-398-7987
website: www.breastisbest.com

Decent Exposures (nursing bras), phone: 800-505-4949
website: www.decentexposures.com

Laura's Closet (breastfeeding apparel), Post Office Box 97, Stoughton, WI 53589;
phone: 888-766-0303
website: www.laurascloset.com

Mama Shark's Swimwear, Inc. (swimwear), phone: 219-289-1248
website: www.milemall.com/mamasharks

Mother's Nature (clothing, slings, pumps), phone: 888-8slings
website: www.babyholder.com

Mother-to-Mother Nursing Wear (catalog of discreet nursing fashions),
phone: 888-580-9399
email: clothing@hotmail.com
website: www.mothertomother.com

Motherhood Nursing Wear (nursing fashions), 456 N. 5th Street, Philadelphia PA 19123.
phone: 800-4MOM2BE
website: www.motherhoodnursing.com

Motherwear (catalog of fashions for discreet breastfeeding), phone: 800-950-2500
website: www.motherwear.com/

The Nurtured Baby (maternity and nursing bras and underwear),
phone: 888-564-BABY
website: www.nurturedbaby.com

Simply Delicious Nursingwear, Post Office Box 5191, San clemente, CA 92674-5191;
phone: 800-637-9426 (USA); 949-361-1089 (oustide USA)

Slightly Crunchy (nursing bras, clothing, pumps), phone: 877-CRUNCHIES
website: www.slightlycrunchy.com

Yummy Mummy (nursing wear, bras, slings), phone: 888-301-2266
website: www.nurture-parenting.com

Nursing Pillows
Double Blessings (EZ-2-Nurse Pillow), phone: 800-584-TWIN
website: www.doubleblessing.com

Four Dee Productions (NurseMate nursing pillow), 13312 Redfish Ln. #104, Stafford, TX
77477; phone 800-526-2594 or 281-261-5510; fax 281-261-5442
email : 4dee@ghg.net
website: www.fourdee.com/

Family Care Company (Nifty Nurser Pillow)
24307 Magic Mountain Parkway, Valencia CA 91355
phone: 800-296-9640

Precious Bundles (The Hugster), 10 Sparrow Ct., Moraga, CA 94556, USA;
phone 800-459-0461

Zenoff Products, Inc. (My Brest Friend nursing pillow), phone: 1-800-555-5522

Other Products

Multiples (Miscellaneous)
Four Dee Productions (general items), 13312 Redfish Ln. #104, Stafford, TX 77477;
phone 800-526-2594 or 281-261-5510; fax 281-261-5442
email: 4dee@ghg.net
website:www.fourdee.com/

Double to Quadruple Strollers and Prams
Baby Jogger (double and triple models), phone: 800-241-1848 (USA)
website: www.babyjogger.com/products.htm

Inglesina, c/o Pali USA, 77 Eisenhower Lane S., Lombard, IL 60148
phone: 630-953-9519
email: paliusa@paliusa.com;
website (international): www.inglesina.com/products/main.html
list of distributors by country: www.inglesina.com/distributors/main.html

Maclaren, c/o AHC (also, pelvic support device) phone: 800-327-4382; website:
www.ahcproducts.com/ or Kidco, Inc. (also, doorway gates), 300 Terrace Drive,
Mundelein IL 60060-3836; phone 800-553-5529
email: kidcoe-mail@aol.com or info@kidcoinc.com
website: www.kidcoinc.com/index.html

Peg-Perego (USA), phone: 800-671-1701
email: peregoservice@perego.com; website: www.perego.com/
Canada email: info@pegperego.on.ca
International/Italy phone: 039/60881; website: www.pegperego.it

Runabout™ "Minivan" (double, triple and quadruple "add-a-seat" models), c/o MOST
(Mothers of SuperTwins) or The Triplets Connection (also carries Peg-Perego; has pre-
owned stroller listing); see Association for Parents of Higher-Order Multiples, page 330.

Baby Slings/Carriers
Baby Sling, c/o Nappies Direct, PO Box 11709, London SE14 5ZR England;
phone: 0171-635 7900 (UK); fax: 0171-635 5051
email: info@nappies-direct.co.uk
website: www.nappies-direct.co.uk/slcarry5.html (illustrations with directions for how
to wear with twins)

Gemini Carrier (twins) and MaxiMom Carrier
(twins or triplets; photos demonstrate use),
c/o Tot Tenders, Inc. (also toddler-preschooler backpack with safety tether/leash);
phone: 800-634-6870 or 619/679-2104
website: www.babycarriers.com/products.html

New Native Baby Carrier, Post Office Box 247, Davenport, CA, 95017, USA;
phone: 800-646-1682
website: www.cruzio.com/~NewNativ

No Jo (The Original Baby Sling), phone: 800-440-NOJO; 800-541-5711

Over the Shoulder Baby Holder (twins discount), Post Office Box 5191, San Clemente,
CA 92674-5191, USA, phone: 770-396-4747; 800-637-9426 (USA); 949-361-1089 (outside
USA)
email: parentspal@aol.com
website: www.atl.mindspring.com/-robert/w/index.html

Parenting Concepts (Sling Ezee Baby Sling), phone: 909-337-1499

Prenatal Cradle, Inc. (Natural Embrace baby sling); phone: 800-383-3068

Prenatal Pelvic Support
CMO, Incorporated (Loving Comfort Maternity Support), PO Box 147, Barberton, OH
44203; phone: 800-344-0011; fax: 330-745-5913

Prenatal Cradle, Inc. (pelvic support devices), phone: 800-383-3068

Smith Orthopedics (Mom-Ez Maternity Support), PO Box 19007, Topeka, KS 66619;
phone: 800-279-7711; fax: 800-289-1903

General

Arm's Reach Bedside Co-Sleeper(tm), c/o Arm's Reach Concepts, Inc., 5699 Kanan Road-Suite 330, Agoura Hills, CA 91301-3358; phone: 800-954-9353 or 818-879-9353; fax: 818-991-5999
website: www.armsreach.com/one.html
list of distributors by country or USA: www.armsreach.com/stores.html

One Step Ahead (multiples discount/catalog—double strollers, co-sleeper beds, childproofing devices, gates, expandable play yards, etc.), PO Box 517, Lake Bluff, IL 60044; phone: 800-274-8440; fax: 847-615-7236
email: osacatalog@aol.com

Information for Parenting Multiple-Birth Children

Books

Bryan, Elizabeth M. (1992). *Twins and Higher Multiple Births: A Guide to Their Nature and Nurture.* London, England: Edward Arnold.

Clegg, Averil & Woolett, Anne (1983). *Twins: From Conception to Five Years.* New York: Ballantine Books.

Gromada, Karen Kerkhoff & Hurlburt, Mary (1992). *Keys to Parenting Twins.* New York: Barron's.

Noble, Elizabeth (1992). *Having Twins: A Parent's Guide to Pregnancy, Birth, and Early Childhood* (2nd ed.). Boston: Houghton-Mifflin.

Novotny, Pamela Patrick (1994). *The Joy of Twins and Other Multiple Births: Having, Raising, and Loving Babies Who Arrive in Groups* (rev. ed.). New York: Crown Publishers.

Rothbart, Betty (1994). *Multiple Blessings: From Pregnancy Through Childhood, a Guide for Parents of Twins, Triplets or More.* New York: Hearst.

Tinglof, Christina Baglivi (1998). *Double Duty: The Parents' Guide to Raising Twins, from Pregnancy through the School Years.* Chicago IL: Contemporary Books.

Magazines

Twins Magazine, 5350 S. Roslyn St., Suite 400, Englewood, CO 80111-2125; phone: 888-558-9467 or 303-290-8500; fax: 303-290-9025
website: www.twinsmagazine.com/

Videotapes

Double Duty: The Joys and Challenges of Caring for Newborn Twins (1998) (30 min.) (15 min. edited version avail.). Two by Two: Four Dee Productions, see "Other Products: Multiples."

Your Multiples and You, Conception to Six Months (27 min.). NOMOTC, see Organizations for Parents of Multiples: International Associations: USA above.

Related Parenting Books

Most of the following books are available at local bookstores or through the La Leche League International (LLLI) Mail Order Catalogue. Call 1-800-LALECHE for a free copy or check on-line at www.lalecheleague.org.

Breastfeeding

THE WOMANLY ART OF BREASTFEEDING (1997)
Available through LLLI No. 297

BREASTFEEDING PURE AND SIMPLE (1991) Gwen Gotsch,
Available through LLLI No. 251

HOW WEANING HAPPENS (1999) Diane Bengson
Available through LLLI No. 256

Nursing Your Baby (1991) Karen Pryor and Gale Pryor
Available through LLLI No. 329

So That's What They're For! Breastfeeding Basics (1996) Janet Tamaro
Available through LLLI No. 385

Growth and Development

The Baby Book (1993) William Sears, MD and Martha Sears, RN
Available through LLLI No. 381

Growing Together (1987) William Sears, MD
Available though LLLI No. 273

High-Need Baby/Children

The Fussy Baby (1985) William Sears, MD
Available through LLLI No. 289

Parenting the Fussy Baby and High-Need Child (1996) William Sears, MD and Martha Sears, RN
Available through LLLI No. 3014

Raising Your Spirited Child (1991) Mary Sheedy Kurcinka
Available through LLLI No. 395

Raising Your Spirited Child Workbook (1998) Mary Sheedy Kurcinka
Available through LLLI No. 3951

The A.D.D. Book (1998) William Sears, MD and Lynda Thompson, PhD
Available through LLLI No. 3046

Other

Infant Massage: A Handbook for Loving Parents (1989) by Vimala Schneider McClure (available LLLI, No. 360)

Kangaroo Care: The Best You Can Do to Help Your Preterm Infant (1993) by Susan M. Ludington-Hoe and Susan K. Golant (out of print)

Mothering the Mother: How a Doula Can Help You Have a Shorter, Easier, and Healthier Birth (1993) by Marshall Klaus, Phyllis Klaus, and John Kennell (available from Perseus Press)

Appendix
Storing Human Milk

The milk you express from your breasts for your baby is a precious fluid. It combines the best possible nutrition with antibodies, live cells, and other substances that protect babies from infection and help them grow and develop.

Human milk's anti-bacterial properties actually help it stay fresh longer. The live cells and antibodies in the milk that discourage the growth of bacteria in your baby's intestines also guard against bacterial growth when the milk is stored in a container.

The guidelines that follow apply to milk that will be given to full-term healthy babies; guidelines vary for premature or sick babies.

Containers For Storage

You can use either hard-sided containers for storing milk or plastic bags. Hard-sided containers, either glass or plastic, do the best job of protecting the milk. Plastic milk storage bags, designed for freezing human milk, offer convenience and take up less room in the freezer.

Some mothers use the disposable plastic nurser bags designed for bottle-feeding to store their milk. These are less durable and are not designed for long-term storage. They may burst or tear, but double-bagging can help prevent accidents. With either kind of bag, squeeze out the air at the top before sealing, and allow about an inch for the milk to expand when frozen. Stand the bags in another container on the refrigerator shelf or in the freezer.

Put only two to four ounces of milk in each container, the amount your baby is likely to take in a single feeding. This avoids waste. Small quantities are also easier to thaw. You can add fresh milk to a container of frozen milk as long as there is less fresh milk than frozen. Cool the fresh milk for 30 minutes in the refrigerator before pouring it on top of the frozen milk in the freezer.

Be sure to label every container of milk with the date it was expressed. If the milk will be given to your baby in a day care setting, also put your baby's name on the label.

How Long To Store Human Milk

How long you can store milk depends on the temperature. Follow the guidelines in this table.

Previously frozen milk that has been thawed can be kept in the refrigerator for up to 24 hours. Thawed milk should not be refrigerated. It is not known whether human milk left in the bottle after a feeding can be safely kept until the next feeding or if it should be discarded, as is the case with infant formula. Recent studies have shown that human milk actually retards the growth of bacteria, so it may be safe to refrigerate unused milk for later use.

Where	Temperature	Time
At room temperature	66-72°F(19-22°C)	10 hours
In a refrigerator	32-39°F(0-4°C)	8 days
In a freezer compartment inside a refrigerator	Temperature varies	2 weeks
In a freezer compartment with a separate door	Temperature varies	3-4 months
In a separate deep freeze	0°F (-19°C)	6 months or longer

To keep expressed milk cool when a refrigerator is not available, place it in an insulated container with an ice pack. It's a good idea to use ice and an insulated container when transporting milk home from the workplace or to the babysitter's, especially on warm days.

Using Stored Milk

• Human milk may separate into a milk layer and a cream layer when it is stored. This is normal. Shake it gently before giving it to the baby to redistribute the cream.

• Human milk should be thawed and heated with care. Just as freezing destroys some of the immune properties of the milk, high temperatures can also affect many of the beneficial properties of the milk.

• Frozen milk: Containers should be thawed under cool running water. Gradually increase the temperature of the water to heat the milk to feeding temperature. Or immerse the container in a pan of water that has been heated on the stove. Take the milk out and rewarm the water if necessary. The milk itself should not be heated directly on the stove.

• Refrigerated milk: Warm the milk under warm running water for several minutes. Or immerse the container in a pan of water that has been heated on the stove. Do not heat the milk directly on the stove.

• Do not use a microwave oven to heat human milk. If the milk gets too hot, many of its beneficial properties will be lost. In general, milk for babies should not be heated in the microwave. Because microwaves do not heat liquids evenly, there may be hot spots in the container of milk, and this can be dangerous for infants.

Photo Credits

Index

About La Leche League

La Leche League International is a nonprofit organization founded in 1956 by seven women who wanted to help other mothers learn about breastfeeding. Currently, there are La Leche League Leaders and Groups in countries all over the world.

La Leche League offers information and encouragement primarily through personal help to those women who want to nurse their babies. A Health Advisory Council comprised of medical consultants from all over the world offers advice and assistance when necessary.

La Leche League is the world's largest resource for breastfeeding and related information, distributing more than three million publications each year. THE WOMANLY ART OF BREASTFEEDING, a basic how-to-book, has helped countless mothers through almost any nursing crisis. Other books published by La Leche League International are sold in bookstores and through the LLLI mail order catalogue.

For further information, we urge you to locate a La Leche League Group in your area by checking your local telephone book or by calling 1-800-LA-LECHE or 847-519-7730 in the USA (800-665-4324 in Canada) or by writing to LLLI, P.O. 4079, Schaumburg, IL 60168-4079 USA (LLLI, 18C Industrial Drive, Box 29, Chesterville, Ontario, Canada K0C 1H0). Or you can visit our website at www.lalecheleague.org/